WALKING WITH JACK

ALSO BY DON J. SNYDER

A Soldier's Disgrace

Veterans Park

From the Point

The Cliff Walk

Of Time and Memory

Night Crossing

Fallen Angel

Winter Dreams

The Winter Travelers

Walking with Jack

A FATHER'S JOURNEY TO BECOME

HIS SON'S CADDIE

Don J. Snyder

DOUBLEDAY

New York   London   Toronto

Sydney   Auckland

www.doubleday.com

DOUBLEDAY and the portrayal of an anchor with a dolphin
are registered trademarks of Random House, Inc.

Book design by Michael Collica
Jacket design by Michael J. Windsor
Jacket photograph © John Dolan/Trunk Archive

Library of Congress Cataloging-in-Publication Data

Snyder, Don J.
Walking with Jack : a father's journey to become his son's caddie / Don J. Snyder
p. cm.
1. Caddies—United States. 2. Golfers—United States. 3. Golf—Scotland—
St. Andrews. 4. Saint Andrews Links (St. Andrews, Scotland). I. Title.
GV964.N5S69 2012
796.352092—dc23
[B]
2012031447

ISBN 978-0-385-53635-6

MANUFACTURED IN THE UNITED STATES OF AMERICA

1 3 5 7 9 10 8 6 4 2

First Edition

For Colleen, who brought Jack into this world and then trusted me to be his father, and his caddie, even though she always wanted him to be a baseball player instead of a golfer

WALKING WITH JACK

As far back as I can remember, when my son, Jack, was still putting his shoes on the wrong feet, golf was always drawing us together, and we were always making one last long putt across the living room floor or one final great shot in the backyard for the championship of the world. Even then all I wanted was never to lose him the way my father had lost me, and so the two of us pledged that no matter what happened, he would become a pro golfer someday in the bright future of our time, and I would be his caddie so that I could walk beside him for as far as the game might take us.

BOOK ONE

All last night a nor'easter battered the coast here in Maine with high winds and heavy snow. This morning I was outside shoveling our driveway two hours ahead of dawn, putting my back into the work, feeling strong and fit. In the harbor behind me a shabby parade of lobster boats motored through the cove for the open water while I worked in the half-light of this new day, breathing the salted air beneath a bright sickle of moon. I was trying to clear my head of yesterday. Jack's eighteenth birthday. Two daughters had come home from college to join the third daughter to celebrate the occasion. I went into town for candles and ice cream in advance of the storm and when I returned, I found two of the girls plugged into their iPods, another at the computer, and Jack on the couch in the family room, staring at a poker tournament on TV. It was one of those unremarkable moments in the life of an American family that in itself has no meaning or consequence until you imagine it replicated in ten thousand other moments that somehow add up to hours, days, and even years of your life together as a family that you will never get back, and you're left wondering how it could be possible that after having four babies in six years and falling blissfully in love with each of them at the moment you first beheld them, and spending every waking and sleeping hour building your new world around them and holding that world together with a love so profound that the joy or sorrow of one of them was registered deeply in all the others—you wonder if all of that is gone forever, and if there's nothing you can do to get it back.

I found Colleen in the kitchen, where Jack's birthday cake sat on the counter. She asked me if I had remembered the candles. What I wanted to do was climb up on the dining room table and shout: Okay, everyone pack your bags. In one hour we're moving to Africa!

Soon the storm was upon us. We gathered for cake and ice cream, and the day passed away.

Shoveling snow this morning made me feel real again. And I wasn't worried about the girls; they had a strong sense of themselves. It was Jack who concerned me. He had been one of the most talented golfers in Maine from the time he began his freshman high school season, and he believed that by his senior year golf coaches at the Division I colleges and universities would be interested in him. When no one was, he began losing faith in himself. And I couldn't look at him without thinking that my life as a father had really been a long run of fixing things. First it was the little things that break—gluing wheels back on, and dolls' heads. Then bigger things, bicycles, skateboards, cars. Now I wondered if it would be stuff inside them, stuff that I couldn't fix. I knew that I wanted to do something to reassure Jack that a light still shone on him. I had no idea what I might do, but this morning at sunrise while he slept in his room just above me, I got the idea of clearing the snow off a patch of grass in the front yard and setting up the big net I had bought him one Christmas.

The whole time I shoveled snow I was thinking of all the miles we had walked together, side by side, on golf courses from Canada to North Carolina. Then I went up to his bedroom and woke him.

"What time is it?" he asked, squinting at me.

"Almost six," I said.

"What are you waking me now for?"

"Golf," I said.

"Golf?"

I had everything set up by the time he came outside. I hit a few balls into the net while he tried to figure out what planet he was on. "I still don't feel like I'm getting my shoulders turned through the ball," I said.

"You're not," he said miserably. "You're swinging like Nanny. What the hell are you using for a tee?"

I told him proudly of my invention. The ground was frozen too hard to get a wooden tee in it, so I'd cut off the tip of a rubber nipple from one of his cousin's baby bottles, and it worked perfectly. "Pretty good, huh?" I asked.

"Jesus, Daddy," he said, shaking his head. "You're crazy and I'm going back to bed."

He began walking toward the front door.

"Wait," I called to him. "Just try a few, Jack."

He thought for a moment, then came slouching down the steps across the driveway. I watched him hit a couple of drives—crushing, fluid blows that far exceeded my ability—before he handed the club back to me. "This is stupid, man, I'm freezing," he said. When he got to the door, he called back to me, "Go to bed, Daddy."

He was gone before I could say anything. I stayed out for a while longer hitting balls into the net while the sky over the cove filled with pink light, but my heart wasn't in it after that.

DECEMBER 27, 2006

Somehow in my sleep last night I was given nine years back. It was 1997 again, and I was flying across the Atlantic with Colleen and our children to take them to Ireland so they could walk through the village their great-grandmother left at the turn of the twentieth century to make her way to America.

Jack sat beside me on that flight. He was still wetting his bed then, and sometime during the night he'd awakened to discover that he had soaked his seat on the 747. He woke me, crying softly. I told him it was nothing to worry about. I opened the half-empty bottle of Chardonnay from dinner and poured a healthy splash onto the seat while his eyes widened. "The pilots will think somebody spilled their wine, that's all," I told him. He smiled at me, crawled into my lap, and fell peacefully back to sleep in my arms.

We are going to be crossing the ocean again together in a few weeks to play golf in Scotland at a place called Carnoustie, on the Championship Course, because to play that track in the dead of winter is the toughest challenge in all of golf. It is the Mount Everest of the game, and I want us to do something hard together—to try to give Jack something to believe in again now that he no longer believes in himself. Something that will mark the long arc of our lives in such a way that as I grow into an old man, whenever he comes to see me from wherever he has ventured in this world, I will ask him as he steps through the door, "Well, Jack, have you met anyone yet who ever played the Championship Course at Carnoustie in the dead of winter?" And he will always say, "Nobody but us, Daddy."

As I write this, it is seven below zero here in Maine. A balmy twenty-nine in Carnoustie, according to the Internet. Ever since I bought the plane tickets, I've been afraid Jack was going to tell me that he was too busy to make the trip.

JANUARY 14, 2007

KLM flight 1279 out of Boston's Logan Airport. Five hours ago we took off from a sleeted runway for Amsterdam, where we will catch a flight to Edinburgh tomorrow morning. Everyone is asleep around me, including Jack, and I am thinking about history. I consider reading, but I'd rather think. When was the last time I'd read to Jack? It must have been *Curious George*. How many years ago? Twelve, fourteen? In a small room with a painted red floor, under the eaves in a beach house we were renting, I read to him in the room where I put him to bed with his Batman figures. I always stopped in the threshold each morning to watch him sleep, on my way back from the kitchen with my first cup of coffee at 4:00. On one of those mornings while he was sleeping, I strung fishing line across the ceiling from the corners of the room, then glued a paper clip to Batman's arm so he was hanging in the air above Jack when he awoke.

His eyes are closed now as the plane sails toward the morning light of a new day. He has the hood of his sweatshirt pulled up and his iPod plugged into his ears. I can't see even a trace of the little boy I recall, and in his absence I wonder why I stopped reading to him at night, sending him off into his sleep with a story. I had once known his bedtime patterns so well. The way he rubbed his eyes to try to stay awake. Then the last deep breath he took just before he conked out, as if he were going underwater until morning. I had delighted in learning his routines. There was a stretch of time when he would awaken in the night and come looking for me, wobbling like a little drunk as he weaved his way down the hallway to my room, dragging his blue blanket behind him. There were nights when I let him climb into bed and sleep between Colleen and me. I guess those nights ended after his younger sister, Cara, arrived. He must have known then that his time had passed and that he was on his own. I never thought of this before, but now as I close my eyes, I can picture him at the side of my bed, his eyes pleading for the chance to climb in beside me. How could I have ever disappointed him when all he wanted was to be closer? How do we do this as parents, how do we pull away? I'd probably been standing on some principle that seemed important then: How can my son go on to conquer the world if he can't learn to sleep through a night in his own bed? Now that seems ridiculous. It is all just guesswork anyway, isn't it, being a parent?

And why wasn't I prescient enough to realize then that a time was coming when I would have given away all my earthly possessions to open my eyes in the night and find my son standing there beside me, wanting to be close?

And let me write this here so I can read it again someday to remind myself: if you get to live in this world and have the privilege of a little boy wanting nothing more than to be close to you, you have no right to ask for anything more ever again. Or, to put it a different way: if you have been loved by a girl who pours her desire upon you and then places one stunning baby after another in your arms, then you have shared the sacred time and been granted immortality.

JANUARY 15, 2007

The Edinburgh Airport . . . By the time I discovered that I was in the wrong line for the car I'd rented on the Internet, I had forgotten what I was waiting in line for.

The man behind the counter seemed to sympathize with Jack when he said he couldn't believe I'd neglected to write down the name of the rental company.

"Well, it says Auto Europe right here," I said, showing the man the printout.

"That's not the name of the rental agency," he remarked.

"Yeah," Jack chimed in, "that's just the company that booked it."

How does he know these things? I wondered miserably as we went from desk to desk inquiring if anyone had a car reserved under our last name, Snyder. Sometime during that aimless walk, I sent Jack to buy us something to drink so I could take the morning stomach pill I'd been taking for seven years that never failed to dilute the heartburn that was presently spreading through my chest. By the time he returned, I had found our place, and the woman working on my forms was asking me for the second time if I was sure I didn't want the additional insurance at £20 a day. I'd booked the car from America in U.S. dollars, $220 for the week. Twenty pounds insurance a day, with the pound equaling $2.22, would mean that the insurance would end up costing more than the car. It seemed like a racket to me.

"No insurance," I said again. Then, with what I intended to be humor, "The insurance companies in this world are making fools of all of us."

She raised her eyebrows at Jack with an expression that said, Not the wisest father for a lad to be stuck with, as she said, "Okay, then. If you have an accident, you'll be required to pay the full value of the automobile."

"I understand," I said. "We're just going to Carnoustie. It's not too far from here, is it?"

"Where's that?" she asked. And her colleague beside her had never heard of the place either.

Jack gave me an exasperated look.

"There's a famous golf course there," I said, "and you must have someone here who can tell us how to get there. And where's the rental car from here?"

"You'll have to take a bus," she said.

"A bus to the car?"

"That's right."

Just before a young man from the back room began giving us directions to Carnoustie, I realized that I had mistakenly swallowed not my morning stomach pill but the pill I had to take every night to put me to sleep. I'd consolidated them for the trip into one container.

"You take a bus from outside to lot number [*number what?*]. Then you'll go out the [*what?*] exit. Take the [*oh God . . .*] northbound to the [*are you kidding me?!*] motorway, which will take you to the [*Jesus, Mary, and Joseph*] across the [*we're screwed*] Bridge."

I was watching his lips move as he talked, but his words weren't reaching me. I turned to Jack. "Did you get all that?" I asked.

You know that feeling when someone gives you a photograph he's taken of you recently, maybe at a party, and you look at it and think, This is how I really appear to the world? It's the cold proof that each of us lacks the ability to see ourselves the way others see us. At the wheel of the little Fiat that Jack began calling "the Death Machine," I wanted to look cool, debonair, even a little defiant as I drove on the left side of the road for the first time in my life and used a stick shift for the first time in twenty years. But my last decade of life spent cruising suburbia in the living room of a minivan had emasculated me to the point where I could sing castrato in a musical about Mario Andretti.

And I had wanted this to be my big moment, my chance to lift the value of my stock in my son's eyes. Golf cap on backward, cigarette clenched between my teeth, hands pounding the steering wheel to the drumbeat of a blaring radio, cup of black coffee steaming beside me, power shifting through the corners. Instead, I was hunched over the wheel like Nanny before the state took her license away.

"At that last turn," Jack said somberly, whipping his head around from where he'd just surveyed the damage out our rear window, "you almost killed two people."

"I did not," I protested. But I knew it had been close. Blame it on a lost night's sleep, bad food, not enough food, too much food, nothing to drink, and the damned sleeping pill, whatever; I was not adapting to this new driving experience. "I need you to get into my golf bag," I said to him. "Find me a pill for my stomach."

It was funny and it wasn't funny. I could usher Jack through the Elysian fields of golf here in Scotland, but if I failed to deliver him back home safely into his mother's arms, all bets were off.

"I've got really bad heartburn," I said as he crawled over the seat for me.

"You should have put me down as a driver," he complained.

"Cost too much."

"I thought we weren't going to worry about money."

"I don't want to argue about it," I said. "I've got to pull off and get some coffee. My eyes are *closing*." This wasn't my finest moment.

The sign said there were services up ahead, three miles. I had plenty of time to prepare for the turnoff, but when I entered the parking area outside the gas station, I kept getting beeped at. It was like something out of an old Peter Sellers movie. "You're going the *wrong way!*" Jack screamed at me.

That was it. I floored it and sped back out onto the highway, where driving like a madman was acceptable.

"Jesus," he mumbled.

"How could I have been going the wrong way?"

"Okay," I heard him say calmly. "From now on I'm going to shift for you so you stop trying to shift with the door handle."

I looked down at his hand on the shifter. "Now," I said as the engine ramped up. He shifted into fourth.

At each roundabout he turned in his seat and surveyed the oncoming traffic, until he started calling, "Not yet . . . Not yet . . . Not yet . . . *Now!*"—then I would goose it.

Soon I was enjoying myself, driving forty miles per hour over the speed limit like everyone else.

"Carnoustie," I said just above a whisper as we pulled in to town and made our way along High Street, passing the two-story stone flats joined together at the shoulders, the modest storefronts and pubs drowsing under a low black sky. It was 11:30 in the morning on January 15 and almost impossible to imagine that in July a hundred million golfers around the world would be tuned in to the British Open taking place here. Today the streets, blackened by rain, were empty. Windswept waves off the North Sea pounded the shore in a thunderous concussion. It was dark and desolate everywhere you looked. There was nothing—no bright splash of paint or color—to relieve this darkness and the feeling that we had wandered into an abandoned town or some ancient film set that no one had taken the time to disassemble and cart away. Even the open fields slanting away from the village center were pale and featureless, just as they must have been in the early eleventh century, when this land was part of the Kingdom of Alba and most of England had been overtaken by Danes who were attempting to conquer the rest of the country. Here in this dark, foreboding place they ran into formidable opposition when warriors from nearby territories led by Malcolm II, king of Scots, got into the fight. It was brutal, and rumor has it that the river that winds through the center of town and pours into the sea at the railway station was red with blood for three days. The name given to this place, Carnoustie, means resting place of heroes. It is also attributed to "Crow's Nestle" because of a plague of crows that once infested the area.

This morning there were no crows and no heroes in sight. I watched Jack scowling at the empty streets as we crossed the black river. You could see the hardness of people's lives in the stone cottages stained by age and weather. Nothing could be pretended in a place like this. It was what it was, and as the golf course first appeared to us, a treeless, windswept plain standing beside an angry, boiling sea, I fell in love with its unwelcoming style, its cold shoulder. It was just a barren stretch of ground with a few flags waving and giant craters filled with sand. Throw in some rotting corpses and you'd have a perfect battlefield.

"Look at this place," I said. "Isn't it spectacular? A true public relations nightmare. Can you imagine the suffering here? Can you picture the fat-cat businessman from Texas who arrives here with his big cigars and his cell phone and all the latest golf technology only to get the piss beaten out of him in such a forlorn outpost?"

It was just as I had imagined it and I was excited.

"Calm down," Jack said.

Maybe I took this the wrong way. "Nobody in this place ever heard of a 401(k)," I said. "I heard you and your buddies talking about them once when you were playing poker in our basement. You're not even out of school, for Christ's sake. There's a real barbarity to the cosseted life everybody in America desires so badly. You should run in the opposite direction of a 401(k)."

He just shook his head at me. "We're here to play golf. Golf? Plaid pants. Knickers. Country clubs. Lives of privilege. It's all the same. Golf is part of the world you're always ranting against."

Smart-ass, I said under my breath. "Hotel first, or the golf course?" I asked as I picked up speed.

"Golf course," he answered.

I turned and watched him taking it all in. "Sergio García just turned pro when he came to play in the Open here in 1999," I told him.

"I know," he said, still looking out his window. "He was thirty over par after the first two days. He left the course and cried in his mother's arms."

"You're going to beat him today," I said.

He nodded thoughtfully.

We pulled in to the parking lot, and when we stepped out of the Fiat, the wind nearly tore the doors off the car. The rain was just turning to sleet. Watching Jack pull his golf bag out of the back-seat, I offered the lines of dialogue that he and I used to say to each other from the *Band of Brothers* series: one paratrooper from the 101st speaking to his buddy, the morning of the invasion of Normandy, when weather was threatening to cancel the drop again. "I think it's clearing . . . Do you think it's clearing? . . . I think it's clearing."

I asked him if he remembered. "Yeah," he said, but he wasn't listening. He was striding into his zone. His expression had turned stoic as he traded his jeans and hooded sweatshirt for a layer of Under Armour, black slacks, a long-sleeved turtleneck, and his black rain gear. I had packed my blue suit, the one-piece long johns that zipped from ankle to neck, my standard bottom layer in the days when I still played goalie with him. The last time I wore the suit was three winters ago, when one of his slap shots had struck me in the throat and I'd blacked out on the ice and sworn off ever being a goalie again.

It took me a while to put on my layers. "You should have some of these gloves," I heard him yell to me over the wind.

"I'll be fine!" I yelled. I stood up, grabbed my clubs, and slipped into the shoulder straps of my bag. He was walking away by then, his game face on, his mind already focusing on what he'd come this far from home to achieve.

"Jack!" I hollered. "Come here a minute!"

When he was just a few feet from me, I began to deliver the speech I'd been rehearsing in my imagination for months. "Can you hear me!"

"Yeah!"

"Okay! I just wanted to tell you that iPods aren't real either!"

"iPods?"

"iPods aren't real!" I yelled again. "Just like 401(k)s! Neither are cell phones, laptops, the Internet, user names, passwords, or PIN numbers! CNN isn't *real*! This is real! The wind! Weather! The sea! This ground! Whenever you get lost in your life, remember that!"

His expression was priceless. "You're so predictable!" he yelled to me.

I bowed at the waist. "I take that as a compliment!" I yelled back.

I hadn't quite delivered the speech with the charisma I'd hoped for, no triumphant call to arms from a marbled arch; but still, I'd said pretty much what was on my mind. And with that, we proceeded to the starter's shed at the Championship Course to play some golf from the back tees.

We startled the woman inside the starter's shed. She told us that she hadn't expected to see any golfers today. The instant she opened the sliding glass window so she could hear me, rain soaked her face like a wave breaking over the bow of a boat.

"We just flew in from America," I yelled to her above the wind. "Just got off the plane!"

"You're on holiday then," she said, ducking her head out of the rain, which was coming down harder now from a low black sky. "Are you sure you want to go out in this?" You could hear a dull concus-

sion of waves pounding the beach in the distance and shells explod-
ing on an artillery range along the shore.

"Do we have the course to ourselves?"

"You do indeed."

I caught up to Jack. When I set down my golf bag, a gust of wind
knocked it over and blew it off the tee box. The wind and rain were
blowing sideways, left to right at about forty knots.

"You're up," Jack called to me as he put on his rain gloves.

In my eagerness I snap-hooked my drive and lost sight of the ball
as it peeled off hard left over some lime-green dunes in the direction
of the beach. I hit a second shot the same way, then managed to get
my third ball into play.

A moment later I watched Jack marching up the 1st fairway after
hitting his drive a mile straight through the wind and rain. His
shoulders were back, and there was confidence and purpose in his
stride.

"Look at us!" I yelled to him. "The whole place to ourselves! That's
why we had to come in the winter!"

As a last-minute precaution when we were heading out the door at
home, Colleen had suggested we pack the neck gaiters that the girls
used when they went snowboarding. All I could see of Jack's face
now was a narrow slit for his eyes and nose.

Unlike most of the world's golf courses, which are laid out with
parallel, out-and-back holes, Carnoustie plays all over the map.
When we reached the tee for the 337-yard par-4 number 3, all the
wind off the sea was immediately behind us. "If the green is out there
somewhere straight, that ball is on it," Jack said after he put all he
had into his drive.

"You must always strike the ball with a downward glancing blow,"
I said as I prepared to take my turn, mimicking the words of Bobby
Jones from an old instructional movie I'd watched a dozen times on
the Golf Channel.

"You're not doing it," Jack said. "You're still sweeping the ball up in
the air. That's why they're just blowing off the course."

"I know," I said.

"You can't feel yourself coming *up* at impact?"

"Yeah, I can."

"You have to tell yourself to swing *down* and *through* the ball," he went on. "Not *up* at the bottom of the swing."

I thanked him as I looked around and thought, I could sleep here. Just crawl behind the gorse bushes to block the wind, lay my head down, and sleep here for about twelve hours.

Then a train went by just across the fairway with the familiar blue and yellow markings of British Rail. "Passenger train," I called out. "British Rail. The same train your mother and I took to Scotland when we eloped. We ended up in a little village called Pitlochry. That's where we called home and told Nanny and Papa the news."

"Let's get going," he said. "No more talking!"

His ball had traveled better than 337 yards from the tee and had rolled off the back of the green. He missed the putt from there for an eagle and then the birdie. "Good par," I told him.

He snapped back at me. "When you hit a drive like that and only end up with par, it's never good. If I'm going to get anywhere in this game, I have to make birdies."

"Hey, you got to Scotland," I said. I was feeling a little disoriented from the cold. I reached into my pocket for the list of things I planned to talk with Jack about. The wind whipped the slip of paper out of my hand and blew it into the dark sky.

I had lost three balls and was ten strokes over par by the time we reached the 6th tee. Ahead of us lay the famous hole named Hogan's Alley. The legendary golfer only ever competed in one British Open Championship, and that was here at Carnoustie in 1953. Ben Hogan had heard so much about how difficult the course was that he arrived two weeks early and played practice rounds every day. I started reading the description of the hole to Jack. "Out of bounds all the way down the left side. Bunkers in the middle and rough on the right." Then the little course guide blew away too.

"How far are those bunkers?" he asked as he walked up to his ball and glanced down the narrow fairway one last time.

"Maybe three hundred yards," I said.

"You had the book," he said.

"It blew away, Jack."

He shook his head at me. "I'm going over them," he said.

He did. Even into the teeth of the gale, he hit his drive far enough to fly over all the sand traps and land on safe ground.

"Not far, but straight," I said after I'd hit my drive. I was hoping he would say something encouraging, but he was already walking out ahead of me.

I ran to catch up with him.

"Your hands are blue," he said when we were nearing my ball, which had dropped seventy or eighty yards short of his and run off the fairway into the weeds down the right side.

Down and through the ball, I said to myself as I planted my feet. *Swing down and through*, I told myself again as I took one practice swing.

"You lifted up again," he said after I sprayed it to the right. "If this was summer and the rough was grown, you would have just lost your fourth ball of the day. Did you bring enough balls to last a week?"

"Why don't you pull for me instead of against me," I said.

"I'm just telling you what you're doing wrong," he said.

Another train went by. On the Night Rider from London, twenty-two years ago, his mother and I had chosen to sleep under a table because we could be closer to each other on the floor than in our seats.

I followed Jack down the fairway after finding my ball and hitting two more decent seven-irons to the edge of the green. He stuck a five-iron to five feet and captured an easy birdie. A moment later I made my first par of the day. "Maybe we could sit out of the wind for a while," I said.

"Why do you want to do that?" he asked as he began walking to the next tee.

"So we can talk," I called to him.

"I didn't come here to talk," he said. "I already told you. I came to play golf."

I watched him walking away, his black rain jacket and pants snapping in the wind. Fair enough, I thought.

I named it Hysterical golf. House of Horrors golf. The wind howling in our ears and blowing us back half a step for every step forward. Hands blue. Feet numb. Our yardage book blown away into the sea and with it the only map we had of the course, so we were blind on almost every shot. Driver cover blown away into the thistle. Balls blown off the wooden tees. And me having to search for my ball every other shot and losing the feeling in my hands. It went on like that to the 18th hole, the famous home hole, a 444-yard par-4 with the Barry Burn winding through a narrow fairway bordered by horrible thistle bushes running down both sides, where you could spend the rest of your life searching for your ball and never find it.

As we climbed up to the tee, a man and a woman walking a black dog appeared in the rain, the first people we had seen in hours. "Teddy would love it here," Jack said, referring to one of our golden retrievers who had been born in our living room four years earlier with eight brothers and sisters. Having a litter of pups was the fulfillment of a promise I'd made years earlier to Jack's sister Cara. My idea all along was that we would sell all the pups, but we kept Teddy.

"When you leave home, Teddy's going to have a broken heart," I said as we both watched the black dog chasing seagulls.

"Yeah," Jack said, nodding.

"The day you leave, he's going to start spending the rest of his life waiting for you to come back."

Jack nodded and teed up his ball. I watched the couple stop and turn toward us. It was another amazing drive, straight down the middle of the fairway and so far I couldn't quite believe it.

"I think that cleared all three of the farthest bunkers," I said.

"I'm probably in the last one," he said.

"I think it's over," I said.

The wind carried my ball a long way as well, and straight for once. "Remember me teaching you to curse in wind like this?" I said as we walked on. "Sailing in our little boat?"

"I remember," he said.

"Each time a wave soaked us."

"Son of a bitch," he said.

Halfway up the fairway I got such a violent cramp in my right leg that I had to stop for a few minutes. We lay against a bunker blocking the wind. I apologized and lit a cigarette. "Par this last hole and I'll shoot 77," Jack said as he went over our scorecard.

"Amazing in these conditions, and from the championship tees."

He didn't say anything.

I unzipped a pocket on my golf bag and took out my father's army diary from boot camp that I'd found in his closet the last time I saw him almost two years earlier. I had decided at the last minute to bring it with me on this trip. I opened it and read aloud:

Thursday December 7, 1944. The Army dentist pulled all my lower teeth yesterday, and all my uppers this morning. Miserable. Then two hours on the rifle range in the rain. Nothing good to write about this day. Glad it's over.

"What's that?" Jack asked.

"My father's diary that he kept in the army," I said. "I found it when I was in Pennsylvania a few years ago."

"Why'd you bring it here?"

"I don't know," I said. "Something told me to bring it with us."

We were up and walking again when he asked, "Why'd he have to have all his teeth pulled?"

"He grew up during the Great Depression, and even after it was over for America, his family was still poor. They didn't have any running water. All his teeth were rotted."

I hit a low six-iron that flew the river in front of the green and rolled to a stop near the flag. "Best shot I've hit all day," I exclaimed.

Jack's tee shot had landed only eighty yards from the green. From there he hit a soft wedge, and his ball fell out of the dark sky right next to mine.

"Better," Jack said to himself.

"Two putts for birdies on the final hole," I said.

We marched the rest of the way to the green. Jack made his birdie putt; I missed mine. Back in the car I looked at my face in the rear-view mirror and said: "Ladies and gentlemen of the jury, behold the face of a 107-year-old golfer accused of swinging like an old woman."

I turned to Jack. "There are things about growing old that no one tells you. For example, right here on the rims of my ears I started growing fur about a year ago. If that happens to you, don't shave it off like I did. Now I've got little mustaches growing on both ears."

I saw him smile at this. I can still make him smile, I thought.

"How old was he when he was in the army?" he asked.

"My father?"

"Yeah."

"Your age," I said. "He was exactly your age when he was writing in that diary." I wondered if that fact was more startling to Jack than to me. "He and his buddies graduated from high school and went right into the army. They'd been waiting to get in since Pearl Harbor, three years earlier. They were being trained for the invasion of Japan."

He began to untie his golf shoes, and I started the car.

In the center of town we had to stop for a train to pass. "You played well, given the conditions," I said.

"I putted like an idiot," he said. "But can you believe we had Carnoustie all to ourselves?"

It thrilled me to hear him say this. "Day of days," I replied.

"Day of days," he said.

JANUARY 16, 2007

Drink enough pints of Guinness on an empty stomach after twenty-four hours without sleep and you can banish even the darkest thought, even the small pain I had felt at the end of our first day when Jack fell asleep without thanking me. I guess I had imagined that each day in Scotland would be a grand victory march along the seaside fairways, serenaded by deep, thoughtful conversations and marked by stunning golf shots that I would remember until the last days of my life. Jack had provided several brilliant shots, but our walk in the deafening gale winds and freezing rain resembled more a retreat from Leningrad than any kind of victory march.

So I drowned my sorrows in a couple of pints. Then, upstairs in our room, I stood at the tall window listening to the wind and rain. "I think it's clearing . . . Do you think it's clearing? . . . I think it's clearing," I said.

Jack crawled under his down comforter without brushing his teeth.

I lay down on my bed across from him and took out my father's diary.

"I may join the Marines," Jack said.

I tried to conceal the fear that settled in my chest and vocal cords. "I didn't know you were considering the military. You'd go to Iraq."

"I know," he said. "But if we're really at war. I mean, if this is a real war we're in, and it matters, then I'd like to do my part."

"War instead of college," I said. I told him that I'd had a lot of friends from high school, a lot of the boys I'd played football with for four years, who went to Vietnam instead of college. When they came back, some of them weren't the same. "I think you have to be careful about fighting in a war where you have to kill a lot of innocent civilians in order to get the enemy. Everyone says we have to fight the terrorists over there so we don't end up fighting them over here. But I think maybe it would be better to fight them over here, where, at least, our soldiers could tell them apart from the innocents. I knew this one boy who got drafted to Vietnam. He was a math geek, the shiest person I ever knew. If there was one person on this earth who was distinctly *not* a soldier, it was this poor kid. He wore Coke-bottle glasses, and he came to school each day with a handkerchief pinned to his shirt pocket. And he got drafted right out of MIT. When he came home from Vietnam, all he could do was live at home and spend his days marching the perimeter of his parents' yard. He spent every day just marching along the edge of their property."

After a moment Jack said, "You didn't go."

"No. I got a deferment to play football and baseball on a college scholarship while a few hundred boys a week were dying in Vietnam. Not to mention the thousands of innocent Vietnamese."

"But what if you'd been drafted, would you have gone or run away?"

"I would have been too scared to run away. Scared of what people would think of me," I said.

This made me think about my father, so far from this place, cared for by strangers in the assisted-living facility where I'd moved him three years earlier. I had visited him there only once since then. I wrote to him two or three times a year and gave him the rundown about each of my children. He couldn't see well enough to write letters, and the only time he went out was when my brother, who lived an hour away, picked him up and took him somewhere.

I had turned eighteen in college my first semester, and because my father still claimed me as a dependent, I had to go to his hometown in Pennsylvania to register for the draft. I rode a bus from Waterville, Maine, to Philadelphia, where he picked me up and drove me to the selective service office. I was pissed off about everything by then. Out in the parking lot we got into a fight. I said something about America not being a country worth fighting for. A rage rose in him that I had never seen before. "I had friends who died for this country!" he yelled at me. "Yeah," I said sarcastically, "they died for nothing." He tried to hit me across the face, and I blocked his hand and swung back.

I watched him kneel down to pick up the pieces of his glasses. Then I couldn't watch, and I couldn't help him. I turned and walked away, and I knew then that I had ruined our chance of ever being close.

Tonight I wished that I had been wrong about that. I wished we had found a way back from there.

Before I dropped off, I listened to Jack fall asleep the way he had from the time he was ten months old—one big yawn, then one long sigh, then out cold. I sat up and looked at his face in the dim light, and for an instant I could see him when he was little, in the days when Colleen was falling in love with him. I used to catch her just gazing at him. Tonight I wanted so badly to have him back as a little boy. Just for twenty-four hours, one day, then I'd let him return to being who he had become.

I got up and drew the covers over him. His feet hung over the end of the bed by four inches.

When he began snoring and I knew he was conked out for good, it was safe for me to open the small pocket on the right side of my golf bag, to take out the ball I'd brought to Scotland secretly. Back in October, when he was preparing to play his State Championship Golf Match in Maine, I surprised him by giving him a special golf ball I had found in Canada at the Algonquin, searching the woods along the fairways where he and I once played eighty-four rounds together one summer and where the young boys working there taught him the game of golf. It was a Pro V1, Jack's ball of choice, with the Algonquin logo on it. Jack had posted the second-lowest round in the state the week before for the qualifying match, but then his game fell apart in the State Championship. At the end of that day he gave me the ball back. I put it on the mantel above our fireplace in the living room, where it stayed. But as I was packing my golf bag for Scotland,

I put it in the side pocket with the idea that once we were in Carnoustie, I would tee it up for him to drive into the North Sea, putting his lost high school championship behind him once and for all.

Now the pocket was empty. First I just felt around with my hand, but then I looked into the black lining with disbelief. It was one of those moments when you think maybe you're slipping. I knew I had put the ball in this pocket. I checked again, and then the other pockets, from which I took out sixteen balls and held each of them to the light, hoping to see the Algonquin name. Nothing. I sat on the floor of our room with the entire contents of my golf bag spread out before me. How could I have screwed this up? In the hysterics of our round today, deprived of sleep and food and water and dazed by the weather, I must have simply reached into the pocket by accident and lost Jack's ball.

I looked over at him, oblivious to all this. I won't tell him, I said to myself. He'll never know the difference. I lay down in bed, listening to the wind. The smell of the coal fire burning downstairs carried me back twenty years to Ireland, to the whitewashed cottage off the gravel road in Rathdrum, county Wicklow. It was there where I learned how to build a proper coal fire in the hearth that would keep the babies warm through the night. If I did it right, there would still be enough coals left when I got up at 4:00 in the morning to get the fire roaring again. I think for the rest of my life I will remember the satisfaction I felt standing on the stairs as the heated air rushed past me, up to the bedroom, where we all slept together, knowing that I had created the heat that kept my family warm. We had no car then, and every two days I walked five miles into town with the babies' dirty laundry in a pack on my back, and then back from town with their laundry clean and neatly folded. Even in the rain I loved this journey. All our needs then were elemental, and I could meet them. Our life was thoughtful, unhurried. We had no car, no car insurance, no health insurance, no cell phones or credit cards, no telephones of any kind, no computers, no lawn mower or dishwasher or television or video recorder, no coffeemaker or gas grill or microwave, no house or homeowners' insurance. Our life was no more complicated than keeping the fire going. I remember dropping down on my knees at the hearth each morning in the darkness and blowing on the coals until they burst into flames. Now I feel like I am doing the same thing with my son, trying to ignite the old closeness that he and I had shared.

JANUARY 17, 2007

Out in front of me, a gold morning light poured over the golf course. It looked as if it was going to be a good winter day for golf. I began to breathe easier, standing there. What appeals to me most about these Scottish golf courses by the sea is that you cannot see the impression of man upon them. They look as if they have been created by nature and time. I love how you can see the whole course in a single glance. There are no trees to seclude one hole from another, and so the solitary sport seems less solitary. You can look out in any direction and see other golfers, comrades-in-arms, fighting the same battle. And there are the colors. The impossible green of the fairways set against the golden-brown fescue of the rough and the darker green gorse bushes until they burst into a riotous yellow, and all of that set against the blue sea at the border. I also love the fact that nature is in charge: the rough grows according to the weather patterns. It is a reflection of the elements. Man takes the land and builds the course, then walks away and gives the golf course back to nature.

It was a perfect morning that even the Englishman sharing the dining room with us for breakfast could not ruin, though he tried his best. He was a lanky, garrulous fellow from Manchester who had fought in the first Gulf War as a sniper, and he told us that America had opened a Pandora's box in Iraq and that it was only a matter of time before the whole Middle East was in flames and the United States was drafting its citizens into the army. Jack was bleary-eyed, eating his Frosted Flakes, while the man proclaimed, as he spread his toast with marmalade, that people he knew inside the Pentagon were already making plans to initiate the draft. He was still talking when he walked across the room to get more coffee.

I got Jack's attention. "Let's get the hell out of here," I said.

I yanked my first drive out of bounds left, just as I had the day before. It was a combination of the narrow fairway, the flag on the green so far off in the distance that you could glimpse only the top of it, and a moonscape of mounds and bunkers in the middle distance that proved too intimidating.

I hit my drive out of play again on the 2nd hole but managed to reach the green with my fourth shot. Jack was just off the back of the green in light rough after a long drive and a blind eight-iron. I watched him take a wedge from his bag and then hit a shot much too hard that rolled thirty feet past the hole. This was the same shot he had missed four times in the State Championship almost exactly the same way, by putting too much strength behind it. "Fuck," he said as he dropped his shoulders in defeat. It is eating at him, I thought. The memory of that day in October is still hurting him.

"My uncle Page was the first person I ever heard say *'fuck,'*" I said.

"Who's Uncle Page?"

I looked up at him, a little stunned by his question.

"What?" he asked.

"Nothing," I said. "It's just that I can't believe I never took you to meet my uncle Page."

He didn't seem to think this was worth talking about and began walking. I watched him for a moment, then called to him to wait. We walked side by side while I told him how Uncle Page had inspired me as a boy. He'd come home from World War II, married my father's older sister, Jean, and settled into a tiny ranch house with an open field in back where he built a baseball diamond for the neighborhood kids. He put up a backstop behind home plate and mowed base paths so that it was the closest thing to a real ball field I'd ever seen. I loved being there so much that when I wasn't there, I was dreaming about getting back. Because he worked the night shift, he was free to spend his days watching us play baseball, sitting in a rusted lawn chair behind the backstop, drinking cold beer and smoking.

"He was one of those men who little boys love to be around," I explained. "He was always up for anything. He had one of the first television sets I ever saw, and I remember the day he called me into the living room to see something he was watching on TV. My father was there with him. It was a news bulletin of some kind, with black-and-white images of Russian tanks rolling through Budapest, Hungary. This was 1956. I had just turned six years old. There was a revolution in Hungary that had begun with students demanding an end to Soviet occupation of their country. The Soviet army crushed them right in front of our eyes. The tanks were rolling over the people in the streets. Uncle Page said to my father, 'What the fuck are we doing here, Dick? We should be over there helping those poor bastards.'"

That was my uncle Page.

At the turn after the 9th hole Jack had a 38 on his card, and I was at 43. We played the tenth and then I called to him, "Let's get a cup of coffee." He set his bag down without saying anything, and I followed him to the little cottage.

Two men, shivering with cold, were running the place. I ordered coffee for Jack and me. "You must be the Yanks who were out here yesterday in that misery. Only two people on the course, I heard," one man said.

"That's us," I said.

"How'd you play, lad?" the second man asked Jack.

"Not bad," Jack said.

"He was five over par from the back tees," I told them.

Both men looked at me, then at each other, then at Jack. "How old are you?" one asked him.

"Eighteen," Jack answered.

"I'll tell you what," the man said. "You make it into the Open someday here, and I'll caddie for you."

Jack thanked him. "That will be my father's job," he said. "But thanks anyway."

Both men held out their hands for Jack to shake, and when he stepped toward them, everything seemed to suddenly shift into slow motion so that I was watching it like frames of a movie. *It's going to come true . . . someday I'm going to be caddying for my son on a pro tour, because he is good enough at this game to play anywhere, against anyone, in any conditions.*

Those words rang with certainty inside my head.

I was standing on the 11th tee when Jack came lumbering toward me. "Where did Uncle Page fight?" he asked.

"All over Italy," I said.

"How old was he?"

"Just about your age, I guess."

"And your father? Where did he end up?"

"He was on a troopship headed for the invasion of Japan when the atomic bombs were dropped on Hiroshima and Nagasaki. That was the end of the war."

He thought about something for a minute, then said, "I've only seen your father four or five times in my life."

I told him that I was sorry for that. I watched him turn and gaze up the fairway. "So was it like the Springsteen song between you and your old man? A darkness in the house that got the best of you?"

Sometimes words have a weight to them that we can feel across our skin. "I guess so," I replied. "It's a long story."

I was filled with sadness the rest of the round. As we walked side by side to number 16, Barry Burn, which is called the hardest par-3 in all of golf, I said, "Right here, in two British Open appearances, the great Tom Watson never made par. Eight rounds and he never parred this hole."

Jack hit a high-arcing six-iron that traveled majestically across the sky, carrying the three bunkers on the right side and drawing left to fall just above the pin.

"Great shot," I told him. "I do feel bad that you never got to know my father. Forgetting our differences, I should have made sure you knew him."

While we walked to the green, I thought about my dad. Jack knew the story. My old man was just back from the war, in love with an eighteen-year-old girl named Peggy. He was her first love, and she was his. They had been married nine months when she gave birth to me and my twin brother, then died two weeks later. For the next month my father slept on her grave, under his army blanket. His buddies would pick him up each morning and take him to the coffee shop and try to get him to talk. I never knew any of this until I was almost fifty years old and my father was struck down by a brain tumor. The real story of my mother had been kept hidden from me and my brother so we wouldn't have to go through our lives knowing we had killed his bride. I had written a book about this some years earlier, but it hadn't really pulled us any closer.

While we walked, I told Jack that I had never really known him. "He used to sit inside his Chevy and smoke. I guess that was the only place he could get away from us."

Jack didn't say anything. By now he was getting a read on his putt. I stood behind him. "What do you see?" I asked him.

"Maybe a cup out to the left," he said.

"I see it a cup to the right," I said.

"Left," he said.

He rolled the putt. I was right. He made a tap-in par, and we moved on.

We were making our way up the 17th fairway after I hit another lousy drive. I told him that if he did decide to go into the military, he might want to join an elite unit like the 101st paratroopers on *Band of Brothers.* "Maybe in one of the special units, you have the best people fighting beside you."

"If I go to war," he said as he set his clubs down alongside his ball, "I'm going to be like Speirs in *Band of Brothers.* I'm going to tell myself I'm already dead. Nothing to lose, you know?"

A flock of geese flew overhead, so low in the sky that you could hear their wings creaking like rusty hinges. He hit a seven-iron right, up high into the wind, which he thought would steer the ball back to the left. It didn't and he landed in a deep pothole bunker. When we reached his ball, we saw that it was right up against the face of the bunker with no chance for a shot. I watched him think over his options. Then he climbed down into the bunker with his pitching wedge and addressed the ball as if he were left-handed, turning his club backward in his grip. He struck the ball with the toe, and it flew up out of the bunker, leaving him twenty feet from the hole. From there he ran the ball into the cup to save par.

"Just a routine par," I said to him. Then I apologized for gabbing so much. "You'll have to forgive me," I said. "I'm just worried that this might be the last chance you and I are ever going to have to really talk about things."

He nodded.

"I know what my uncle Page would say if he was here," I said. "He'd tell us both that we should laugh more."

When we reached the car, I told him he was lucky. "You're way ahead of where I was when I was your age."

"No I'm not," he said. "If I'd won the State Championship, things might be different. I don't have any colleges coming after me. Nobody knows who I am."

"You just played the toughest golf course in the world, under brutal conditions," I said. "Five over par yesterday. Two over today. You've got a gift, Jack, like Roy in *The Natural.* You just need to take some time to develop it, to see how good you can become."

While we drove back to the hotel, I decided it would be best to tell him about the Algonquin golf ball. "I can't believe I lost it," I said. "I'm sorry."

I awaited a reaction, and Jack shrugged. "I don't really care," he said.

That night I lay in bed reading to him from my father's army journal. When I finished, he said, "We were going to walk this course at night, weren't we?"

My first thought was that if he was going to insist on going back out into the cold right now, when all I wanted to do was curl up like a dog, he was going to have to carry me. Across the room the window was streaked with rain. Outside the dark trees were bending low again in the gale off the North Sea.

He didn't carry me, but he took hold of my arm above the elbow and steered me through the darkness, because I kept wandering off in the wrong direction and he was afraid I would drop into the river. He was using the light from the movie camera to find the way. The wind was ripping across the dark sky and it was raining on us, but out over the bay there were stars. You could see the Little Dipper.

As we started walking back through the storm, I felt his hand on my arm again. That's when I told him what I had imagined back in Maine, that for the rest of my life, whenever he came to see me from wherever he had ventured in the world, the first thing I was always going to ask him when he walked through the door was if he had met anyone who ever played the Championship Course at Carnoustie in the dead of winter from the back tees. "And you'll always say, 'No, just us.'"

In the car when I turned on the radio, Neil Young's song was playing. "Old man take a look at my life . . . ," which seemed perfect for the moment.

JANUARY 18, 2007

We drove to St. Andrews, about an hour away, early this morning. Somewhere before the Tay Bridge, Jack took out my father's army diary and began reading to me by the light of the glove compartment.

"Listen to this part," he said:

> Wednesday November 29, 1944. Was today inducted into the U.S. Army at Philadelphia, 32nd and Lancaster. Left 30th street station Philadelphia at 5 p.m., and arrived New Cumberland Induction Center about 7:30 p.m. Assigned to barracks 315, Area 3, Roster 2958. Went to bed about 9 p.m. following a few instructions about camp and army in general. Raining hard as nails all day.

He turned through the yellowed pages.

> December 15. Arose at 6 a.m. Formed platoons and started to drill. Were interviewed and told I'm in the infantry and can't get out. 17 weeks of basic training and then across. A bit sad, but finally got over it. Eye exam. Chow and evening was good. Got twelve letters and two packages. Feel swell!

"Feel swell, exclamation point," Jack said.

"Can you keep reading?" I asked him.

"Sure," he said.

I listened as this picture of my father at Jack's age formed in my imagination. It was someone I had never known, and with each sentence Jack read to me, I felt something falling away, something that had drawn my father and me apart.

This morning when we pulled in to the parking lot behind the Rusacks Hotel in St. Andrews, I watched Jack as he climbed out of the car, walked across the lane, and stood looking out at the Old Course. It was brilliant green even in the middle of winter. Its fairways rolling like swells at sea. The flag on the 18th green blowing stiff in the wind.

Jack stood there a long time with all the history of the place running through his mind, mixing with all his personal dreams for the game. A pilgrim.

I walked up to him. "What do you think?" I asked.

"Let's play," he said.

We threw our things into room 220 at the Rusacks, then headed to the starter's shed. I recognized the young man working at the counter and hoped he would remember me from four years earlier, when I first came here and lived in this hotel that winter writing my novel, but he didn't.

The wind was howling, and the rain was coming sideways into our faces, a mirror image of our first round at Carnoustie.

No one else was playing. We had the Old Course to ourselves.

"It doesn't get much better than that," I said to Jack.

We put on our neck gaiters and walked to the 1st tee. As Jack stood up to his ball, I looked into the broad windows of the Royal and Ancient Golf Club, where the proper gents were gathering for their lunch. I was sure at least a few of them were watching when Jack hit his first drive. It was 313 yards to the Swilcan Burn at the edge of the 1st green, too close for him to use a driver in normal conditions. But with the wind coming straight at us at thirty knots or better, he swung away freely and hit a perfect shot that cut straight through the wind. I pulled my drive left and had to hit a full four-iron to the green, though I was only a hundred yards away. Jack two-putted to make his par, and I took a bogey 5.

Jack parred the first three holes with ease, and though it was quite a trick to drink my coffee, run the movie camera, piss in the bushes, light my cigarettes in the gale, and play golf, I was having the time of my life watching my son eat up the course.

I was thrilled when one of the groundskeepers tracked us down on the 4th hole. J.J. had seen my name on the starting sheet, and he remembered me. We shook hands. "Did you finish your book?" he asked me.

"I did. And I brought a copy for you boys," I told him.

"I'm delighted," he said.

I took a picture of him shaking Jack's hand, and then he helped me light my cigarette in the wind after I kept failing. "It takes a knack in this," he said.

We laughed as he recalled how I had played the course for a week in bedroom slippers because I'd been so eager to get out the day I arrived, I'd forgotten to change out of the thick wool socks I wore on the plane over. By the time I finished the last hole, I had bloody blisters on both heels.

"You're remembered here for that," he told me.

"To be remembered," I said happily.

On we went, having the time of our lives. With the wind in our faces on the way out, the best I could do was make bogeys and double bogeys, but Jack was attacking each hole, turning golf into an easy game by hitting nothing but fairways and greens. Because the novel I'd written here had required me to know the ground well, Jack was counting on me to remember the locations of the 113 pothole bunkers, many of which were so deep and treacherous you could ruin your score for a round if you landed in them. It didn't really matter where the bunkers were; Jack just swung as hard as he could, flying over them and reaching safe landing areas that most golfers were never able to reach even on a calm day. It was amazing to watch. On number 4, Ginger Beer, the 419-yard par-4, Jack chose the dangerous alley down the right side bordered by rough and bunkers, rather than play it safe to the left. When we reached his ball, it was sitting up on a mound as if we'd placed it there, only 120 yards from the green. In all that wind, I said to myself as I aimed the movie camera at him. He hit a knockdown nine-iron low through the wind as if he'd been playing these conditions all his life.

I couldn't make a par on the way out to save my life, but the way I was playing bore no resemblance to how I felt inside. Some men take their children to church hoping to point the way for them toward a light they might follow through the darkness of the world. I had brought my son here for the same reason.

Jack was two over par when we made the turn to the 10th tee. I was ten over. The rain had stopped, and we rested for a few minutes before we hit our tee shots. In the sky over the Eden Estuary, fighter planes from Leuchars Air Force Base climbed through the clouds. I told Jack the story of how the Germans had tried all through the war to bomb the base but it was so well camouflaged they could never find it. Finally, out of frustration, near the end of the war they bombed all the schools instead, killing many of the children in the town.

"Do you think it could really happen again?" he asked me. "Another big war, a world war?"

"I don't know, Jack," I said. "If there is, though, I think they should send all of my generation. The baby boomers. And I don't mean the guys who had to fight in Vietnam, but the rest of us who've had things pretty much our way all these years. Instead of gated retirement communities, we get boot camp."

"You notice how the people who start wars are never the ones who have to do the fighting," he said. "Someone makes a decision, and then the little guys get screwed. Guys like your father."

"I think he wanted to get in that war," I said.

"I don't mean the war," he said.

I turned and looked at him. "What then?"

"Hit your drive," he said. "We'll talk about it later."

Standing on the tee to number 12, Heathery In, a 316-yard par-4, I told him I was going to hit one shot for the highlight reel. "With all this wind behind us now, watch this drive." I nailed it right to the edge of the green, chipped it close, and made an easy birdie. That started a good run for me, and I finished with a back-nine 40 to post an 86, respectable under the conditions. Jack shot three over par, 75. Before we walked to the 18th green, I made him stand on the Swilcan Bridge for the movie camera, in the spot where Jack Nicklaus had stood two summers before, when he played his last Open.

The whole round I had been looking forward to a few beers in the Chariots pub, the point of origin for this journey, but the place was closed. Four years earlier, inside that pub late one winter afternoon after I stripped off all my wet clothes from a round on the Old Course, a tough old Scot said to me, "You should try Carnoustie on a day like this."

I asked Jack to pose beside the mural outside of the beloved Scottish runner Eric Liddell, who was portrayed so beautifully in the film *Chariots of Fire*. "Only if we eat in the next five minutes," he said.

He ate a mountain of sausages and mashed potatoes, an order of wings, a bowl of mushroom soup, and half a loaf of bread, before he finished my fries.

"I'm glad I only have a few more months of paying for your food," I told him.

In our room we found golf on television. The pros playing a big-money event in Abu Dhabi under a warm sun, on a perfectly mani-cured course. Feeling self-righteous after what we'd been through, we began yelling at them. "You call that wind! What kind of wimps are you?"

Jack was sleeping when I went out for a walk. The skies had cleared. The sun was shining brightly in the day's final hour of light, and I walked joyfully. At every turn there was something I had seen before when I was living here four years earlier, writing a new novel and having no idea that I would return to live this part of the dream with Jack. As I walked, I took in the shadows and the open places where that novel had taken shape in my imagination as if I had dreamed it in another life. I had missed these places, I knew that, but only now that I was back did I realize just how deeply I had longed to return. In a way, it felt as if my life had been suspended for the four years since I'd left here and only now had its progression and reason been restored.

Back in the room, I found sand in the empty tub from when Jack had climbed down into the Hill bunker off the 11th green. That was the bunker that got the better of the great Bobby Jones in 1921 when he took three hacks at his ball and, failing to get out, tore up his score-card and quit. Jack had dropped a ball in there in Jones's honor and knocked it out on the first try.

I was standing in the shower, thinking about this, when Jack opened the bathroom door.

"Where did you go?" he called to me.

"Just took a walk," I said.

"Maybe I won't leave home," he said flatly. "Maybe I'll just go to the University of Southern Maine. Play on their golf team."

I was trying to tell if he had already decided to do this or if he was just testing the water. "That would be the easiest thing," I said. "I think you should do the hardest thing."

I heard him walk out of the bathroom. I listened as the television went on. More of the golf from Abu Dhabi. I walked into the room, wrapped in a towel. "I've been riding the stupid exercise bike for ten years," I complained, "and I still have this pathetic potbelly."

He looked at me and then away.

"It won't be forever, Jack," I said to him. "You can just give it your best for a year—it's worth going for it."

"I know."

"What's wrong?"

"Nothing."

"It was a great day here, wasn't it? It was a great day for me."

"Yeah."

"My father and I never did anything like this."

He looked at me for a moment. "What if I never make it as a golfer?"

"What if you fail, you mean?"

"Yeah."

"Most people fail, Jack. Look at me. I wanted to write books that would make the world better in some way. Take a look at the world; it's gone to hell on my watch. You'll never fail as badly as I have. You just keep trying, that's all."

"Yeah, but some dreams die," he said. "You have to let some dreams die."

"Maybe," I said.

"I don't know what's harder," he said, "holding on to a dream or letting go."

An hour later we were lying on our beds heckling the professional golfers on TV again. "These pins are in very difficult locations today," the announcer said gravely.

"They should be!" Jack hollered.

We laughed about my former student who wanted to revolutionize professional golf by lining the fairways with wind turbines and Welsh longbowmen who would shoot arrows at the players to make the game more challenging and more dramatic for TV.

Just before we fell asleep, I heard a gust of wind rattle the windows across the room. I got up and looked out over the rooftops. A narrow band of moonlight lay along the shore. I watched some stars appear and disappear behind the drifting clouds.

"I think it's going to be cold out there tomorrow, Jack," I called to him. I wasn't sure he was still awake. Then I heard him roll over and face me in the darkness.

"You've blamed your dad all these years for not being there for you after your mom died," he said. "But if you read his army diary, you can tell he wasn't a strong enough person to be a real father after Peggy died. It wasn't his fault . . . People do the best they can. I just think it's too bad for the two of you that there wasn't any forgiveness."

This struck me as a remarkably thoughtful comment. "Well," I said, "you're right, Jack, I should have forgiven him, but there were a lot of things that happened—"

He cut me off. "That's not what I mean," he said. "I mean *you*. You should have asked him to forgive you, man. You killed his wife and ruined his life."

I have thought for many years that our lives come down to a collection of moments. After all our planning and trying, there are only a handful of moments that really matter. Some of these moments tell us what we might have been, others what we might still become. Standing there in the darkness, I was sure that this was one of those moments. In all the years I had examined it and dreamed it, I had never seen things between my father and me as clearly as my son had.

This morning I was raring to go. It was only twenty-four degrees Fahrenheit, and the wind was already strong and rising out of the west, but the bright sun lay in gold bands along the fairways when we walked to the 1st tee.

Jack hit one of his big drives toward the horizon beyond the 1st green, but rather than admire it, he turned his back disdainfully and walked to his bag. Something was wrong. He had barely spoken over his breakfast. I watched him a moment, trying to figure out what it was. He looked handsome in the new black jacket with the Carnoustie emblem that I had bought him.

I hit a miserable drive on number 4. "Hit another one," Jack said.

I had been asking him for lessons for at least five years, and his response was always the same: "I can't tell you how I hit a golf ball; I just hit it." But now he was offering instruction, and I accepted it eagerly.

"The trouble is you're not releasing your hands at impact. Look, your clubhead is square like it should be, but you're coming *up* because you're not turning your hands over. Your right hand—there, you just did it again. The palm of your right hand is facing *up* when you swing through the ball. It should be *down*, turning over. Releasing. Try it again."

I hit a perfect drive. And then a perfect five-iron from the fairway. When I saw Jack smile, it made me think just how complicated our relationship was. The son wants to beat the old man, needs to beat him, and it's a thrill when it happens the first time. It sets off a chain reaction of things the old man is no longer better at than the son.

Golf, driving, using the remote control. It goes like that until the son has taken almost everything there is to win, and then he starts to get scared because there's his father unable to beat him at anything anymore and it hits him that a certain immunity has now been lifted from over his head. His old man has reached a dark turn in the road. And he's next.

If I was right about this, then Jack was angry at me for playing so poorly, for making the same mistakes again and again, for giving golf away to him without a fight.

So I began to fight hard. Fighting to release my hands. I softened my hands on the club, then took it back low just until my wrists had cocked before I started down and through the ball. When I raised my eyes, I saw the ball climbing and then falling from the sky. All right! I thought.

I fought to par number 8 with the wind mercifully behind us at last. Jack made a brilliant birdie after hitting an eight-iron to within four feet. "Well," I said, "I'm going to really have to light it up the rest of the way." Jack was already walking to the tee, a little too victoriously for my taste at that particular moment.

Which brought us to number 9, End, the short, 307-yard wide-open par-4 that I had birdied on our first time around. I took out my driver, swung easily, and caught a nice roll across some of the only open, flat ground on the course.

I found my ball in perfect position. Meanwhile, I watched Jack climb into the bushes and hack out his ball with a wasted stroke.

I ran a seven-iron the rest of the length of the fairway onto the green and made two putts for par to Jack's bogey.

That was the end of the front nine. With a double-bogey 7 and a quad 8, I knew my score was high. I added up 48 strokes to Jack's two-over-par 38. Slaughter. When you're losing like that, golf can be a hard, hard road of humiliation and despair. Or, occasionally, it can lift you up if you can just manage to hold on.

And I did. Though it was back into the wind, we both were on the green in two on the 10th hole after hitting safe drives to the right of the deep rough. My drive had come to rest eighty-five yards from the green, right at the edge of the malevolent Kruger pot bunker. It could just as easily have rolled down into it. But my luck had turned. Or I was turning it. I made par. Jack made birdie and was up by another stroke.

We both parred 11 and 12.

Number 13, Hole O'Cross (In), bears the stamp of the hideous Coffins bunkers down the left side of the fairway and then the Cat's Trap and Walkinshaw bunkers farther up the fairway. The best landing area is a narrow path straight over the Coffins.

We both hit fine tee shots, but I pulled my second shot left into trouble and took another bogey while Jack made par.

We both parred the long par-5 14 and the par-4 15, and drove our tee shots over the round-killing Principal's Nose bunkers on 16 and went on to make par there as well.

So we walked to the most difficult hole on the course, the 460-yard par-4 17th, Road Hole, where so many great golfers have met their demise across the years. To hit a great drive, you have to stand on the tee and hit a line that runs so close to the broad flank of the Old Course Hotel that if the drive is off to the right by four or five yards, you're going to go right through the windows. There's no place to hide. You have to go for it. If you play safely left, then you'll catch the rough down that side, and it will seem like forever to the green. Each time I played this hole four years earlier, I used to say to myself as I stood on the tee, the faint of heart need not apply.

I did the same today and hit a perfect drive. So did Jack, outdistancing me by eighty or ninety yards. I took out a four-iron for my second shot. I saw Jack up ahead of me waiting. Swing easy, I told myself. Down and through. Down and through.

It was another shot where I didn't feel the club strike the ball. Pure. Pure! I watched it climb in the sky, on a path straight for the pin. It landed short of the green and started rolling straight again. Then I lost sight of it in the little gully in front of the green.

I watched Jack face his Achilles' heel. The short wedge to a tight green. He swung effortlessly with a smooth turn of the hips, about as handsomely as anyone could hit a golf ball, but from where I was walking, I knew he had given it too much again. I saw his ball hit the green and bounce off the back out across the road.

From there he made a bogey 5, while I rolled a seven-iron straight up onto the green and right into the cup for a birdie. A birdie on the Road Hole.

On 18 we both hit straight, deep drives, though without the wind blowing hard to the left from over my right shoulder, I might have flirted with trouble down the right side. Jack hit another wedge with too much behind it and flew his ball past the pin to the back of the green. I left my nine-iron short and watched the ball lose its momentum and die in the Valley of Sin in front of the green. I waited for Jack to make his par. But he three-putted for only the second hole of the day to take a bogey 5. I was doing the math in my head by then, and I knew that if I saved par, I would beat him on the back nine 37 to 38.

With this in mind I putted out of the Valley of Sin with much too much force, and my ball rolled across the green, passing the pin on its way to stopping four feet in the fringe. It was a terrible shot. Just terrible, but I thought if I could tie my son on the back nine of the Old Course, that would still be something.

Jack stood on the green about to pull the pin. "Leave it in," I said to him as I walked to my ball. There were a few people with cameras, watching us now, the only two people left on the course again. I put my putter back in my bag, took out a seven-iron, and hit the ball right into the center of the cup. It made a marvelous sound as it rattled against the iron pin on its way down into the hole.

We shook hands. "You played the last five holes at one under par," Jack said generously.

"Thanks," I told him. It was the first time I'd beaten him at anything in so long I couldn't recall when it had last happened.

Back at the hotel I was settling in to watch soccer with Jack, when he announced that he was going out for a while. "Is everything all right?" I asked.

"I just want to take a walk," he said. "I have five months before I graduate."

I was certain that he was feeling what it was going to be like to leave everything that was familiar to him. I think he had a sense of what this would be like for him.

The minute he left the room, I started to miss him. I ran down the back stairs to the lobby and out the front door. I reached the sidewalk just in time to see him disappear around a corner way out ahead of me. Take all the times I'd stood at the window at home watching him drive away, feeling helpless, and worrying if he would make it back safely. And all the times I'd watched his sisters do the same thing. What I felt now was worse. It seemed as if everything I knew was wrong.

Lying in bed, waiting for Jack to return, I recalled the nightly "knee football" games we used to play before his bedtime when he was little. He was still wearing the pajamas with feet, and I could almost hear the little scuffing sound they made on the floors. If you get that in your life—a little boy in your arms laughing as you tackle him to the floor, and then begging you to do it again, and then pleading with you to lie beside him in his bed until he falls asleep—you don't have the right to ask for anything more. Even if you end up alone in the end, you've lived. You've really lived in this world, and you have no right to ask for more. But I had. I was always asking for more.

JANUARY 20, 2007

The final day of our trip, and it turned out that I had not lost Jack's high school ball at Carnoustie. It had slipped inside the lining of my golf bag. I took a butter knife from breakfast to bury the ball on our last round at the Old Course.

As we walked up the 9th fairway, I told Jack that before we left home, I had spent an afternoon reading my old journals, and I'd found something I had written about him when he was four years old. "It went like this," I said:

Tonight I had to scold you for the first time because you had punched Mommy in the nose. When I went into your room later you were curled up in your blankets. How are you, Jack? I asked you. I'm going to die, you said, No, you're going to live to be as old as Batman. As old as Bruce Wayne? Older. As old as the old man who takes care of him in the bat cave. What's his name, Daddy? Albert. Yeah. Albert. Because you're a great boy, Jackie, and it's just that sometimes the Joker gets inside you and he makes you do bad things. I punched Mommy. No, it was the Joker who punched Mommy. I'm still scared. Why? Because I don't have any money. Why do you need money? To buy you a present for your birthday. When is your birthday, Daddy? In the summer. Don't tell anybody what I'm going to get you, okay? Not even Mommy. What are you going to get me? Black undies like Batman wears. He wears black ones? Yep. And they're going to have a little button on them so when you push it a light will come on so you can see in case you have to get up in the night to go pee. How much money will I need, Daddy?

"I really said all that?" Jack asked.

"You did. You used to talk all the time, and I wanted to live forever to hear everything you ever had to say."

Standing on the 10th tee, I looked around. "Finding my way to this place," I said, "is something I'm always going to be thankful for. And now you know how to get here if you ever want to come back."

We chose a spot off the 14th tee box along the base of the ancient stone wall that runs between the Old Course and the Eden Course to bury the ball. We both wrote our names on it, and then I handed Jack the knife and turned on the movie camera. He cut out a square of sod. "The past is past now," I said to him. "You're going to go as far as you want to go in this great game. And with some luck, someday I am going to caddie for you on your first pro tour."

He nodded solemnly, and we shook hands on it.

We played our way in from there. Another good round for Jack, and he finished with a 75 to my 88. He wanted to get to a hotel at the airport in Edinburgh so we wouldn't have to face the drive in the morning and risk missing our flight home and his hockey game Monday night.

I didn't expect to ever return here and so, on the 18th green, I took one last look around to remember the ground while Jack waited for me to pick up my clubs. And then we started walking away together.

JANUARY 21, 2007

Flying home at forty thousand feet. Jack had a movie playing on the little screen attached to his seat, and I thought he was done talking to me. But after a couple of vodka tonics, he wanted to know what else I wrote about him in the journal that chronicled his boyhood.

"Let me think for a minute," I said. I had kept a journal for each of my children and I decided a long time ago that I was going to give the journals to them to take with them when they left home. "You were a great eater," I told him. "There was one morning when you were six months old. We were letting Mommy sleep in, and you and your sisters were in the kitchen, where I was feeding all of you pancakes. You kept eating them as fast as I put them down in front of you. When your mother came downstairs, I said, 'Look at your little boy wolfing down these pancakes.' She said, 'He doesn't eat solid food yet, Don. Nothing but breast milk.' 'Well,' I said, 'he sure loves pancakes.' There was no turning back after that."

His smile encouraged me to go on. "That winter when you were five years old and I was working construction, you waited at the door for me to come home each evening. You would take my carpenter's belt and say, 'I've got a knuckle sandwich with your name on it.'"

I laughed and closed my eyes, recalling how I had hurried home from work each day to see him. "You were a real character," I said. "I was teaching you to ride a bike when you were four. The safest place was the beach at low tide when the sand was packed hard. The day you finally figured it out, you just rode straight into the Atlantic Ocean."

"I remember that day," he said.

"We had a lot of good times," I said. "And look, I'm sorry about all my speeches on this trip. I really should be disqualified from talking so much. I'm going to try to stop making speeches as I grow old."

"Okay," he said. "I'll believe it when I see it."

He asked me what the highlight of the trip was for me.

"Finding your ball," I said. "And seeing you walking those fairways. What about you?"

"Getting the car back without an accident."

"Come on," I said, "I had it under control."

I listened to him laughing at this. I told him that it was good to hear him laugh; we hadn't had a lot of laughter between us in a long time. "Things slip away," I said. "It's no one's fault. They just do."

I asked him if he remembered our days in upstate New York when I was teaching at Colgate University and we would all go sledding down the big hill on campus.

"Not really," he said.

"I never thought those days would end. We spent all winter sledding. I used to love pulling you and your sisters up the hill. I was forty-one, forty-two maybe; I guess it made me feel strong and young, you know? And then one time you wouldn't let me pull you up the hill. You wanted to climb up yourself. You were all bundled up in your snowsuit and boots, so you could only take these tiny steps. It took you forever to get up the hill, and I kept trying to explain how much better it would be if you just let me pull you to the top because you could save all that time for going down. But you had made up your mind. And you just marched up like a little soldier. That was when I knew."

"Knew what?" he asked me.

"Knew that I wouldn't have you forever," I said. "It was that way with your sisters too. There was a moment with each of you when I realized the same thing. Part of falling in love with all of you when you were babies was believing that I would have you forever. And then there was a moment when it came clear to me that I wouldn't. I remember telling your mother how sad it made me feel. I said, 'He's starting off now, on his own.' She didn't understand. 'He's only four years old,' she said, 'we'll have him a lot more years.' Something like that. But I felt it. And it's gone so fast, I'll tell you that, Jack. So damned fast."

He didn't say anything more. I had my eyes closed, and I was dreaming back that sledding hill and him in his powder-blue snowsuit.

JUNE 18, 2007

Five months have passed since Carnoustie. A former student of mine from when I was teaching at Colgate for four years in the early 1990s, Jim White, had grown up in Toledo, Ohio, and he had opened a door for Jack to work for the summer at the fabled Inverness golf club, with the goal of trying to make the University of Toledo golf team in the fall as a walk-on.

Three months after we returned from Scotland, Jack flew to Jim's home in Columbus to begin a golf trip that few people ever get to take. They played the famous Scioto Country Club, then the world's greatest golf course, Pine Valley, then Jack Nicklaus's course at Muirfield Village, and then Inverness, where Nicklaus played his first U.S. Open when he was seventeen years old. The head pro there, David Graf, offered Jack a job for the summer working in the bag room.

Jim White grew up just a few miles from the course, and while they were in town, he set up a meeting for Jack with the golf coach at the University of Toledo.

"Day of Days," Jack wrote to me in an e-mail from there. The coach couldn't offer Jack a place on his Division I golf team, but he walked him around campus and told him if he was willing to play in some collegiate golf tournaments that summer and managed to hold his own against the Division I players, he would give him a shot.

"I'm going to do it, Daddy," Jack said to me. "This is my chance."

And so he applied to the University of Toledo, was accepted, and began making plans to leave home on June 14, three days after his graduation from high school. He spent the spring at the practice range, and in the evenings he and I would walk a few holes together at Prouts Neck, sneaking onto the course there again as we had when he was four years old with his puddle boots on the wrong feet.

It came down to last night—Jack's last night at home. We played five holes as the sun went down.

"Why do some people want more?" he asked me. "Why can't I just stay here?"

"This isn't about you wanting more, Jack," I told him. "It's about finding out what you want so that you don't have to wonder for the rest of your life. It's going to be the hardest thing you've ever done."

"It already is," he said.

I told him to remember two things when he played in his first tournaments in Ohio. "First, don't hold anything back. And second, you are a person who can make par from anywhere."

This morning before he awoke I slipped a letter into his golf bag and a scorecard from our first round at Carnoustie that I had laminated for good luck. In the letter I wrote what I had told him once before: "Just don't ever do anything that will break your mother's heart. It's simple. I believe in you, Jack."

We were at the airport at 5:30 a.m. waiting for his early flight to Ohio. In the next five days he is going to have to start his new job, move into a room he has rented in Toledo, sight unseen over the Internet, buy a used car, and drive to his first college tournament four hours from Toledo in upper Michigan. I told him that when he felt weak or scared, he should think about all the boys his age who were flying out of airports for the war.

I shook his hand and let him have a few minutes with his girlfriend to say good-bye. I could feel myself already waiting for him to return home.

JULY 23, 2007

I bought Jack new golf shoes for his graduation present, and when I got back home from the airport the morning he left, I hung his old pair in the garage, over the doorway to the living room. I soon made it my habit to reach up and touch them each time I passed through the threshold. I fell off the wagon for a stretch in early July, when I missed him so much I began wearing his shoes each day, though they were four sizes too big for me. And though I had promised myself not to visit our old stomping ground at the Prouts Neck golf course, from time to time I would weaken and go out there and search for balls in the woods as he and I had done so many times when he was little. I was really searching for him, but whenever I found a dozen good-as-new Pro Vis, I put them in an egg carton and mailed them out to Ohio.

I was wearing his shoes, looking for golf balls, when he called me on my cell one evening. He was driving home from his tournament in the car he had bought. "Are you okay?" I asked.

"I'm not going to make it, Daddy," he said. "I can't get my game going."

He had finished near last place, he told me. For the third time in as many weeks.

"It takes time, Jack," I said. "It's going to take some time."

I knew he must be wondering why he was putting himself through this disappointment when all he had to do was come home and have his old, comfortable life reinstated, everyone and everything waiting for him exactly as it had always been.

"How's work?" I asked.

"Work's fine."

"How far did you have to drive for this tournament?"

"Four hours. I left at three in the morning."

"Well, it's tough to play well when you don't get any sleep, Jack."

"Maybe," he said. "Have you spoken to your father?"

"I've been writing him letters," I said. "It's a start."

"Good. I've got another tournament next week. I'll call you."

I thanked him and told him to keep fighting as hard as he could.

JULY 29, 2007

Jack was sky-high when he called this afternoon just before 5:00. He finished another tournament, this time in seventh place in a field of sixty-seven college players.

"I could have won the damned thing if I hadn't putted like an idiot," he said.

I could hear the confidence in his voice as we talked. A few minutes after we said good-bye, he called again.

"Day of days, Daddy," he said. "The coach at the University of Toledo just called me. He saw the results of the tournament. He said, 'Congratulations, Jack. What size shirt do you wear? I want you on my team.'"

Tonight I wrote Jack a letter and told him what I had not dared to tell him in Scotland:

Most of us have a dream that our life will be exceptional in some way, Jack, that we will do something extraordinary, that we will mark our life with greatness. And if we fall short, then we find out that we are just like all the rest. But if we can accept this with grace, accept the ordinariness of our life without becoming bitter over our failure, then a certain dignity will attend everything we do. So, there would have been no harm in falling short if you had.

Colleen and I are planning to fly out to Ohio in August, the day he moves into his dormitory. She wants to meet him at the house where he's been living all summer so she can finally answer the one question she's been asking since he left home: "Where is he doing his laundry?"

AUGUST 22, 2007

It was a dark, depressing place that smelled as if old meat had been left under the wall-to-wall carpet. Cars sped past on a busy highway maybe ten yards away. Jack had done well to survive here, but he was packed and eager to move when we arrived. He looked lean and fit. Colleen rode with him in his car, and I followed them to the campus. It was 3:30. We had left home that morning at 5:30 for an 8:00 flight out of Portsmouth, New Hampshire, which took us to Columbus, where we rented a car and drove three hours to Toledo. I added up the distance between me and my son in real terms now for the first time. I could be here in eight hours, standing right beside him, if he needed me. I felt that I could live with that.

He was very busy, but we had a few dinners together, including a special one with Jim White and his father. Looking at them across the table, I was struck by the passage of time. Seventeen years earlier Jim had been my student at Colgate when Jack was just two years old. Ten years later, I had spoken at his wedding. Now he had two little children of his own, one of them a son who looked a lot like Jack had at the same age.

When Jack arrived, he looked handsome as he strode across the room in his golf shirt and pants. "How did you do today, Jack?" Jim asked him as he sat down.

"Came in first," he said.

Jim smiled at me and nodded.

The day before we left, Jack treated me to a round of golf at Inverness. It was late on Sunday afternoon, and with the weather threatening, we had the place to ourselves. He surprised Colleen by getting a cart and insisting that she drive around with us. I was amazed by how steadily he played. He had taken his game to a new level since he'd left home. When it began to rain, he smiled at me and said, "Just like Carnoustie."

The next morning he had his first class, an English class in a building named Snyder Memorial. We laughed about that as we said good-bye. I watched him hug his mother, and then we drove off. The only thing I wanted to do before we left town was walk the course where he was going to be playing his challenge matches all fall, a lovely place called Stone Oak, about ten miles from the campus.

It was raining again, and Colleen sat in the rental car reading while I walked alone. I was memorizing the layout so I could picture Jack there when I was back in Maine. Houses lined the fairways, and I thought about the people who lived there, who might glance out their windows some afternoon and see my son walking by.

I had tears in my eyes when Colleen caught up with me. I hadn't noticed that the rain had stopped. She had brought me a cup of coffee. "It will warm you up," she said.

I told her that I hated leaving Jack. "Nell will be in Boston soon. Erin in Spain. Jack's in Toledo. In a few years Cara will leave too. How can life ever make sense again when our children are scattered around the world like this?" She took my hand in hers as we walked and said, "Give it time. It will make sense again. You'll see."

FEBRUARY 2, 2008

Five months have passed and I have not stopped missing Jack. I have missed him so much that even when he was home at Christmas for five days, sitting beside me on the couch or at the dining room table, I never stopped missing him. This winter I have been spending a lot of time in front of the television, and that was where Colleen found me today watching an old British Open Championship at St. Andrews on the Golf Channel. "You're wearing Jack's shoes again," she said as she sat down beside me.

"I just miss him," I told her.

She looked at me a moment, then said, "You need to do something different. Go somewhere. Where would you like to go?"

I was staring at the TV screen when I answered her. "Right there."

That's how it began. I wrote to Jack that night and told him that I had decided to go to Scotland to learn to be a caddie so that in three years, when he finished college and played on a professional tour, I would be ready to meet my pledge to him to carry his bag. It was as if I were resurrecting a whimsical childhood dream, the kind that evaporates with the passage of time, but it suddenly seemed real and tangible to me.

Later he wrote back to me. "You go to St. Andrews, Daddy," he said. "Learn all you can and we'll meet up someday, before you know it."

BOOK TWO

Elie, Scotland. Almost three weeks ago, I flew to Scotland and took residence in the village of Elie, just up the road from St. Andrews, because there is a golf course here open through the winter where I can get back to the game and into decent shape. For the last ten days I have walked two rounds a day at the Elie Golf House Club, carrying rocks from the shore in my golf bag for extra weight, always marching at a good clip and pacing off the yardages in my head. Not an easy task for a fifty-seven-year-old, but the exertion feels productive. "I'm in training!" I yelled to a groundskeeper during the gale last week when the wind knocked me to my knees twice.

"You're mad!" he yelled back at me.

I've been thinking maybe he's right. During that gale, the town had to plow two-foot sand drifts off the main street, and I began wearing my headphones day and night to block out the noise of the wind. Some of those winter days I was so cold as I dressed to start my first round that I put on my three layers of clothing right over my pajamas.

This morning I waited out a downpour with a couple of the green-keepers inside a shed off the 13th fairway that looked as if half of it had blown off its foundation in the storm. Both guys had such weathered faces that it was impossible to believe they could look so old and still be standing up. They spoke with thick accents, and I couldn't understand a word one said, and only about 30 percent of the other. What was curious about them was that the large fellow's clothes were too small and the small fellow's clothes were too large, so I was distracted from our conversation at first by the ridiculous thought that maybe they'd accidentally dressed in each other's clothing.

When I told them that I was going to the Old Course in a few days to sign up as a caddie in training, they told me about some lads they knew who had worked there long ago. A fellow called "Shell" because he often passed out and spent the night in the Shell bunker off the 11th green. "Ringo," who allegedly played the drums better than Ringo Starr before he had one hand mauled by a pit bull. "Soap," who never washed, and "Rotar," who had worked the grounds crew at an RAF base and learned to roll his cigarettes *inside* his pocket in the gale winds. When I explained that I was down to my last pack of American cigarettes and at the equivalent of almost $12 a pack would not be replenishing them, they took out their papers and gave me a lesson in rolling my own. I was surprised to see that they used little white filters. "We're tight," the one I could understand said. "You can't smoke the last wee bit of tobacco, so you end up wasting it without a filter."

That began a conversation about the cost of living and the Yanks who came to Scotland "on holiday," as they put it. I pointed out right away that I was not one of them. "I've got four kids in college at the same time," I explained. "I need to earn every penny I can and send it straight home." They nodded with sympathy and together explained that at the Old Course I would average two rounds a day at £60 per round. I did the math inside my head. In a season that lasted around two hundred days that was around forty grand in U.S. dollars. Music to my ears, and I immediately set down two objectives for the six months ahead of me—learn to be a damned good caddie for Jack, and earn $40,000 for my family.

The rain, which had been coming down in sheets, suddenly got even heavier, peppering the metal roof above us like machine-gun fire. "Get yourself some good waterproofs, tops and bottoms," one fellow said. "Gore-Tex. Nothin' else works in this shite."

The whole time we were in the shed I wondered how difficult it was going to be for me to be accepted by the other caddies. Tonight I made up my mind that I'm not going to tell anyone that I'm a writer. If someone asks, I'll say that I was a teacher before I came to Scotland. I won't say I was a college professor, just a teacher. Wherever Americans go in the world they think they're better than everyone else, and if word gets out that I've been on the *Today* show, and chumming with Hollywood stars on the set of a movie I wrote, and riding through Chicago in Oprah's limo, I won't stand a chance. In truth, those things are faraway memories now, just things that happened to me across the years and don't have anything to do with why I'm here. And none of these boys I will work with comes from a more modest childhood than my own, and so I have earned my humility.

MARCH 26, 2008

I rode the number 95 bus to St. Andrews this morning, a journey of maybe twenty miles from Elie that takes just about an hour as the coach sails past the North Sea and oceans of rich farmland at a pretty good clip, then crawls through the narrow streets of villages named St. Monans, Crail, Pittenweem, Anstruther, and Kingsbarns before it reaches downtown St. Andrews. The ride took me past five golf courses, counting the new Castle Course, which is still under construction on a cliff just outside the town of St. Andrews.

From the bus station I walked four blocks to the caddie pavilion just off the 1st tee of the Old Course, where I waited outside in the rain with half a dozen on-duty caddies who glanced at me and nodded their acknowledgment when I moved in next to them under the overhanging roof. I figured all of them to be younger than

I by anywhere from ten to forty years. Dressed in clothes that had seen better days, smoking their hand-rolled cigarettes down to their knuckles, they glanced up at the low gray sky from time to time like sailors or fishermen looking for a break in the weather. There was a weary dignity about them that I found instantly compelling. I couldn't understand most of what they were saying to each other, but just being in their presence for half an hour, I realized that they were not merely talking to each other; they were telling stories. I've never been around caddies. I never hired one in my life or ever really gave the profession any thought one way or the other, but this morning as I watched and listened, I felt as if I had known these men before I saw them. These men who immediately made me wonder if they were not like the porters on the great old passenger trains. They work for tips. They rub shoulders each day with people from all over the world, people who occupy a higher station in life than they do. They learn to walk a certain way with the contours of the train track and to carry their heavy trays a certain way. And I imagine when they're off duty, they share stories about the people they've met.

It took half an hour this morning for me to decide that all I want is to spend the next six months with these guys, learning as much as I can from them, and walking the ground of the Old Course and glancing up from the 1st fairway, and then again coming up the 18th to the windows of the Rusacks Hotel, where I lived as I wrote my novel in the winter of 2002 and where Jack and I stayed just over a year ago. Every day I will get to walk past the place where we buried his golf ball last winter and took our pledge. I have a history here with Jack that has already taken its place in the wide and luminous history of this old golf course.

I had a real stroke of good luck this morning after I rode the bus back to Elie. I walked to the golf course and met up with an old fellow named Pete who had worked twenty-three years as a caddie at every golf course in the area, including the Old Course. He was the only person in sight, and he was thoughtfully rolling putts on the empty 18th green and pausing to share his mince pie with a tiny squirrel when I walked up to him and introduced myself. "You're a long way from your kids," he said as he took out his wallet and showed me photographs of his young school-aged daughter. Then he told me that he hadn't seen her since before his wife ran off with a furniture salesman from Dundee and moved somewhere in Turkey, he believed, though he'd only heard that as rumor in local bars. That was seven years ago. The story he told me was that he was working all day as a caddie and then driving taxis all night to support his family. One night he left the taxi company he normally worked for when his cab broke down. His boss sent him to help out another taxi company whose driver had failed to show up for his shift. So there he was driving the new taxi, and the first call he got was to pick up someone on a back road that ran along the river Tay outside Dundee. He pulled to the side of the road. He saw a guy and a girl walking up arm in arm from the riverbank. The guy had his hand up the girl's dress. And then he recognized the dress. He had bought it for the girl on their sixth wedding anniversary. "There was a lot of mayhem," he said sheepishly.

"You'll see your daughter again," I told him. "She'll want to find you."

"Aye, maybe," he said. "But she'll be grown up. Old enough to see her father's flaws." His eyes were fixed on the photograph as he put it back in his wallet.

I wrote an e-mail to Jack about this. "What a damned story. And the way he told it made me understand a little something about the relationship of caddies. I had told him that I was just signing on as a trainee, but apparently this was good enough for him to trust me. And because he trusted me, I had no difficulty telling him that I was very uneasy about the road ahead as a caddie here. He told me that after fifty loops I would know the place like I'd spent my life here."

When I told Pete that I was most worried about the putting, he walked me to the practice putting green, where he pointed to one hole about fifteen feet from where we were standing and asked me if I could see the break. I saw nothing. "Well, it's there, right at the hole, a wee hump that will move the ball to the right." I knelt down and took another look. Nothing.

Thus began my first lesson in reading putts, with Pete saying, "I'm going to tell you everything you need to know."

In the first place it was not going to be only a matter of me learning the terrain of the 18 greens on the Old Course. On any given day I might be sent to caddie on any one of the other three courses that lay alongside the Old Course—the New, the Jubilee, or the Eden—or up on the cliff to the new Castle Course when it opened. So that means 90 greens to learn. And on any given day the hole will be cut in one of 7 pin positions on each green, meaning I will need to learn how the ball rolls from 630 locations.

Pete's advice was to focus my mind on the essential truths about reading putts. First, the pros read their own putts and only rarely ask their caddies' opinion. Why? Because only the golfer knows *how hard* he will be rolling the ball toward the hole. If he dies the ball into the hole, then it will break dramatically along the contour of the green. But if he rolls it with authority, it will go through some of the break on a straight path. But for us, we are almost always asked by our golfers to read every putt. Meaning it is at best an imprecise science. I will make mistakes. I will misread putts. The important thing is to admit it when I'm wrong. Too many caddies who read the break incorrectly then tell their golfer, "Well, you pushed it," or "You pulled it." It's better to be honest and admit your mistake and tell the golfer you'll get that stroke back for him if you can. It is all about trust between the golfer and his caddie. Break the trust and you'll never get it back.

And there's more to remember. If most of the break is at the beginning of the putt, remember that because the ball is almost always moving faster at the beginning, you don't want to read in all the break. That's important.

Next. When the ball rolls uphill, it loses steam and takes more break. Conversely, when it's rolling downhill, it picks up pace and rushes through some of the break. When the greens are wet and the ball slows down, you have to factor this in. And you do all this in no more than thirty seconds and then deliver the verdict to your golfer in no more than five seconds. If you take longer than this, you are slowing things down out on the course, and this is something a caddie must never do.

Note to myself: One thing Pete said that I really have to remember is to start reading my golfer's putt long before I reach the green. As soon as I can see his ball on the green from the distance as I'm walking toward it, I must use this perspective to view the contour of the green between his ball and the hole. Never waste this time, because you usually get a better read from the distance as you approach the ball than you ever get standing right on top of it. And do not read anything into the putt that isn't there. Trust yourself. Eighty percent of the time your first read is the most accurate. Once you start changing your mind, you are in trouble.

And one more thing. If you look at the putt from behind the ball and it breaks one way, and then you look at the putt from below the hole and it looks completely different, treat it as a straight putt. Same is true with a double-breaking putt. Find the straight line through both breaks.

Holy Moses. A lot to remember. And here's the most important thing of all. Try to get your golfer onto the green in a place where he is *not* putting downhill. Uphill putts are infinitely easier.

So, before I left the Old Course today, I paid my £100 to the assistant caddie master. I am to report for my first class in forty-eight hours. Which gives me all day tomorrow to practice putting and reading putts on my own. I'm going to test everything I learned today from Pete.

MARCH 27, 2008

It is just after 2:00 in the afternoon, and I am writing this one letter at a time into the memo file on my BlackBerry inside the clubhouse at the practice center by the Eden Course to get out of the rain, where I have just been putting for more than four hours after taking the bus into town again early this morning. I stopped at the pro shop on Market Street with the blue door, and a gregarious fellow named Jamie sold me a proper set of waterproofs. Gore-Tex. Tops and bottoms. Black pants with a black-and-white jacket manufactured by Callaway, for which I paid just under £300. A lot of money. Setting aside £460 for next month's rent due on the fifteenth, I have just over £100 left. My goal is to never use credit cards or have money wired to me from home. Meaning I cannot spend a dime outside rent and food. With this in mind, I brought my coffee with me this morning in the small thermos that Nell got me for Christmas from Starbucks. And two peanut butter sandwiches to last me through the day. Breakfast was oatmeal and shall always be oatmeal and a half glass of orange juice. Supper last night was a can of pea soup for seventy pence and two hard rolls for fifty pence. I find that I am not hungry. I think I miss Colleen too much to be hungry.

As for the BlackBerry, I can send and receive unlimited e-mails, and since I arrived, I have kept it in my shirt pocket, right over my heart, so that when it buzzes, I imagine it is a message from someone who cares about me, going straight into my heart. No calls are allowed and no texting because of the prohibitive price. A few minutes ago I wrote to Jack asking him if he could actually believe that in twenty-four hours I was going to be reporting to the Old Course to begin my training as a caddie. I am five hours ahead of him, but he was up for his early class and wrote back, "Sweet, Daddy." He's a man of few words, though as a little boy he never stopped talking and he spoke with such enthusiasm that he stuttered. I know that his golf season has begun at UT, but I am not going to ask him how it is going. I don't want to put pressure on him. When it starts going well, he will tell me, I'm sure. Each Monday, Tuesday, and Wednesday, the team of ten players has challenge matches with only the top five making the weekend tournament. So far, though Jack has been in the top five after every first and second round, he has always collapsed in the final round and finished just out of the running. Whenever he brings this up in an e-mail, I just keep telling him that he will get there. It all takes time.

10:00 p.m. Jack, you won't understand this for another forty years, but in the hours I spent the past few days at the Old Course, I have felt for the first time in my life that I know where I want to grow old. Standing outside the caddie pavilion with the caddies, I felt like I had finally found my tribe. Hard to explain really. Deep inside, it feels as if I have been returning here my whole life. Enough of that, though. The important thing I wanted to write to you about is that I know

I have come to the right place to learn to be a caddie so I can
be of use to you when we meet up someday on a pro tour. If
you are going to learn to be a caddie in this world, you have
to learn here in all the Scottish weather so that you can
learn how to play the game in the worst possible conditions
that you and I will ever encounter. Truth is, it has rained
ever since I arrived, and the wind! Well, you remember the
wind at Carnoustie last winter. I was out in a gale the other
day playing the Elie Course. I was about 130 yards from the
green, dead into the wind. I hit the best five-iron I've ever hit,
and the ball went on a straight line to the flag, then, halfway
there, started blowing back toward me. Amazing. It reminds
me of when I was first learning to sail a small boat in French-
man's Bay in Maine. George Shepherd, the old skipper from
across the road, told me that the only way I was going to
learn to be a real sailor was to take my boat out into the bay
when the small-craft warnings were flying and everyone else
was coming back to the harbor. I think the same is true for
becoming a caddie. I have to learn how to manage my golfer's
game in weather so foul that you just want to dig a hole and
crawl into it. Tomorrow is my first day, Jack. My first real
step to prepare myself. Wish me luck. I'm five hours ahead
of you, so you will be sound asleep when I do my first loop. I
love you and miss you tons. Daddy

MARCH 28, 2008

I was much too excited to sleep well, and in order to be certain I wasn't late for my first day on the job, I took a bus this morning that got me into St. Andrews two hours early. I took a walk out to the farthest point on the course, the 11th green, where Bobby Jones had met his demise. The sun lay in gold bands across the fairways as I made my way back, dreaming about what it was going to be like walking the same ground each day where Jones and all the great players had walked. There was still no one in the caddie pavilion or standing outside, so I killed some time looking in the windows of the handsome gift shop behind the 18th green, deciding what I might buy Colleen and the three girls at the end of my first day of work. I had my face pressed to the glass, searching for some little thing I could send them to mark the beginning of my journey as a caddie, when a reflection appeared. Two people just behind me, walking up to the 18th green, where the white flag was blowing in the rising breeze off the sea. Rather than turn around and face them, I let myself imagine that Jack and I were coming to the green together and it was our reflection in the glass. Not the two of us last winter, but on some day in the near future when I would be carrying his bag. The possibility of this felt so close and real and I was zinging along with it when my BlackBerry zapped me in my heart. It was much too early for anyone from home. That is what I was thinking when I took the phone from my pocket and saw an incoming e-mail from the caddie pavilion. No lights were on there, and no one was standing outside. I clicked open the e-mail and found this message: "This is Rick Mackenzie, the caddie master. If you're the writer, I cannot take you on as a caddie. I won't have any writers working for me."

A few minutes later at the window of the pavilion, the assistant confirmed this and handed me back my £100. So much for my life here as a caddie.

MARCH 29, 2008

I was on the 4th tee at Elie yesterday playing my final round before I packed to return home when, to make matters worse, I got an e-mail from Jack telling me that several members of the Inverness Club whom he has gotten to know are coming to St. Andrews to play the Old Course this summer and they plan to look me up to caddie for them. I wrote back and said nothing to Jack about what has happened. He doesn't need any bad news from me.

I played fifty-seven holes of angry golf today trying to get it out of my system. Out on the course I sent Rick Mackenzie an e-mail telling him about Jack and me and our dream and asking if he would reconsider. He wrote back immediately with two words: "Sorry. No." I birdied the next hole and the one after that while my blood was boiling. Something about anger focuses the mind, I suppose. I felt as if there were no hole on the course I couldn't birdie. Until I made a bogey.

MARCH 30, 2008

My plan was to take the train to London today, spend the night there, and get the cheapest flight out tomorrow. This morning I walked to the maintenance shop off the 3rd tee and presented the head of the grounds crew with a quart of Jameson whiskey as a thank-you gift. I explained what had transpired at the Old Course and said that I was going home. When I delivered the news, there was a look of sorrow in his eyes, as if this reversal of fortune had happened to him. He took a deep drag on his cigarette, and then he told me that he knew the caddie master at Kingsbarns Golf Links, just outside St. Andrews. "His name is Davy Gilchrist," he said. "I'll ring him just now on my mobile if you want."

Ten minutes later I was running to the bus stop to catch the 95, which dropped me in the center of the village of Kingsbarns. From there I walked about half a mile, along the main road for six hundred yards, then down the long curving entrance road through a farmer's fields. I was so nervous that I kept counting my paces just under my breath. When I walked through the stone pillars, past the practice range, and got my first glimpse of the place, it stopped me in my tracks. The golf course lay along the sea in a kind of splendor most golfers will never see in their lifetimes. Out in front of me for as far as I could see were pale green fairways sweeping through wild, honey-colored dunes with the kinds of dramatic elevations that are uncommon in links courses anywhere in the world. My first glimpse of the place was breathtaking. Like something from a dream. If caddying at the

Old Course was going to be like working every day in a museum, Kingsbarns was an art gallery.

I met Davy Gilchrist in the small stone cottage just behind the parking lot that served as the caddie shed. When he shook my hand, he narrowed his intense blue eyes as if he were trying to see inside me. I told him in one breath why I had come to Scotland and what had happened to me at the Old Course. He told me about his own kids and his grandkids, who all lived within fifty yards of his house. "They're fantastic! They rob me blind," he said with a wide grin. He told me that Kingsbarns trained the best caddies in all of Scotland. Then he outlined the terms of employment. He had around seventy caddies, and I would be starting at the bottom of the list, meaning I wouldn't go out each day until all of them had. But he gave me his word that he would get me as much work as he could, and because I was living in Elie and was familiar with the course there, he would send me there as well when there were requests. Until I learned my way around, I would be a "shadow" walking beside one of the real caddies and paying that caddie £2 per round for the privilege of learning all that I could from him. The season opened in three days and would run for six months, and I was expected to be there every day.

That was good enough for me. We shook hands again, and he said, "I can always use a hardworking caddie."

I walked back into the village in the rain and was soaked to my skin by the time I got under the roof of the bus stop. I didn't care. I couldn't have been happier if I had just been elected the mayor of Kingsbarns. Inside the little hut was a guy sitting on the bench with boots caked in mud. A middle-aged man, he was hunched over, smoking a cigarette and looking out at the rain with a baleful expression. "Are you a farmer?" I asked. He gave me a sideways glance, then resumed glaring at the weather without answering my question. "I feel sorry for the farmers in this country, working outside in this weather," I said a little too cheerfully. He got a pained look on his face as if my tone of voice had offended him in some way.

Then without looking back at me, he muttered, "Try working as a bleedin' caddie."

MARCH 31, 2008

Opening day is tomorrow. In four hours I will be caddying my first loop at Kingsbarns for the management of the course. Davy told me that I would be carrying the bag of David Scott, the director of golf operations. I won't be paid, but I will be given my tea (lunch, I suppose) in the clubhouse after the round. Fair enough. I'm taking one of Jack's University of Toledo golf balls to present to Mr. Scott on the 1st tee. And I've been awake since 4:00 a.m. studying my yardage book. I walked the course once, taking notes, and I've written those notes into the book. But when I close my eyes and try to picture the holes, it is all just a blur to me. A pale green field of mounds and valleys rolling beside the blue sea. I am going to pretend that I am caddying for Jack today and that we are trying to qualify for an important tournament. And no matter how nervous I am, I'm not going to forget the hazards you can't see—the hidden stream at the back of the 6th green and the hidden bunker up the left side of the 14th fairway. And the stream behind the 16th green. And the only out of bounds on the whole course, up the right side off the tee on number 11. Since I woke up this morning, I have been trying to think of the worst thing that might happen to me today.

I think the other caddies in my group are also new. I think that's what Davy told me. Many of the experienced guys are still in Florida, where they work during the winter months. They won't be back for another few weeks. Something I didn't realize until yesterday is that we host the last event on the European Tour, the Alfred Dunhill Links Championship. So if I make it through the next 187 days in good order, I will have a chance to caddie with the pros, and Jack will be able to watch on TV.

MARCH 31, 2008

10:00 p.m. In my thirty-one years of living a writer's life, I have inhabited the world on one level with everyone I've ever known, including the lady at the fruit and vegetable shop in Elie across from the bus stop who sold me my banana this morning and the people who rode the bus through the fog with me. I belong to this world just as they do, and I endure my share of the same joys and hardships, pleasures and sorrows that they do. But for the hours when I write each day—normally from 4:00 a.m. until 10:00—I inhabit a different world, on a layer of existence maybe three levels below the real world. From the very first time I ever wrote, it has been this way. The moment I close my eyes and wait for the first words to come, I can feel myself dropping down the elevator shaft to the world that awaits me. It is a world of made-up stories and invented characters, a world that feels more real to me than the real world outside my door. And on the mornings when I am writing particularly well, all the reference points that lead back to the real world have vanished. The coffee cup beside me is part of the made-up world. So is the lamp. There is no way back. And I have the grand illusion that I have become a citizen of this made-up world with a passport that can never be revoked, granting me the right and the privilege to travel there until the end of my time.

The important word here is "privilege." From the first page of fiction I ever wrote almost exactly thirty-one years ago living in a cabin in the mountains of Maine, I have felt privileged to occupy what I have always called the *deep down world*. It is a world of stillness and extreme contrast, so that colors and emotions and sounds are dramatically defined. All I have to do is turn and face them, and there they are waiting for me to absorb and then to find words to describe. It is also a world of surprises and stunning reversals of fortune, where roads take unexpected turns without warning and blizzards blow in from nowhere, and so I must always be alert and on my toes.

Until this morning if anyone had ever asked me if the landscape of my made-up writing world could be matched anywhere in the real world, I would have said no. An unequivocal no. But I found it at work today out on the golf course, after I had met my fellow caddies beside the starter's hut and introduced myself to my golfer. Just as Mr. Scott addressed his ball on the 1st tee, I felt all the sound fall out of the world around me. And when he glanced up the fairway one last time at his target, I began to drop down to the same level of concentration that has characterized my writing world every morning of my life for more than thirty years. I saw Mr. Scott's eyes narrow. I saw the wind move his hair. I saw the TITLEIST 4 on his golf ball. He seemed to suddenly be cast into slow motion, so that there was plenty of time for me to finish taking in every detail of the ground ahead of us. The light brown fescue down the left and right side of the fairway bending back in the breeze that faced us. The mounds and hollows outlined in shadow and light. I could not see the bunker at 256 yards up the right side, but I knew it was there without having to remind myself. It was no longer just part of the landscape; I had claimed it as part of my known world. Just as the green and the flag blowing in the distance belonged to me. I had laid claim to them in my imagination. I had made them real. And as I took my first steps beside Mr. Scott after he hit his shot, cleaning the face of his hybrid club with my wet towel and then sliding it back into the bag as we began our long walk, I felt the same privilege I always feel in my deep down world of writing. Somewhere in the real world people were driving in traffic or yelling at each other or worrying about the balance in their checkbooks. I was in a deeper world where nothing mattered more than the slant of the ground beneath my feet and the direction of the wind. When I bent down on the 1st green to get a read on our first putt, I was concentrating so deeply that I could see which direction the blades of grass had been cut to form the grain. "What do you see in this, Don?" Mr. Scott asked as he looked down the line of the putt. The truth is I saw nothing. No break at all. I should have trusted this, as Pete had told me. But I was too nervous. And the longer I looked at the line, the more break I saw in it. First right to left. Then left to right. I was lost. Everyone was waiting for me to give a diagnosis; instead, I gave a prediction of sorts. "I think it will break a cup right to left," I said. The other three caddies heard me. Mr. Scott and the other three golfers heard me. And now there was no place to hide. I held my breath as the ball began rolling toward the hole. It held a perfectly straight line, stopping just short. "Pretty straight," Mr. Scott said as he tapped it in for par. "I got that one wrong," I said. "That's all right," he said as he handed me back his putter. "It's never the caddie's fault. I'm the one with the putter in my hands. I should have seen it straight."

I was kicking myself as we walked to the 2nd tee. The truth is I never recovered from that bad read. I lost my nerve to the extent that I spent much of the next four hours just following my golfer around as he explained to me how to play each shot. All he really needed me for was to carry his bag. So I was a bag carrier, which doesn't even come close to being a caddie. I see the difference clearly. A competent caddie walks slightly out ahead of his golfer like the maître d' at a fine restaurant, leading the way, using the fairway yardage markers to count the paces in his head so when his golfer reaches the ball, the caddie can deliver in about five seconds the distance to the flag on the green, as well as the distance to the front edge of the green, and the back edge of the green, and the distance to any hazards lying between him and the green. Not just the distance to reach the hazards, but equally important the distance to carry them. All this became a jumble in my mind. The one time I tried to be clever was when we were standing in the 4th fairway with the wind blowing steadily. I could feel the wind, but when I looked ahead to the green and saw that the flag was hanging straight down, not moving at all, I volunteered that there was no wind at the green. As Mr. Scott chose his club, he reminded me as graciously as possible that the flag was not moving because it was still wet from the morning dew. Lesson learned for me. I will never again make this mistake. But I wonder how many mistakes there are like this that I might make before I can reach some level of competency. Like, what do you do with your waterproofs when it turns into a lovely, hot summer day, as it did by the time we reached the back nine? I was sweltering, on the verge of a heatstroke, it seemed, before one of the other caddies, new like myself, Jimmy Hughes, kindly showed me how he had tied his around his golfer's bag. Later, when we were side by side, searching for his golfer's ball, Jimmy told me that this was his first round as a caddie too. He spent forty years fishing the North Sea, and he'd had enough with waterproofs, which he called "skins."

As we searched for that ball, Jimmy told me something I am going to remember. When I show up for work each morning, if I see the small boats out at sea, then I know the weather forecast is fair. The small boats won't go out if there is awful weather ahead.

David Scott is what Jack hopes to become someday, a PGA pro. And what I learned from him today as he shot two over par was that he did not *play* the golf course. Instead, he took possession of it with fierce conviction. I mean, he was smiling and chatting with his pals and giving me pointers, but beneath the pleasantries he was on fire with determination. Tall and lean, he marched in an even, effortless gait, then stood his ground as he took the measure of the next shot with his feet firmly planted like an explorer who had just jumped down from the bow of a ship to claim this land for himself. And each shot was a blunt but poetic assertion of will as he struck the back of the ball with a downward glancing blow, trapping it for a millisecond against the hard-packed ground before it sizzled off into its flight with enough backspin to hold it on a straight line all the way to the target. It was just after eleven o'clock when we made the turn and I had time to take my BlackBerry from my pocket and send an e-mail to Jack, who at that same time was at golf practice:

> I'm out here caddying right now for David Scott, the direc-tor of golf at Kingsbarns, who is making this course look as simple as the track you'd lay down in your backyard when you have the grandkids over to play with their Fred Flint-stone plastic clubs. Everybody talks about how you have to stay focused ONE SHOT AT A TIME. Well, here's how you do that, Jack. You break the golf course into pieces. And claim ownership of it one piece at a time. I'll explain more later. Love, Daddy

What Mr. Scott was showing me today was how to play to safe ground from wherever we stood. This will be my job as a caddie this summer. To take my golfer from one piece of safe ground to the next. "You don't need to stand on the tee and tell your man that there is a bunker 245 yards up the right side," he explained. "You tell him if he hits his shot 200 yards up the left side, after it rolls another 40 yards, he'll be in fine shape to take a mid-iron into the green. All positives. No negatives."

APRIL 4, 2008

I am not a real caddie. I am only a "shadow." There are six of us out on the course each day, walking beside the real caddies and their golfers, keeping our mouths closed, trying to stay out of the way and to do no harm when asked our opinion, following the golden rule of caddies, which is "Show up, keep up, and shut up." "Would you call this a three- or four-club wind!" old Kenny yelled, as I stood behind him and his golfer stood behind me, all three of us holding on to each other to keep from blowing off the tee box on number 13, the wee par-3. "At least four!" I yelled back through the gale. Kenny took the fellow's driver from his bag. "All we got!" he said, handing it to the man. Then he whispered in my ear, "In wind like this, don't hold back!"

I may be only a shadow, but I am a shadow in Scotland. And I'll say this about golf in Scotland. It is such beautiful ground, and the people are modest, clever, and honest. Already I think of eager Jimmy Hughes, the fisherman with his thick shock of white hair, and silent Scan, who caddied on the European Tour, lean and elegant in his movements, and intense Kenny, retired from the army, and laconic Paul, with his salt-and-pepper beard, once a barrister, as some of the finest people I've ever met. Kim, who once managed supermarkets, taught me how to light a golfer's cigar in the wind. A small but necessary talent. But this country is cursed by weather. Absolutely cursed. And if it is true that golf was invented in this country, then it is also true that it was never intended to be more than a test of endurance and a lesson in humility. Try hitting drivers into 145-yard par-3s and *not reaching* the green! Maybe humility is golf's greatest lesson. And maybe this is why I never cared for Tiger Woods or raised Jack to emulate him. Instead, I held Ireland's Padraig Harrington up for Jack when he was a little boy. There was something marvelously humble about the way Harrington walked with that slight limp. We followed him for years, and then like magic he won the Open at Carnoustie right after Jack and I went there and played on those brutal winter days. And as he stood on the 18th green and was presented with the Claret Jug and named the Champion Golfer of the Year, the first words from his mouth were "I was never meant for anything like this." So, if Tiger Woods is the greatest practitioner of the game and yet he has failed to learn the game's greatest lesson—humility—then what does this say about him as a man?

Not sure.

Right now humility is not Jack's problem. He lost another team challenge match yesterday, failing to finish in the top five to play the tournament this weekend. He took two triple bogeys in the final round and finished last. It happens, I wrote to him. It can happen to anyone. I told him to just hang in there. His time will come. This is the spring of his freshman year. I don't expect him to really come into his own until he's a senior. He started late in the game. And he doesn't come from the golf pedigree with parents who could hire coaches to help him with his swing. In the world of golf, Jack is definitely from the wrong side of the tracks. He worked at a gas station to pay for his clubs. In fact, he was scrubbing the floor of the men's room at that gas station the night before he played his State Championship match. And I always tried to make him see that this was a point of honor. He was not a country-club golfer. I told him about Lee Trevino, who grew up with one club and used it to hit stones because he couldn't afford a golf ball. "We're the kinds of guys that the country clubs are trying to keep out," I always told him. "You'll be a renegade golfer."

Over here the game belongs to everyone, including the renegades. There is no country-club golf for the locals. That is reserved for the guys who can afford to fly here to play. For example. A round at Kingsbarns is £150, or approximately $250. But if you are a resident of St. Andrews, you pay £170 a year, and you get to play all seven courses of the Links Trust, including the Old Course, as many times as you like. You could play the Old Course twice a day every day of the week, except Sunday, when it is closed. Golf belongs to everyone here, no matter his station in life. Somehow, when the game was hijacked to America and Japan, it was transformed into a game for the elite. Like the fellow I was out with from Germany the other afternoon. Handsome, arrogant, dressed to the hilt. He listened to none of his caddie's advice, though Brian, who used to be a chef in Paris, delivered this advice with the greatest respect, as if he were talking to someone on the PGA Tour instead of someone who should have been banned from ever swinging a golf club in public. He made one horrendous shot after another, and each time his ball disappeared into the rough, he turned and glared at his caddie and me, even though he knew I was only a shadow, as if we were to blame. After a few hours of the man's abuse, Brian whispered to me: "That's why those boys lost the war. Twice."

Somewhere in the dunes on the right side of the 16th fairway I was searching for his ball after he insisted we try to find it, even though Brian had already delivered that great Scottish aperçu with a "Sir" at the beginning: "Sir, Lassie wouldn't find that ball if you wrapped it in bacon." The German was only a few feet from me taking a piss when he called out, "Are you not a little too old to be a trainee in anything?"

True, I thought. "I'm training to caddie for my son on his first pro tour," I replied. "So you see, I'm out here with you right now, but really I'm with my son. And that's why it's so important that we find your ball." All this was true. The only part I left off was the last wee bit: "Personally, I couldn't give a flying fuck if we ever found *your* ball, and my best advice for you is that you give up this sport and take up some equestrian event."

The great thing about this job is that in four hours (five on an exceptionally long round) it is over. I think of each round as a blind date. Perfect strangers meeting up on the 1st tee. And if things work out, best friends, hugs, and photographs four hours later. It is really quite something to observe. The other day I stood beside big Gary as he and his golfer eyed a shot of approximately 170 yards. Gary was recommending a five-iron. His golfer was unconvinced. "Trust me, sir," Gary said softly. "We'll need all of the five-iron to get there."

"But this is only the 3rd hole," the man objected as his voice rose in an arc of incredulity. "How can you know my game already? I haven't even hit a five-iron yet."

With utmost diplomacy, and a self-deprecating little shrug of his big shoulders, Gary replied, "Well, sir, I watched your seven-iron on number 2. You struck it well. We're going to need a five-iron here."

With that, Gary handed him the club he had already withdrawn from the man's bag. The five-iron. And then Gary stepped aside. When he had my attention, he silently pointed his finger to his eyes and then to the man's ball. While the golfer took his practice swings, Gary's eyes remained fixed on the ball. Right through the man's shot, his eyes never moved until after the ball had taken flight. The three of us watched as the ball rolled up onto the green. "You were right," the man said. "Good call."

Gary just nodded. Then he put his hand on my shoulder, and we waited until the golfer had marched out ahead of us and joined his buddies. "I like to let my man enjoy a good shot without me," he said. "God knows there's enough misery in this game." Then he asked me if I had noticed his practice swing. I confessed that I hadn't noticed anything really, and he pointed out that the man had taken two miserable practice swings but the third was spot-on. His club-head came down and brushed the grass. That practice swing is what set up the good strike. "When you're out here with a golfer who is really struggling, show him the importance of a good, solid practice swing. And the other thing is I watch the club hit the ball so I can tell if it was a good shot that got us 170 yards or a poor shot. If it was a poor shot, then I gave him too much club, and I know if he'd hit it pure, he would have airmailed the green and sawed my head off for it."

I have a lot to learn.

APRIL 7, 2008

Today I was out with wry, lanky Johnny from London, who might be in his mid-forties but still has the build and the face of a boy in his twenties. He led around four Spaniards who were trying to save money and could hire only one caddie. This happens from time to time. Instead of each man paying sixty quid for his own caddie, the four of them will pay twenty each, making it a good payday for the caddie and a real savings for the golfers. So there I am on the 1st tee, really bearing down, dropping down to the *deep down world*. George, the starter, tells us the pin positions so we know exactly where the holes are cut today. I've got the four men's names in my head, and which golf ball each is using, while I follow their tee shots across the sky and mark their landings in my mind. The golfers don't speak any English, and Johnny and I know about ten words of Spanish between us, but somehow Johnny conveys that two of the drives are in deep trouble, we might not find them, so it would be best to play a provisional. They do. Now I have six golf balls in my mind.

Up the fairway we go. Johnny will take the two who have sprayed their drives to the right, and I'll take the two who have hit hooks. "Keep them moving," Johnny tells me. "We've got foursomes right behind us."

This is a problem. I find five golf balls in the crap, but none of them are the balls these fellows have hit. Everywhere I turn I keep stepping on golf balls in the thick fescue. No luck. Both men are happy dropping balls in the fairway and playing on, but I feel like a failure. If I am out with Jack in a tournament, that is a penalty for a lost ball.

On we went. Things are a bit more complicated with the Spaniards because they need their distances in meters instead of yards. You do the simple math in your head, deducting 10 percent. So a 150-yard shot turns into a 135-meter shot. On the 4th green Johnny tells me it's my turn to tend the flag. This is the caddies' main performance. Center stage. Tending the flag if the golfer is so far away with his putt that he needs it in the hole to find the hole. Pulling it out and holding it so that the flag doesn't blow in the wind. Standing so that your shadow doesn't fall in anyone's line. A shadow without a shadow. You sort of dance around the green, and if you are doing your job correctly, no one notices you. That's the key, to blend in and disappear. I read both putts perfectly and watched both balls drop into the center of the hole. "Well done," Johnny said to me. I thanked him and then, in my excitement, proceeded to march halfway to the next tee still holding the flag.

By the time we stood on the 11th tee box, the empty blue sky had been replaced by clouds so thick and black that it felt as if night were descending. Our golfers were playing like piss, losing two or three balls on every hole (balls we were no longer even trying to find) but laughing and drinking whiskey and apparently having the time of their lives. I wanted to do something to help my two fellows, and I was trying my best, but as soon as I had one of them straightened out and back on the fairway, the other was in trouble again in the rough or a bunker or a river. It was as if I were babysitting two rambunctious toddlers in a fine house filled with priceless antiques. Every time I turned my back, there was another catastrophe. One moment they were knocking over the Ming vase in the foyer. The next they were banging the keys on the Steinway. Suddenly a hailstorm was upon us, and we all went trotting after Johnny, who led the way to a ditch beneath a tree where we pulled our jackets over our heads and curled up in the fetal position. The hail was large enough to feel as if someone were throwing rocks at us. All we could do was curse and then laugh. One of the Spaniards passed around his flask. When I declined, Johnny told me he had noticed that I never went to the pub after work with the boys. I had hoped that my absence was going unnoticed. When we all sat outside the caddie shed, there was always a lot of banter about what had happened or failed to happen the night before in the pub. It was common for caddies doing two loops a day to spend all the money earned from one loop in the pub that night. The other morning I'd heard one senior caddie say, "I had a hundred quid with me when I went to the pub. Then I woke up this morning with only eight quid left." There was no accounting for this; at £1.50 for a pint, he would have had to drink sixty-six pints. I had already taken my pledge to send all my earnings home and to never spend a dime in the pubs, and I had my wee white lie ready for Johnny, the one lie that would excuse me in a country where so many men had wrecked their lives with the drink. "I've had my troubles with booze," I said. Johnny nodded immediately with understanding. "I hear you, mate," he said. He worked for a while to roll his cigarette inside his jacket to keep it dry. When he had it lit, he looked up at the sky and said, "Lovely spring we're having. Whenever you're out here in shite like this, you want to pray that it gets *worse, not better*, so the blokes will quit."

"I'll remember that," I said. Then I remarked that when we were all following him off the fairway into the ditch under the tree, we looked like ducklings following their mother. "It's a matter of trust, isn't it? I mean, a golfer has to trust his caddie?"

"If you want to get philosophical about it, yes, it is about trust," he said. "I suppose that's why I do this job year after year. Each time out is the chance to earn the trust of a complete stranger. And in this world where nobody trusts anybody, that counts for something. We know the ground and the weather. These blokes would have followed you and me right off a cliff."

I thought about this for a while as we lay in the ditch until the storm had passed. I wondered if Jack would trust me as his caddie. And what it would take to earn his trust.

The sky clears. The wind falls off. And there is a moment on the long par-5 12th when it all becomes clear to me. One of my golfers wore a red porkpie hat, the kind I remember seeing Bing Crosby wear when I was a kid. Through the round, he was often wandering off by himself, and on several occasions I found him just looking around, taking in the surroundings thoughtfully as if he were trying to memorize the course. He was the last to drive on number 12, and he was so deep in thought that he forgot to hand me back his driver after the shot and began walking down the hill from the elevated tee box following the flight of his ball. It took a while for the other three golfers to convey to me that he had been here before. He had played this course before, soon after it first opened, with his wife, who had recently died. His friends had brought him back to Scotland on this trip to try to help him get through his grief. When I caught up to him, he said to me, "I love this hole." His ball had traveled almost two hundred yards, then caught the right-to-left slope of the fairway and rolled to a stop just before the thick dune grass that ran along the shore all the way up the left side to the green. "We should make a birdie here," I said to him. He laughed off this suggestion, but when I told him that I was serious, our eyes met and I could see how much the idea appealed to him.

I handed him back his driver and showed him how to play the ball back in his stance. The goal here was to keep the ball low, maybe two or three feet off the ground, so that it would roll forever if we caught the slope of the ground just right. Then I showed him where to aim. And he did it. Not once, but twice. The first shot with the "driver off the deck" went almost as far as his drive from the tee. We made the same shot again, only this time with his rescue club, catching the right-to-left slope off the mound on the right of the green. When the ball came to a stop, it was fourteen feet from the hole. By now the other three men understood what was at stake, and they huddled with Johnny while I lined up the putt. Using my hand, I explained that the ball was going to break right, maybe half a foot in the first half of the putt, before turning back the other way for the remainder. "Just hit it straight at the cup," I said. "Concentrate on your pace."

So he makes the birdie putt. The ball rolls one final revolution in slow motion, collapsing into the hole, his arms go up to the heavens, his three pals surround him in a solemn victory celebration, and I realize this is going to be the highlight of their trip. As we walk to the next tee, he puts his arm around my shoulders and thanks me and insists that I try one of his black cigarettes. The tobacco is so strong that on the first drag my knees buckle, which gets a laugh out of everyone.

I know now what my job will be out here caddying for strangers, and then one day caddying for my son. The governing dynamic in golf is the same as it is in love, or life itself. In order to love and to be loved, you must believe in yourself. In order to live a full life, you must believe in yourself—at least enough to keep going one more day. In golf you must believe in yourself enough to make the next shot. Doubt will destroy you. And so I will be a confidence man. I will convey confidence in a calm manner, never showing any doubt or fear. In addition to reading greens, and tending flags, and carrying bags, and pointing the way to the safe, good ground, and knowing the weather, and keeping his clubs clean and his grips dry, and moving him along to keep the pace going on the course, and lighting his cigar, and keeping his score—I will believe in my golfer, and I will make him believe that he can make the next shot, no matter how difficult.

I tried this out on Johnny as we were coming up the 18th fairway, and he disagreed. "No, mate," he said. "I don't get that involved. If they make the putt or miss the putt, it's all the same to me."

Not me, I thought. I am going to make my name out here as the caddie who fights for every single shot with my golfer whether he's

Tiger Woods or Caspar Milquetoast. Because, to me, every golfer out here will be my son.

APRIL 27, 2008

For weeks now I have been living like a monk. Up at 4:00 to write with a bowl of oats, a half glass of orange juice, and one cup of coffee instead of the three I normally had because more than one and I have to piss out on the golf course. Pack two peanut butter and banana sandwiches and a thermos of tea. Walk three blocks to the bus. Ride the bus to Kingsbarns. Walk the half mile to the caddie shed. Do my round as a shadow. Walk back to the bus. Ride home. Eat two hard rolls and a bowl of soup and drink one tin of lager. Fall asleep in my chair, reading. Wake up at 4:00 in all my clothes and start in again. I am breaking the pattern tonight, eating mashed and bangers and drinking a pint of Guinness to celebrate what happened yesterday. It was a slow day, only a few caddies went out. Everyone had given up and left by around two. Even Davy had gone home. I had almost an hour to wait for the next 95 bus, so I was sitting at the picnic table outside the caddie shed, typing into my BlackBerry. Before I left for work this morning, I discovered the memo file was just like a file on my Mac, and I was sitting there thinking that maybe I would write a new draft of the screenplay of my father and mother's love story while I'm here working this season. It will be my sixth draft. I had just typed in the title page—*American Love Story*—when one of the assistant pros appeared and asked if there were any caddies around.

"I'm just a shadow," I said.

He said that two golfers from San Francisco had just shown up and requested two caddies. He started to turn away.

"I know the course," I said. "I could take them around."

He nodded his approval. "Well, then," he said. "Up you go."

They were brothers in their thirties, one a little stockier than the other, both very friendly and delighted to be in Scotland playing golf for the first time. I put one bag over my shoulder; the other I pushed on a trolley. I was too nervous at first to descend to the *deep down world* or to forget that this was my first time out on the golf course unsupervised by a real caddie. On the 2nd hole, a par-3 along the sea, I failed to calculate the distance to the hole, giving them the distance to the front of the green instead, and left them both short. I admitted my mistake and then made a worse error on the short par-4 5th hole, giving them way too much club when I failed to see that the wind, which had been out in front of us on the tee box, was now suddenly behind us. They both hit their balls right through the fairway into the rough. I walked out ahead of them at a good clip to give myself extra time to find their balls, but even after they arrived to help me, we found neither. If this had been a strict competition or if I'd been caddying for Jack in a tournament, failing to hit a provisional ball would have cost us dearly. They called it even, both dropping new balls, and we played on from there. They took it in stride, and soon enough I felt myself descending into their story as they told me it was their mother, a champion player, who had taught them the game and who insisted that the only gift they ever gave her on Mother's Day was a round of golf together.

We spent a while discussing the physicality of the game, as explained by their mother. If you figure that it takes the average player two minutes to execute a shot, this means that in any given round of golf played to even par in four hours, ninety-six minutes are spent just walking. All this downtime is a problem for most golfers. There is just too much time to think about all the things that can impact negatively on your next shot. Meaning the girl who dumped you thirty years earlier because you weren't quite good enough. Or the promotion that went to the other junior account executive because he was a little brighter. The bad stuff has a way of creeping in, and by bad stuff their mother meant history. "She believed that out on a golf course was where all your small and large failures in your past were waiting for you. They tracked you down and waited for you even in a place as beautiful as this place," one brother explained. "You think you're heading out for a nice, pleasant walk," the other brother said, "and bingo, you're ambushed by history instead." Their mother had taught them to use the time spent walking to observe the natural world around them. Birds and trees. The movement of clouds. To try to become part of the surroundings. "And the way you walk is also of great importance," one brother said. "Most people are much too stiff when they hit a golf ball. Their arms are like blocks of wood. This starts by the way they march to their ball. You want to teach your son to walk with loose joints, like he's made of rubber, and with his shoulders relaxed so the tension dissipates. By the time he steps up to his next shot, he should be half asleep!"

I practiced it myself as the afternoon wore on, walking with a rolling gait while they shared their personal history with the game. Both of them had always believed they would try for the pro tour. They'd played in junior competitions and set their sights on the big D1 college programs, but things hadn't worked out. We were on the 14th tee when they showed me a drill their mother used to work on with them. "Where is the worst place you can drive the ball from here?" one asked me. It had to be down over the steep embankment into the fescue on the side of the hill running along the 12th fairway, I explained. After he hit his first drive up the middle, he hit a second one right into all the trouble. As we walked through the deep grass searching for the ball, he told me that his mother had taught him one of the most important lessons for Jack in competition and for me as his caddie. "Okay, here we are," he said, after we were standing over the ball. "Now is the point in time when you have to give up the idea of getting on the green in regulation. Actually, the instant you hit this drive, you should have given up on that." His point was you are in trouble now and trouble is part of this game. No one gets through a round without encountering trouble. The players who end up at the top of the leaderboard are the ones who deal with trouble better than the rest.

"So, all I want to know from here is where to hit this shot to give myself a decent chance to make my par. This is one of the paradoxes in the game; we all know that we are supposed to concentrate on one shot at a time, the shot right in front of you. But here is one of those exceptions. I have already conceded the second shot. I'm not even thinking of trying to get to the green in regulation. All I'm doing now is setting up the third shot."

It made perfect sense to me. I asked him what he considered his strongest shot into a green. "One-hundred-and-fifteen-yard pitching wedge," he said. I walked back up the hill and out onto good flat ground that distance from the flag. He hit an eight-iron to that spot, then took out his pitching wedge and landed the ball ten feet from the hole. We missed the putt for par, but he had made his point, and it was a point that I will remember. We took a disaster out of the equation by playing for a bogey. My job is to limit the damage.

When we finished, we grabbed one of the groundskeepers to shoot a photograph of the three of us outside the clubhouse. Then they paid me, and we said good-bye in the parking lot. I took the bills in my right hand and stuffed the money into my pocket as I turned away and began walking to the bus. I didn't look at it until I had reached the bus stop. Two fifties and two twenties. It was the first money I'd earned as a caddie.

I had my last smoke of the day outside my back door under the stars. A sky swept with stars. I am now a caddie in Scotland, I said just above a whisper. I am here learning what I need to learn for Jack, and I am also *making money* to send home to my family. One hundred and forty pounds at the current exchange rate is about $250. Not bad for a day's work. Not bad at all for a nice four-hour walk with those two fine young men, who played the course at four and seven over par.

Then sometime in the night I awoke with rain lashing the windows and a terrible feeling in my head. It took me a moment to comprehend that in my sleep I was being reprimanded by Davy, my caddie master. Gone were his bright eyes and quick grin. He was pissed and letting me know in no uncertain terms that there would be consequences for what I had done. First, I had posed as a real caddie instead of telling the golfers that I was only a shadow. This, in Scotland, he explained as his eyes narrowed with contempt, was akin to impersonating an officer, and it carried a penalty. Second, by pretending to be a real caddie, I had earned £140 that should have gone to one of his real caddies.

Unable to get back to sleep, I took a shower and dressed. It was three in the morning when I started drinking coffee, seated at my kitchen table, waiting for the first bus to Kingsbarns at 6:03.

I arrived in the downpour with no place to get out from the rain until the milkman showed up half an hour later and led me to an unlocked garage bay where he leaves his deliveries. "You look like you're lost," he remarked. When he heard my Yankee accent, he asked the standard question: "On holiday?" Which made me wonder what line of logic could possibly have led him to the conclusion that an American on holiday would be standing outside soaking wet in the rain waiting for a golf course to open. There was a certain tone to his voice that annoyed me. I had heard the same tone from one bus driver. It was the spiteful tone reserved by some Scots for the ugly Americans. Their way of telling us to get the fuck out of their country. They were never going to get the opportunity to turn their contempt on Donald Trump, who had recently bought up a hunk of their country for another golf course, so any Yank would do.

You can't blame them really, though I lit a cigarette and waited silently for the milkman to grow bored with me and leave.

Davy was the next person to arrive. I watched him park his small car in the empty parking lot, then sprint through the rain to the caddie shed. The lights went on inside the low-slung stone building, which looked as if it had stood on the land for centuries.

I've been on Oprah's lit-up stage. And the *Today* show. And *Good Morning America*. But I was nervous now in a way I hadn't been before. Here I was a foreigner without a work visa, because caddies are never asked for them, who had overstepped the dividing line separating myself from the real caddies.

I had the money in my left hand as I shook Davy's hand. "I think I made a mistake yesterday," I told him. He cocked his head slightly and looked straight into my eyes. I explained what had happened, then handed him the money.

He looked at it, folded the bills carefully, and handed them back to me.

"I heard what you did for us yesterday, Don," he said. "You helped us out, and I'm grateful."

It was the kind of relief you feel when the cop who has pulled you over tells you he's going to let you off this time with just a warning. "I don't think I should keep the money," I said. "I'm just a shadow, and I made some mistakes out there."

"Aye," he said. "But you dinna make any new ones! And you're not a shadow anymore, Don."

We talked for a while. He gave me the best advice: "Someday you will be caddying for your son when every shot will count. What you want to do now is learn something each time you are out on the golf course. Keep your eyes open and your head up and you will always learn something new."

So here I am in the Chariots pub celebrating with mashed and bangers. And I'm wearing my new handsome vest, dark blue with the gold Kingsbarns crown over my heart. I feel as if I belong here.

MAY 13, 2008

Let it be noted here what a well-trained caddie working in Scotland will carry for himself and his golfer: tees, divot tool, small coin for marker, pencil, extra scorecard, lighter, wool cap for when the wind howls off the North Sea, sunscreen (seldom needed), large towel with one end kept wet to clean clubs and ball, wee towel kept dry at all costs beneath his clothing and used only for grips (often needed), sandwich for when he is sent straight from the 18th green back to the 1st tee for a second loop, small bottle of water he can refill around the course as needed, waterproofs top and bottom, a pharmacopoeia of drugs for aches and ailments because it is a point of honor *never* to call in sick in the 180-day season, pin sheet, and yardage book, though he knows the ground by heart. In addition, of course, he carries his golfer's clubs, and because the game can wreak havoc inside a player's mind, there are those times when he carries his golfer as well and learns what it really means to be a caddie.

These last three days I made a friend for life in a sixty-year-old investment banker from JPMorgan. It began on a windswept hillside just off the par-5 9th tee. He had blocked his drive high into a left-to-right gale, and by the time I climbed down the hill and found his ball, we were so far off course that he was just going to pick up and skip the hole. I persuaded him that we still had a chance. "A chance for what?" he said. "For par," I told him. I handed him his eight-iron. "If you can just get the ball up in the air and over my head, we'll be able to play from there." He agreed to give it a try. I climbed back up the hill to the edge of the fairway, then positioned myself in a spot that took the bunkers out of play. It had taken us so long to reach his ball that his three pals were way off in the distance, already approaching the green. I put my hands over my head like a football referee signaling a touchdown. "Right at me!" I yelled down at him. He sort of shrugged, then settled into the swing. He swung so hard his hat flew off, and though it was not a great swing by any means, it was decent enough for his ball to clear my head by a few feet and land harmlessly in the fairway. When he reached me, he was winded from the climb. "We lie two," I reminded him. "Three strokes left to save par." We missed that par but had two even more remarkable par saves on the back nine, and as we were walking up 18 together, he asked me if I would caddie for him the next two days, when he and his pals played at Elie and the Torrance Course. "Why didn't you give up on me?" he asked as we walked to his car. I gave him my stock answer, every word true, telling him that someday I would be fighting to save par with my son when we were playing on a pro tour somewhere.

Davy gave me permission, and I spent the next two days with him. Late this afternoon as we were saying our good-byes and exchanging e-mail addresses, I said, "Can I ask you something?"

"Anything," he said.

"Well, all my life I've heard that making a ton of money as an investment banker is easy. I've never believed that. I've always thought that for every guy who gets rich, there have to be nine guys who wash out."

He stopped me and turned to look into my eyes. "You're wrong," he said. "Take a look at the four of us. None of us made less than thirty million last year. And believe me, it was easy. A hell of a lot easier than lugging around someone's golf clubs."

We had spent enough time together that he knew my financial situation. I had told him about the $300,000 I'd borrowed from banks so far to put my kids through college. Now as he took his wallet from his golf bag, he asked me if I had any of that money left. "Not much," I said. "Well, whatever you have, you need to get it out of the banks in cash," he told me. "Are you getting any news from home?"

I told him that I had no TV or radio or Internet. "I'm living in a dreamworld here," I said.

"Good for you," he said with a smile that quickly vanished. "Bear Stearns's stock was selling for $133 a share not long ago. Our company is about to buy all their stock for two bucks a share." Then he asked me if I had read my Suetonius. "The writings of the Roman historian who accurately predicted the collapse of the Roman Empire," he explained. "Suetonius was invited to spend an evening reading poetry in the mansion of a nobleman. All in attendance were noblemen, and after two poems they were no longer interested in listening. Here were the nation's aristocracy, and they had become shallow, uneducated people, interested only in their personal gain and their entertainment. After that evening, Suetonius knew that his society was finished. We're right back there again. Trust me."

He took seven $100 bills from his wallet, folded them neatly, and placed them in my hand. "Don't put this in the bank," he said. "Wire it home on Western Union to your wife. Wire home every dollar you don't need to survive here. Tell your wife to put it in a coffee can along with all the cash you have in the bank and on those lines of credit. Max out all your credit cards for cash too. Don't worry about paying it back. And if you own stock, sell it. Have your wife bury the can in your backyard. I'm completely serious about this. A tsunami is coming. It's going to happen this summer. Guys like me already have our exit strategy. You need to do exactly what I'm telling you."

I don't know what to make of this, whether these are the wise words of a man with inside information or the mad, guilt-laden rantings of a jaded banker. Either way, I liked him and enjoyed our connection. As for his predictions, it's a terrible thing to admit, but if he had been a decent golfer instead of a hacker, I think I would take his advice.

After my loop tonight when the course was empty, I sat on a hillside, leaning against a stone wall, and wrote Colleen a love letter on my BlackBerry. I thanked her for each of our babies and for believing in me as a writer. I apologized for being such a slow learner and for never being able to hold down a job across the years. In our twenty-five years together I taught for only eight years, and that was the only time I've had a steady paycheck. I was already fifty years old when we bought our first house. And I was fifty-three when my movie was made and I took my three daughters to Hollywood and bought them their first nice dresses. It just took so damned long for me. And it was difficult. I never had any natural ability. It was all just pure determination for me.

For as long as I live, let me never forget this ride into work along the North Sea with the sun just rising over the blue water, and the tan sheep on the green hillsides, and the ancient stone walls dividing the farmers' fields, and these good people on their way to work with me. The farmworkers from eastern Europe in their muddy rubber boots. The young Scottish nurse with blush in her cheeks, sitting up so straight in her starched white uniform. And the schoolchildren in their blue blazers and black ties.

I climb to the upper deck of this bus and tap these words into my BlackBerry: I could live here forever, and if I can stay healthy and fit, I can march every day as a caddie and take care of Colleen as I grow old. I can do one loop a day for £60, which is £1,800 a month roughly. Four hundred and sixty for rent and utilities. No car. No car insurance. No TV or Internet. No pension. No bank account because since September 11, no foreigners can open up bank accounts in Great Britain. Just throw my money into a drawer at the end of every day and we will have more than we can spend. What we won't need, we will send home to the kids.

Midnight. I can't fall asleep. I miss Colleen. I miss my girls. It seems that whenever I think about them, my eyes fill with tears. I miss Jack. They all seem so far away. I can feel the passage of time carrying us away. I know what it is. All day out on my loop this morning with the three caddies who were half my age, I had to hurry to keep up. The thing that I worried about on the bus this morning was right there in front of me at work. And my right knee is sore. I came down the back side of a hill and twisted it under the weight of a very heavy golf bag. I was trying not to limp through the rest of the round. But for the life of me, I could not catch up. I felt the way you do in a dream when you are trying to run but your legs won't move fast enough to get up any real speed.

And then, to make matters worse, when I walked back to town and stumbled into the little stone hut at the bus stop, there was someone there, sitting on the bench with his head bowed, leaning forward on his knees, as if he were praying or trying to catch his breath. He was wearing a new Titleist cap and brand-new running shoes and shorts that showed his tan legs. I had on my blue vest, and when I introduced myself, it surprised me that he knew who I was. He explained that Davy had told him about me, the guy trying to become a caddie for his son. He asked me how old my son was, and we talked for a while about the road ahead. Then he told me that he had been caddying for almost thirty years, working at private clubs in Florida during the winter and for the last seven seasons here at Kingsbarns during the summer. This winter he had developed some trouble with circulation in his feet, and today, his first day back in Scotland, he had walked the golf course alone, climbing the hills at his own pace, just to test his feet on this ground. "I'm at the end of the line," he said as he glanced up the road into the distance. "I just told Davy that I'm through. I'll be leaving in the morning."

When the bus came, rather than walk to the door with him, I said good-bye. "You're not coming?" he asked.

"No, I'm taking the bus into St. Andrews," I lied.

"You're waiting on the wrong side of the road then," he said.

"Right," I said. "I keep forgetting."

I don't know why I didn't want to ride the bus with him. Maybe because I thought he wanted to be alone with his thoughts. Or maybe because I was afraid to get any closer to him. He looked to be younger than I by at least a few years. I watched him pull himself up onto the bus like an old man. Then he turned back.

"Your boy has to make the cuts to have a chance. Play the early rounds *not to lose*. Then after you make the cut, *play to win*."

"Good advice," I said. "Thanks."

"And if you're going to be on his bag, don't put on weight," he said, patting his stomach. "There aren't any fat, good caddies."

JUNE 10, 2008

This morning I sat for three hours with Jimmy Hughes, my age exactly, a fine man with bright eyes and a quick wit. I feel comfortable talking with him. His father did not want him to become a fisherman, and so that is what he became. For years, each day at work, just off the shore here, he would look at the golf course while he was working and wonder what it would be like to be a caddie. Now he's here. Today I told him the advice that one of the veteran caddies had told me a month ago. The secret is to stay one step ahead of the golfer, meaning, don't wait until you get to the tee to look in your yardage book for the distances to the bunkers ahead of you. Glance at the yardage book and get the distances while you are walking from the green to the tee box. If you are going to be calm and unhurried out there, then you have to stay ahead. This is going to be a job of uncertainty. Each day we don't know if we will go out. And if we do, we don't know what time we will go out. We don't know when we will finish and go home. We don't know what kind of golfer we will have or how he will treat us. We don't know what we will get paid. We don't know what the weather will be like. We don't know if we will screw up in some fundamental way. We don't know if we'll be able to find his golf ball when he hits it into the rough. And then, of course, there is the uncertainty that is intrinsic to the game. Nothing is certain. The caddie must carry through all the uncertainty—with a quiet confidence and calm as if he relishes the uncertainty. Thrives on it! Will never get flustered by it! We are supposed to be the Kings of Cool. Always cool.

After three hours, Davy told us all that we could go home. The rest of the golfers booked for the late afternoon had not requested caddies when they made their reservations. There was always the chance they might change their minds when they arrived, and so I stayed behind and waited another four hours and had the privilege of being the last caddie out on the course with a Catholic priest from Northern Ireland with freckled arms and long red hair who apologized to me on the 1st tee for the weight of his old leather golf bag. When I raised it off the ground, it felt like a ship's anchor. "Take a look," he said. I knelt down and unzipped the large pocket, then counted eight sixteen-ounce tins of Tennent's beer. "If you're feeling like a drink yourself, be my guest," he said amiably. "The more we drink, the lighter your load."

I liked him immediately and tried out the line I'd heard from one of the Scottish caddies on the 1st tee. Because we meet on the 1st tee, we have no idea what kind of golfer the fellow is—more of the uncertainty. I have already been out with a man from Belgium who never hit one single shot in the fairway the entire round. I spent five hours walking through thick fescue with my head down searching miserably for his balls. "Okay, Father," I said as he took his practice swings on the 1st tee. "Tell me how far you can hit your driver, and please don't lie to me."

I liked his smile. And the way he struck the ball. He didn't hit it far, but he kept it straight, which meant a walk in the short grass for a change. We were only 158 yards from the green after his low, drawing drive rolled 60 yards when it landed. This called for his first beer. When I unzipped the bag this time, some clothes fell out. One item was a black shirt with the white priest's collar attached. I am beginning to think that every golfer I will meet this season will have a story. He told me his as we played on. He was here to make a very difficult call on an old friend who had started seminary with him twenty-four years ago but had dropped out, gotten married, and raised a family not far from St. Andrews. Three days ago the man's oldest son had drowned.

It came down to the two of us discussing the existence of God while we huddled on the bench at the 15th tee, him finishing off his last beer and me holding the umbrella to keep the sideways rain from our faces, with the grip of his driver shoved under my jacket and shirt to keep it dry. Across the years he said it had occurred to him many times that the whole story of God and Jesus and the Holy Mother might have been just a made-up story to placate our fears about dying. But he had always renounced these doubts and clung to his faith. But now he was worried. The moment he had received word of the death of his old friend's son, he had begun to sense that this was going to be the end of his belief. "That's why I arrived in time to walk eighteen holes," he explained. "And I never take a caddie. But I knew that I needed to talk with someone this time. I mean, before I go and see my friend."

I told him that I had taken my four children to Northern Ireland in 1997 so they could walk through the village their great-grandmother had left in 1901 to make her way by boat to Ellis Island. "The next summer there was that terrible bombing."

"Omagh," he said. "Horrendous. The worst bombing in the history of the Troubles. It was the anniversary of my ordination of all things. I went to Omagh one year later." He asked me if I was familiar with the band U2 and their version of "Sunday Bloody Sunday" when Bono recites the names of everyone killed in the bombing there. I told him that I was.

"Actually," he said, "a writer from America wrote a book about Omagh. I read it some time ago. A novel that was set against the backdrop of the bombing. He had been at the funeral for a young mother who died in the blast with twin girls in her belly just a few weeks from being born. And her three-year-old daughter holding her hand. All four were buried in the same grave. I don't recall her name just now."

"Avril Monaghan," I said.

He was surprised. "So you know the story?" he asked.

I told him that my son had given me the DVD of Bono singing

the song in her memory. We talked about his faith and loss of faith as we walked in the soft rain while dusk fell. Coming up the 16th fairway, we were only 170 yards from the green in two on the par-5. I handed him a six-iron and explained that we had to land this next shot short of the green. "If the ball reaches the green on the fly or the roll," I said, "it will race all the way across the green and down the slope into the river. Nothing can stop it."

When I handed him the six-iron, I could tell that he wasn't buying it. "You want the five?" I said.

"I do," he said.

A moment later we watched his ball roll right up the front of the green and down off the back.

"That's going to be wet," he said with a pained expression.

"I'm afraid so," I said.

I took the club back from him, cleaned it, and slipped it into the bag as we started walking.

"I should have listened to you," he said.

"Well," I said, "why don't we take a test, Father? If your ball is not in the river, then that will be proof that there is a God and that you have lived a virtuous life."

He smiled and said, "That's putting a lot of pressure on God, don't you think?"

"That's what he's there for," I said.

Of course there was no sign of his ball on the green or in the two-yard band of sloping ground behind the green that fell off into the water. I took an iron from his bag and began fishing around in the narrow river, which had only a few inches of water in it. "A wee burn," I said. "That's what the Scots call these rivers."

A moment later he called to me. "You have to come see this, Bob," he said. So far he had called me Tom, Bill, and now Bob, though my name tag said Don.

Then I stood beside him looking down at his ball, which had rolled to a stop on a sprinkler head that was recessed maybe half an inch in the ground, just deep enough to stop the ball from continuing down into the river. He put his hand on my shoulder. "Can you believe that?" he said.

He paid me too much, and as I carried his clubs to the taxi, I wished him the best. "I'm sorry about your friend losing his son," I said.

I saw the anguish return to his eyes. It seemed to hit him all at once, as if the round of golf had made him forget what was waiting for him.

If he writes me an e-mail, I suppose I will tell him that I am the American writer who wrote the novel about Omagh. All the way back to Elie, I was thinking about that part of my life. I was up writing one August morning in 1998. News came over the radio of the bombing in the town of Omagh that killed thirty-one people, mostly women and children who were doing their back-to-school shopping in the town center where the blast took place. The summer before, when Colleen and I had taken our children on our family trip to Ireland, I fell in love with the Irish children, who all looked so much like my own, and later in the morning, when it was clear that most of the people killed in the blast were children, I knew that I had to go there and bear witness. Six hours later I was on a flight from Boston, traveling alone this time. I walked through the shattered glass and the puddles of blood on Main Street, and for ten days I stayed fifty yards from the center of the blast in the back of a hotel whose front half had been sheared off by the explosion. I attended thirteen funerals that week, joining the long processions from the victims' homes to the cemetery. And I stood in the rain at Avril Monaghan's grave, where she and her three children were buried. It was the only square grave I have ever seen. The following summer I returned for four months and spent time at the site of every IRA bombing in Northern Ireland in the thirty years of the Troubles before I wrote my book. That seems like another lifetime now.

JUNE 19, 2008

My pal Glen Carter, from Canada, arrived today. I was able to get
him a caddying job at the new Castle Course just up the road from
Kingsbarns. Glen is an old veteran from the Nationwide Tour and
the Canadian Tour, and he's been suffering through the loss of his
father, and I've been trying to persuade him to come over and walk
off his grief.

Glen got a flat in Pittenweem. So we are now two towns apart,
both of us riding the 95 bus route to work and back each day. I hope
I get to see him often. When I came off the 18th green, he was
standing there, waiting for me. Glen, the old basketball player with
hands as big around as pie plates and the expressive eyes and sharp
nose that stamp him as a duplicate of the actor Donald Sutherland.
His was the first familiar face for me in three months. For a while in
my life we had been neighbors in the small town of St. Andrews-by-
the-Sea, New Brunswick, Canada, and he played golf the same way
I did, with a deep longing to play better. I had not seen him in over
two years, but as we walked a few holes at Kingsbarns under a high,
bright sun, it seemed as if only a few weeks had passed since we were
last together. He was a veteran caddie but he was apprehensive about
this new job. "On the tour you know your player," he said. "Out here,
you're with someone different every time around."

"A blind date," I told him. "But it comes down to the same thing
you did with the pros. You are just trying to help each golfer believe
in himself enough to make the next shot."

"True, I suppose," he said. "A blind date. I don't know if I like the
sound of that."

We rode the bus into St. Andrews, passing the new Castle Course on our right, hidden beyond big green hills, so he could purchase his bus pass at the station. In the streets of St. Andrews today there were the unique sounds and scenes that mark this town as the home of golf—men walking the narrow streets, carrying their golf clubs. Close your eyes and you hear the clinking of irons on every block. Past the golf shops with the latest technology on display in the broad windows. And then the big surprise, you turn a corner and there it is, the Old Course. It comes on you suddenly and gives you the odd impression that even though you have been streaming through towns and cities and across continents for years, chasing after one enterprise or another, you were really only returning here the whole time.

"Look at this" was all Glen said. "Just look at this." The 1st and 18th fairways an impossible shade of green, as if they were painted. Golfers waiting nervously on the 1st tee. A collection of pedestrians standing at the low green slatted fence watching three players make their final putts, one of them taking a full swing with his putter to send his ball up through the famous Valley of Sin. The granite steps rising from the back of the green to the Royal & Ancient (the golf-governing body of Scotland) with its blue-trimmed windows, where old men in blazers and ties stood drinking tea, enjoying one of the most exclusive views in the world.

"Arnold Palmer shot an 84 his first practice round here," I said.

Glen the historian and sports statistician replied, "He had old Tip Anderson on his bag when he played his first open championship here in 1960," his voice hushed as if we were standing inside a church.

"That's right," I said. "Palmer was making a charge when the R&A delayed the final round because of rain, something that had never happened before. Arnie was furious."

"So he makes an impossible par save from the road on 17, then birdies 18," Glen went on.

"Then loses to Kel Nagle by one stroke. And Palmer still says it was the greatest disappointment of his life."

"Hell, he'd already won the Masters and the U.S. Open that year. He was on his way."

We followed the narrow white path of crushed seashells, passing the short par-4s, talking about all the fabulous history that had taken place on a golf course that was remarkably modest and nondescript. "Kingsbarns is an art gallery," I said. "This is like the course you'd set up behind the barn for your grandkids when you give them their first golf clubs."

"Ah, it's a museum," he said.

We walked out onto the 4th green, and he marveled at the humps, as if someone had buried old trucks beneath the ground. "If you were here," he exclaimed, "how would you roll this putt? To where? Where does it become a straight line?" I surveyed the ground and walked to a spot maybe four feet left of the hole. "I'd putt it to here," I said. He thought about it then walked the line himself. "Yep," he said. "I agree." We were like two old carpenters checking the warp in a pile of boards.

"At sixty-one," he said, "I imagine I'll be the oldest caddie at the Castle Course."

"I think I'm the oldest at Kingsbarns," I told him.

"It's a young man's game," he said gravely.

"You'll be fine," I said. "I've done a few doubles. Walk straight off 18, right back to 1. Turn-and-burn, the Scottish boys call them."

"How are they treating you?"

"Great," I said. "Best people I've ever known."

As we made the turn, I told him about the winter I spent here writing my novel, living in the Rusacks Hotel on the 18th fairway. He had forgotten that I had played the course every day for almost two months. Today I named all the bunkers for him and told him their distances from the tees and showed him the lines on the blind shots. "Someday, Glen," I said, "you and I are going to caddie together here."

"Wouldn't that be something," he said.

There were tears coming down his cheeks then. We were just two more pilgrims who had followed an ever-narrowing path through fading dreams and somehow ended up together here on a luminous afternoon. I showed him the place where Jack and I had buried his golf ball in the sleet that winter morning, vowing that we would return someday and that far out into his future he would bring a son or daughter of his own here to dig the ball out of the turf as some kind of proof that the past was real.

We spoke of Glen's father. His death three months earlier is the reason Glen is here now. He needs the work to try to get through his sorrow. I hadn't known anything about his father before today. Glen, at age eighteen, was the center of his father's life and the source of his greatest pride when he went off to college on a basketball scholarship. And when he flunked out after his freshman season, a wide space filled with regret and recrimination opened between them for years. They managed to reach an understanding and were just beginning to draw close again when they ran out of time.

I rode the bus to Pittenweem to see his flat. He's right in the harbor, just three doors down from a pub, where I bought my first pint in two months. When we told the bartender that Glen was going to be caddying at the Castle Course, he informed us that Prince Harry is going to be on hand for opening day.

JUNE 21, 2008

I am Davy's coverage this summer. Meaning I have volunteered to be here all summer, sitting outside on the lopsided picnic table or in the stone shed that is damp even on sunny days with a cold that insinuates itself right into my bones and joints, so that after an hour of sitting, it requires real effort to stand up straight. None of the other caddies can bear to sit here for longer than three hours waiting for work. But because I am the outsider, the illegal immigrant working in this country, I told Davy that I will sit here every day, all day long if that's what he needs. My little secret is this BlackBerry. I can do my writing here each day. Today I sat under the trees along the side of the practice range and began writing a new draft of *American Love Story*, one letter at a time. I've lived with the story for the three years it took me to write the book and the three years I've been trying to write the screenplay, but it wasn't until Jack and I were in Carnoustie, when he gave me his take on it, that I began to see my mother and father's love story in a new way. I am digging in again.

Here is a note to myself. Golf is distinctly *not* what you see on TV. No breathtaking fifty-foot putts that collapse with one final revolution into the center of the hole. No jarring the ball from bunkers with sand as white as sugar. Golf here in Scotland, where the game was invented, is anguish and slaughter. I was sent to Elie to caddie today, a place I will forever think of as my home course, and I stood on the tee box of the 214-yard par-3, and no man God ever invented, and no driver ever designed, could have reached the green in the teeth of the forty-five-knot wind that was howling in off the sea. What I have already learned here is that trying to play this game at some level of perfection is a dark ride to nowhere you want to be. Which has me worried about Jack. On the one hand, it still holds the elegant governing dynamic of one man against nature. A simple and perfect equation. But I wonder if Jack has the constitution to take the pressure on his mind. And now that I think of it, maybe golf is one of the reasons that the Scottish boys are humble by nature. You sit around with fifty of them day after day, and one thing that is missing from the chatter is the word "I." They don't speak about themselves very much. They love to tell stories, but they are not the central character in these stories.

A few days ago, Kevin, in his thirties with two small children, was asking me why there weren't any great Scottish golfers on the scene. I hadn't considered this before, and I really didn't have a clue. Neither did he. But maybe the golf has humbled the Scots in some way so that they can't summon the arrogance it takes to win at the top and to stay there. If arrogance is required rather than self-confidence, then I hope Jack never wins at this game. And if he does become an arrogant man, then I will rue the day I first placed a golf club in his hand.

JULY 5, 2008

Trouble at home. I had an e-mail this morning from Jack saying that he had failed to make the cut in a tournament. "I don't think I have what it takes to make it here, Daddy. I'm thinking of coming home. Why do we chase our dreams anyway?" he wrote to me. I was sitting on the bench inside the caddie shed when the BlackBerry buzzed across my heart. Beside me was one of the frontline boys, a big-shouldered fellow in his early fifties, I would say. He keeps to himself. I've never seen him speaking with anyone. He just sits with his head bowed until Davy calls his name to go up to the 1st tee.

A week ago or so I asked one of the other experienced caddies about him, and he told me that he had once been a championship golfer who won the Scottish Boys Golf Championship, then went on to make it through the qualifiers to the British Open a few years later. A regular phenomenon and hometown hero who was expected to become one of the greatest golfers Scotland ever produced, until the wrong girl and too much booze got in the way. His life fell apart until he began putting it back together by working as a caddie.

This morning after I read the e-mail, I turned my head slightly and saw that he was just staring at the ground. I thought maybe he was trying to fall asleep and I should leave him alone because it was obvious that was what he wanted, but instead I said, "My son is in his first season at D1 golf in the States. Nineteen years old. He can't make the cuts, and he just wrote me to tell me he is thinking of quitting."

Then I read him the e-mail. When I finished, I said, "I don't know what to tell him. Why do we chase our dreams? What's the answer to that question?"

He never turned his head to acknowledge me, but his eyes narrowed and he drew his shoulders back as if I'd just kicked him in the chest. He never looked at me when he answered. "Tell him we chase our dreams *because we can*. Because we're not in some hospital, dying of cancer."

With this, he stood up and went to look for some privacy, I suppose. But before he could leave, I got to my feet and thanked him. "I'm going to tell him that," I said.

JULY 19, 2008

For caddies in most of the world, the term "double" means you carry two bags, one on each shoulder, caddying for two golfers and dividing your time between them. Here in Scotland the term "double" means you do two loops in one day. And in most cases each golfer has his own caddie. The reasoning for this makes perfect sense: in Scotland the majority of golfers have traveled here from somewhere and are unfamiliar with the ground and need careful supervision in order to avoid disaster. One caddie attempting to provide sufficient attention to two golfers at the same time would be perilous and rather like one man attempting to romance two women simultaneously, with the result being that neither woman felt sufficiently looked after.

I did the back half of a double today with Paul, a retired policeman from Glasgow with a gleaming shaved head and the rugged build of a lumberjack. All summer I have observed a mounting anxiety in all the caddies, even the seasoned vets, as their time to go out approaches. It was a blind date for all of us; one never knew what to expect, and secretly we all feared the same thing—being stuck for five hours with an irredeemable asshole. Paul was the only caddie among us whose calm demeanor didn't change as he made his way to the starter's hut. "Once more into the breach," he said to me as we walked side by side.

"Ah, Shakespeare," I said.

"*Henry the Fifth*. I said the same thing before each shift on the police force." He gave me a handshake and said, "It will be nice to be out here today with someone who knows his Shakespeare."

Paul had the best greeting lines I'd heard so far. On the 1st tee he said, "Gentlemen," then waited for all four golfers to turn to face him. "Just remember. You're not here to have fun today. You're here to play golf."

All four gentlemen smiled and laughed, and we were off on what promised to be an enjoyable loop with four heart surgeons from Los Angeles. But the trouble started on the 1st green when Paul's man glared at him after he missed a three-foot putt for bogey. It was just a glance but enough for Paul to know that a storm was brewing. On the way to the next tee he said to me, "I've got a real wanker on my hands here."

He was right. Over the course of the next three holes the surgeon made a series of horrible shots and found a way to blame Paul for each of them. I watched closely as Paul bided his time and kept his distance, giving the man the line for each shot and the read for each putt without expression before promptly walking away from the man as if he might be carrying an infectious disease. After each shot, Paul reached for the doctor's club, then marched out ahead as he shoved it back into the bag. The whole time I had the feeling Paul was going to walk off the course and leave the doctor to his misery.

And then we came to the 8th hole, and the poor fellow's ball landed in a footprint in a bunker. He looked down at the lie, opened his arms to appeal to the heavens, and cried out, "That's not fair!" By now all of us had gathered around to have a look at the injustice for ourselves. "That's not fair!" he cried out again.

Paul casually handed him his wedge and said, "Life isn't fair, Doctor. And it's a good thing it isn't, or we'd all be in Africa right now starving alongside those poor bastards instead of playing golf in Scotland." A great hush fell over us as Paul stood the man's golf bag on its legs and leaned over it with his head resting on the driver as if he intended to take a nice nap now that he had delivered his sermon. His golfer took three swings to send the ball out of the bunker, then climbed out himself, handed Paul his wedge, and said very calmly, "You're right."

The effect on the doctor was nothing less than stunning. At once he began behaving like a grown-up instead of a child. And within the next hour he and Paul were walking side by side and chatting each other up. At the clubhouse when we finished, he had one of his pals snap a photograph of the two of them with their arms around each other.

Walking back to the caddie shed, I told Paul that I had never seen such a transformation. He smiled and held out his hand to show me what the doctor had paid him. One hundred and sixty pounds.

Paul made more in one round than I made in my double. "That's because you taught him something about life," I said.

"Sometimes we have to," he said. "It's in the job description. In the fine print." He gave me a grin, and we walked on.

AUGUST 3, 2008

It has been raining for so many days and I have been walking in wet shoes for so long that the tips of my toes have turned black with some kind of fungus. Big Gary tells me that I should soak them in boiling alcohol while drinking single-malt whiskey. "The only cure," he says.

Today, a few hundred yards down the 1st fairway my shoes were filled with rainwater again. Even the Gore-Tex waterproofs couldn't stop the rain, and by the time we reached the 1st green, I was soaked through to my skin and shivering with cold. Rainwater sloshing around in my crotch. Each step is a small agony in this kind of condition. You can feel your bones grinding in their sockets when you climb up the hills. And no matter how you try, rain keeps running down the back of your neck, like a cold spark. It was just survival out there for almost five hours.

When it was over, I walked the half mile to the bus stop in rain so heavy that it had strange properties of light and color, almost like spilled milk, pouring down over my head. The bus driver told me that I had to take a seat. "I can't," I told him. "I'm too cold."

So I stood beside him. The bus lurched forward, and I finally allowed myself to imagine stripping off my wet clothes and stepping into the hot shower. We rolled maybe a hundred yards, just coming upon the gates to Kingsbarns, where one of the boys from the pro shop sat in a buggy waving the bus to a stop with both hands. I asked the driver what time it was. Three thirty, he said. I knew the buggy was for me and that a golfer must have shown up wanting a caddie. By eight thirty tonight I will be finished, I told myself. In five hours I will be back on the bus, heading home. In six hours I will have a hot shower, my bowl of pea soup, and two hard rolls with butter. And then I will sleep in a bed under warm blankets.

AUGUST 11, 2008

Today is my fifty-eighth birthday, and all I have to say is this: a good, hardworking caddie doesn't complain if his golfer is an ungrateful asshole or if he's not properly paid or if it is pissing rain for five straight hours or if the wind is at gale force and knocks him back a half step for every step forward or if he spends hours in the rough searching for balls or marching up and down hills to the *wrong* fairways or if his bag is too heavy or if he's hot and thirsty and his back is aching or if he has finished eighteen holes and just rolled a cigarette to relax for a few minutes when he is summoned to the 1st tee to begin another five hours with cold rainwater running down the back of his neck or if at the end of a ten-hour day he misses his bus home by three minutes and has to wait an hour in the pouring rain for the next one. It is a point of honor never to complain and in a 180-day season never to call in sick: this is how one earns the respect of his fellow caddies. And in the end, respect is all that matters to a good, hardworking caddie.

I want to earn Jack's respect out there someday when I caddie for him. His golf team is back at practice again. The start of his fall sophomore season. I hope he has a breakthrough this season and can make the travel squad. He hasn't written to me more than a few sentences in e-mails all summer. He's busy, I know. There is a young girl in town here who reminds me of my Cara at home, and I can't look at her anymore, because it makes me too sad. And the same is true about the golden retriever at the corner who reminds me of Teddy asleep at my side of the bed waiting for me to come back. I've been gone five months now, and I miss Colleen terribly. Maybe this is why I have not had a single putt drop for me in the last week. Not one. And I can't blame it all on the golfers, even though most of them are probably lousy putters. I'm not seeing the lines anymore. I was out with old John the workhorse yesterday, and when I told him that I felt like a blind man and asked him what he *sees*, he said, "I don't see anything. I feel it with my feet." That explains why he walks the length of the putt on each green. He feels the break with his feet.

So last night I fell asleep in my clothes again and then woke at 2:00 in the morning with the room filled with light from the moon right outside my window. I walked across the street to one of the greens on the little public course, which was lit up in moonlight bright enough for me to putt. I dropped balls all over the green, then walked the lines and tried to feel the humps and slopes with my feet. I set my BlackBerry at the hole with its lit dial for my target. I missed every putt by a mile until the moon slipped behind clouds and it was then so dark that I had to rely only on what I could feel with my feet. I began doing better. Much better. And at work today I had my confidence back, and the putts started falling again, right from the 1st hole. I was out with an old World War II vet from Illinois whose left hand was shaking badly when he putted, so I told him to rest his left elbow against his body. It worked like a charm for him. We were sitting on the stone wall at the 10th, waiting for the group in front, when he told me that he had built his little manufacturing company from the ground up. For years he had employed 280 people working three shifts. His son took over the company, and two years ago he moved the operation somewhere in Asia where he could pay workers almost nothing. This enabled the son to earn an extra 11 percent profit a year. "For 11 percent more profit, he put those good American workers out into the street, my boy did," the old man told me. "I don't blame him for being greedy; we all have our share of greed in us. What I blame him for is being unpatriotic."

I'm going to remember him telling me this. When we finished and were shaking hands, I said to him, "Thank you for what you did for America."

AUGUST 22, 2008

I now own the reputation for the biggest caddie fuckup in the brief but elegant eight-year history of the Kingsbarns Golf Links. I am the guy who has lived on a monk's budget all season so that I could send all my money home. Seventeen pounds a week for my food, not a dime more. Which means eating soup and hard rolls six nights a week and splurging the seventh with a hamburger, which they call mince here. Watching every penny. Never going out with the guys to drink at night. I have my BlackBerry with me all the time. It is in my vest pocket on vibrate so that each time it hums, while I'm working, I have the pleasant thought that Colleen or one of the kids is writing me an e-mail. But I cannot use it as a telephone under any circumstances, because the fee would be way beyond my budget.

So today I was out with the nicest group of guys from Oklahoma. They were down to their final day in St. Andrews and had not been able to get on the Old Course. I told them the local secret, that if they showed up just before the last tee time, the starter might let them follow behind the final group and play what they call the Dark Hours. Then I offered to make a call to the one starter I knew there to see how it looked for today. I made the call standing on the 10th tee and got an answering machine. So I left a message, and we played on.

It wasn't until an hour ago, just after nine o'clock tonight, that I realized I had somehow failed to hang up the phone. I had left a five-hour-and-twenty-three-minute message. When I called AT&T, they told me it cost $889.45. The math. I am averaging £63 per loop, which means I will have to do eighty-three loops to earn that money back. Impossible.

SEPTEMBER 2, 2008

"I was never much of a church person," old Burton in his thread-bare plaid trousers whispered to me on the 16th green. "My church was always on a golf course." There were eight of us—four golfers and four caddies—all in hushed silence while one fellow prepared to putt. There is a churchlike nature to the structures and rituals of golf. Kneeling down to line up a putt. Heads bowed over each shot. The searching. The arms opened, eyes turned to the heavens exhorting the gods for some explanation of why we keep thinning our long irons. The dreadful and penitent march to where your ball disappeared hopelessly into the rough, praying for salvation—that you'll be able to get a club on it, or at least find it. All of these transactions conducted in a peaceful quiet that sometimes seems to enter you.

Today I carried my golfer's medication in the inside pocket of my vest. A small plastic box like the kind fishermen keep their flies in. He handed this to me on the 1st tee. "Dynamite," he said. "Nitroglycerin for my angina. Not enough blood flowing to the heart."

He was stooped at the shoulders and he walked with a limp, but he had wonderful, restless blue eyes and a great story. He was stuck in a nursing home by his children somewhere in Missouri where everyone was sitting around waiting to die, and he was just dying to get out and play golf while he still could. "I'd never used a computer in my life," he told me. "And I didn't know the Internet from the interstate, but one of the nurses showed me the ropes." He spent most of a year doing Google searches and Facebook searches, trying to find out if he had any old friends left in the real world. Finally one turned up. "That man right there," he told me, pointing to his pal Nigel. "We were at Stanford together doing graduate work in the 1950s. I hadn't spoken to him in thirty years. But he sprung me from the nursing home. Just drove up in his Lincoln and took me the hell out of there one night. And here we are now." All Burton brought with him were his golf clothes. He was so paranoid his kids would find out and come after him that when they made the reservations for this trip, he used a false name.

What a character! I told him that I was going to remember him as my fugitive golfer. "That's me," he said cheerfully. "On the run. On the lam. Tomorrow we're at Royal Dornoch. Then on to Turnberry. I can't wait. Maybe Prestwick too if my ticker holds up."

We skipped the last two holes so he could catch his breath. It was almost growing dark when we sat on the stone wall waiting for Nigel and the others to finish. Burt couldn't get over how bright the sky was. "That beautiful par-3 where I hit it into the ocean, I sure ruined that hole," he said solemnly. "I tried to bail out to the left like you said, but I blocked it. What a shame. The one that got away, I guess."

I was prepared to bribe someone in the pro shop with a tenner, but the assistant pro let me use the buggy and I drove the two of us back down the 9th fairway through the golden sunlight and the long shadows, up the front side of the mounds and down the back, all the way to the 15th tee, where I handed Burt his driver so he could play the beautiful par-3 again.

"You think I need the big dog?" he questioned.

"It's late," I said. "The air is heavy, Burton."

He nodded and held out his hand, palm up. "I'll take one TNT," he said.

I gave him the pill, and he slipped it under his tongue. "I think we make our own destiny, don't you, Don?" he sang as he teed up his ball.

I told him to take aim at the right half of the bunker on the back of the green.

"One hundred and eighty-seven yards will reach the sand," I said. "Just give me 165, and we'll be in the mayor's office."

"The mayor's office," he said. "I like that. I just want to make one pretty swing, and then I'll tell you about Deidre while we're driving to the green with my putter in my hand."

It worked out pretty much the way he envisioned it. He didn't hit it on the screws, but close enough for the ball to run up onto the front of the green. I handed him his putter (best feeling in the world for any caddie coming off any par-3 tee box), and then he told me that he preferred to walk. So we did while he told me that there was this girl in Palo Alto named Deidre back in the early 1950s when he was there. He and Nigel were both in love with her. "Madly in love" is how he put it. "Intoxicated, to be honest. Nigel thought I was bedding her, and I thought he was. We became mortal enemies. It wasn't until I found him on Google that we both discovered that neither one of us had ever had her. Can you believe it? We found her on Google too. She lives in Seattle. When we get back to the States, we're going to look her up, hats in hand, you might say."

We missed the long birdie putt but captured the par. Burton was describing it to Nigel for the third time while we rode in a taxi to Elie. They had insisted on giving me a ride home. It was ten o'clock, and the moon was floating above the poppy field as we left the course. The taxi driver was talking about the bad economy; his fares were down more than 50 percent from last summer. He'd met a caddie in town who sold his vest to a golfer for twenty quid. He went on and on about the Royal Bank of Scotland—"nottin' but a pack a thieves." It was an old story by now. I was grateful for a day's work, even though I waited seven hours for my loop. We are down from about

130 jobs a day to 30, and it is every man for himself now. The America I left behind seems to be in ruins.

We said our good-byes. I thanked Burton for the good company and the tip and wished him the best of luck with Deidre in Seattle.

He smiled, and nodded thoughtfully. The last thing I heard him say was "Thank God for Google."

SEPTEMBER 9, 2008

Apparently, the big investment bank Lehman Brothers is kaput, and people are afraid that the stock market is going to fail big-time.

Here is my e-mail exchange with my pal at JPMorgan at 10:00 p.m. my time. Five o'clock his time in New York City.

"Donnie. We might be facing the end of our economy. Make sure you can get your kids home from wherever they are scattered around the world. Send them enough cash. Credit cards will be worthless."

"What do you mean, 'the end of our economy'?"

"I mean we will all be growing our food in our backyards."

"When?"

"Immediately."

"All my life I've been told that there are safeguards in the system to prevent another Great Depression."

"Forget that. And don't listen to any of the so-called experts. When the wind blows hard enough, things fall down. You should know that, Donnie—you're a fucking caddie in Scotland!"

"How bad is it going to get?"

"We could be talking about this scenario. You go to the bank on Monday and find the ATM is empty. Your accounts have zero balances—it turns out those figures were only images on a computer screen. Your credit cards are no longer valid. We are cast into a cash-only society overnight. All you have is the cash you have in the coffee can buried in the backyard. When that's gone, you're toast."

"I won't have anything."

"Tell your wife to take all your money out of the bank immediately!"

"Are you sure?"

"Call her *right now.* I am here on Wall Street. It's in the air. Like a plague."

"Okay. And I'm still sorry about that putt I misread on the 11th at Elie."

"I should have taken it out of your tip!"

OCTOBER 1, 2008

Day of days, Jack. I was in the parking lot carrying my golfer's clubs to the courtesy car after my round with a Swedish industrialist. There I was walking beside Padraig Harrington and his young caddie. I told him that since you were eight years old, just falling in love with golf, you and I have followed him.

"Before anyone knew me," he said with his grin.

"Yes," I said. "My son went off to play college golf in the States, and I came here to be a caddie so he and I can meet up again some-day on the tour."

"Where is he in college?"

"University of Toledo."

"In Ohio."

"That's right," I said. "Good luck this week."

He thanked me and we shook hands. As he was walking away, he turned and called to me, "What's your son's name?"

"Jack Snyder," I said.

"Jack Snyder at the University of Toledo," he said. "I'll remember that."

OCTOBER 14, 2008

Home. I awoke this morning knowing that I have been away from home long enough and that it is time for me to leave here. For a month I watched the grandstands and the tee box markers being constructed for the Dunhill Links Championship, like a stage set being built in advance of the actors' arrival. This is what I have looked forward to since early April. And the truth is I never thought I would make it through the season. I have walked about a thousand miles. I turned fifty-eight years old here a few months back. I am going to miss the people I worked with and the ground I walked each day. But I will not miss the waiting. The eight and nine hours of waiting for work.

The world of work seems to be changing now. I have not read a newspaper or listened to a radio or watched the television or surfed the Internet in over half a year, but I have had reports from home in e-mails, and it is clear that America is changing. The news that I hear from golfers has been steady and ominous. Financial leaders from around the world have all told me the same thing all summer long. A real economic collapse could be coming. "Build a shelter," one South African banker told me. A prince from Brazil told me to take all my earnings and buy gold. He took hold of my elbow and said, "I'm serious. Listen to what I'm telling you."

My last loop was with one of the high-and-mighty rulers of Goldman Sachs who chain-smoked his way around the course and never laughed with his mates, though they kept trying to distract him. Coming off 18 at the end, I asked him how bad things are going to get in the world now, and he answered me in one monotone run-on sentence just above a whisper, as if he were passing on to me a precious secret: "The rats are already running for the exits, if you hold any chips, cash them in now, don't delay."

Maybe the world is changing. But it is always changing. It changed for my father when he was a little boy suddenly riding through the Great Depression. He had told me many time how all his cousins, aunts, and uncles moved in together and slept together on the kitchen floor in front of the coal stove riding out the storm of the Great Depression. Every morning his father, my grandfather, left the house and spent the day selling apples on the sidewalks to buy food for the family supper that night and a few lumps of coal for the stove. Twenty-three years ago my first child was born in Iowa City. I remember buying baby things for Erin at a nearby farm that the bank had foreclosed on. A family there was selling everything they owned and losing the farm that had been in their family for four generations. I still remember the father leaning against the fence, watching people carrying away his possessions in the rain. I bought a wicker changing table for our new, first baby. His changing table for one of his babies. In his eyes you could see that he had been shattered and that he would never believe in himself again. He was only a few years older than I, but his life was over, you could tell. My life was just beginning, and his was ending. I wonder whatever became of him. I wonder if we are all going to *be him* next. Perhaps it will all fall down, and then a new and better America will begin. The corporate lawyers and the Wall Street princes will learn to make trousers and coats in the formerly abandoned textile plants. Insurance executives will plow fields, and hedge fund brokers will fire up the steel mills. I hope that

I am a caddie in the new world. I would do this job for nothing, just for the chance to be out on this wonderful ground, walking beside the caddies who have taught me so much this season.

OCTOBER 16, 2008

I rode the early bus to work through the morning darkness, watching the fishing boats out on the North Sea as we passed through St. Monans and Pittenweem, thinking of Jimmy Hughes, who fished this sea before he began caddying with me. Jimmy, whom I relied upon for weather forecasts and who became a great reader of putts, much better than I.

At the gate to Kingsbarns, the big blue Dunhill signs waited for me. There hadn't been a single day in the last six months when I hadn't looked forward to this, and suddenly there I was, nervous at first, but soon fighting for each stroke with my golfer, marching up the fairways as I had 140 times before, only this time I shared them with Padraig Harrington and Paul Casey, the two pros my son has always admired most. The moment I will always remember came as I walked off the 6th green, making my way through the gallery to the 7th tee, when Glen stepped out of the crowd and shook my hand. He had taken a day off to watch me work my first professional tournament. We didn't say anything, but when I looked into his eyes, I knew that he understood. I still had a long way to go to measure up to him and the veteran caddies I had worked with all season. But I thought I just might get there.

OCTOBER 17, 2008

Logan Airport, Boston. In the Edinburgh Airport before I boarded my plane, I received two e-mails. One from Jack with word that he is in the NCAA Bridgestone Golf Collegiate tournament. His first tournament. It starts on the twenty-seventh.

And an e-mail from Nigel. The name meant nothing until I began reading: "You caddied for my friend Burton earlier this summer. We all took a taxi together."

Then I remembered. He was writing to say that Burton had passed away a week ago.

I was in line to board the plane when I remembered that Burton and Nigel were going to Seattle to find their old girlfriend, Deidre. I e-mailed back: "Did you find Deidre?"

I had to wait seven hours for the answer. Yes, they had found her.

OCTOBER 27, 2008

I am at the Forest Oaks Country Club in Greensboro, North Carolina, standing fifty yards behind Jack, who is competing in his first NCAA Division I event. I drove seventeen hours from Maine to be here, and I am typing the hole-by-hole action into my BlackBerry so that I can e-mail it to Colleen. I want to talk with Jack. I want to carry his bag and tell him that it is okay for him to be wondering now if his dream of playing D1—that old dream he's had for so long—has been real or nothing more than a dream all along.

Hole 1—230-yard par-3. He misses green to the left. Misses four-foot putt for par. Bogeys 1st hole. One over after one.

Saved par on 2.

Saved par on 3.

Putting from twenty feet for birdie now on 4. He has his blue Toledo sweater on now. Two feet short. He hit a beautiful drive and wedge on this hole. Makes par.

When he walks past me, I say, "Fight for your team now and you'll be in this until the last stroke."

"I will," he says.

One over after four.

Fifth hole—525-yard par-5. Lovely drive past everyone. Two hundred and thirty-four yards left into this par-5. Here we go. He yells, "GO!" Yes to twenty feet! Eagle putt coming up! He's taking the long walk with his putter. The other two boys are not even close to being on in two. Beautiful putt. A tap-in birdie. Even after five.

Sixth hole—471-yard par-4. He just blasts his drive 40 yards past everyone right down the heart of the fairway. Eric, on the grounds crew, gives me a package of Fig Newtons. I ask him if he can find me some whiskey. Jack has 110 to the pin on center of green. A choked-down sand wedge for him. Mississippi strikes his second shot to two feet. Here goes Maryland—beautiful shot to eight feet. Here comes Jack. Hits fifteen feet from the pin and spins back to twenty feet from hole. Should be an up and down. But this first putt is a big break five feet left to right and downhill for the final eight feet. I am looking at this from below the hole and it is a tough breaker and he's going to have to die it at the crest before the final eight feet. Just rolls past the hole. Almost drains it. Thirteen inches for par. In the jar! Even after six—and leading his group right now.

He makes an easy par on 7.

Hole 8—552-yard par-5. Dogleg right uphill over water. He nails it! Right down the center. I just paced it off—he's 251 from the flag for his second shot into this par-5. Uphill into the wind. Pin is guarded by a deep bunker. He must play right onto good flat green. Maryland is in the woods. Jack outdrives everyone by 40 yards. Mississippi lays up to 60 yards. Maryland lays up to 70 yards. Here's Jack going for it in two now. Fairway metal. It's drifting right. Fifteen feet off the right side of green. Buried in deep Bermuda rough. I am standing right over the ball and can barely see any white. But he's here in two on the par-5, so all he has to do is get on the dance floor even if he can't hear the band. Pars are good enough out here now. It's freezing cold, and all the southern boys look as if they want to be at the waffle house on Route 40. Excellent wedge—high and landing soft. Ten-foot putt for birdie now. He's the only one on the green putting for birdie. Okay, Jack for birdie now—it's uphill and will break only a cup right to left. Makes the birdie! He is now one under after eight.

Hole 9—409-yard par-4. Tight driving hole. He can hit fairway metal. But he has driver out. Two birdies in last three holes. I would take the driver out of his hand here. But here goes—oh God, he PIPES it right down the highway. Okay, I just ran to this ball. He hit that drive 351 all the way over and down the hill no more than 50 yards from the green. Downhill wedge into bright sunlight now. The whole surface of the green is painted with shadows from the trees. Here he goes. Safely on—he's hitting too much spin on the ball—it hopped back eight feet. He just cursed. He's twenty-four feet from the hole now. Okay, a good lag putt. And a par. One under through nine.

Hole 10—a little par-3. He has the honors. Waiting for the group ahead to clear the green. I am halfway up the right side. Okay, it's high and short, into the bunker. It's a deep bunker, but he's got ten feet of green between his ball and the pin. And he's now singing as he walks past me. Bunker shot to ten inches. Makes par. One under after ten.

Hole 11—448-yard par-4. Jack has honors leading his group. He looks very relaxed now. Just put on his white sun visor. It's a massive big drive down the center. He's 123 from front of green. Light breeze behind him. He's 20 yards ahead of everyone. Mississippi is on in two and tight. Maryland is on at fifteen feet. And Jack hits a perfect wedge. A high cutter. He's nine feet from the hole for birdie. It looks like a makeable putt. But pars are so good right now. Jack will putt third here. Blue sky above. This morning it was hailing on this green. Okay, Jack is putting for his birdie now. Pars are good, I am saying under my breath. He misses. Makes par. He's hanging very tough. One under through eleven.

Hole 12—short 370-yard par-4. Jack has driver out. He's leading his group at one under par. Sun is lowering now, and it's getting colder. I lose his drive in the sun, but I think he's turned it left toward the bunkers. A better caddie would have seen it land. Wait! He's carried the bunkers 310 yards. Only 60 yards to the center of the green. He's outdriven everyone by miles again. Mississippi is lost in deep grass. Here comes Jack's wedge. Just left off edge of green but he's putting only fourteen feet from the hole. Maryland is to ten feet. A long wait for Jack. Mississippi is off the green in deep rough. Jack is using wedge. I would give him putter. But he could run this in. Not a great wedge. Two feet short. Should have putted it. Will he save par and keep his streak going? Hasn't bogeyed since the 1st hole. All pars and two birdies. I still can't believe he's here playing with the best D1 players in the country and holding his own. He's got a long way to go. But he's learning something about himself today. He's lining up the putt now. He misses it. Bogey. Even par after twelve.

Hole 13—553-yard par-5. Can he get that dropped stroke back now? He must stay out of the trees here. Yes—right down the center. That is how you fight back from a dropped stroke on the last hole. How far to the green from here? Two hundred and twenty-six yards to the front edge. A four-iron in his hand now. Oh my God, he flies it to the pin in two on this par-5. The ball misses the hole by five inches. Rolls past. Twelve feet for an eagle. Every stroke to help his team. He doesn't need eagle here. A birdie puts him back at one under par through thirteen and right at the top of the leaderboard for the round. But this eagle putt will pick up a lot of speed at the hole and will be tough to stop for an easy birdie putt. Here he goes—to ten inches, great eagle putt. Should have this birdie. Yes, birdie. Back to one under through thirteen.

Hole 14—441-yard par-4. Jack leads his group at one under par. He fought right back from the bogey on 12 and birdied 13 to take the lead again. Turning very cold now. Narrow landing area. Okay, drives it up the left side. Close to tree line. Have to run ahead and see. No, he's fine—drives it 327. Just over 110 into the green. He's 40 yards past everyone. What a lovely wedge. Right on the pin but thirty feet short of the hole. Must play to save par and hold his lead here. Still a few balls of hail on the green from this morning. This is a long difficult putt. Pushed it right of hole. Two-footer to save par now. No one else saved par. I just need a beer and a cigarette. Two beers maybe. Yes, beautiful par. One under through fourteen.

Hole 15—202-yard par-3. Very narrow through the middle. Uphill over a ravine. No sunlight on the green. Four holes left to play at almost 5:45; might not finish in daylight. Dark here in forty-five minutes. A brilliant five-iron on the green. Fifteen feet from the hole. All he needs are pars the rest of the way in. He hasn't hit one poor shot this whole round. And has birdied three of the long par-5s. He moves his head and pushes the putt right again by two feet. Another tester to hold par here. And the lead going to the 16th tee. Yes, on to 16. One under after fifteen.

Hole 16—357-yard short par-4. Tee shot. He's trying to carve the corner on this dogleg. Why? It's short from the middle. A mistake. He pushes the drive too far right into the Bermuda rough again. Mistake number one with three holes left. This is where you have to think straight and close the deal. Pars are all he needs. He drives to 10 yards short of green, 347 yards. That was a hell of a drive. But he's in Bermuda grass again. He chips it out. Okay, a ten-foot putt for birdie. Should save par. But he got ahead of himself on this hole. Feeling his oats. This will be a fast putt, and it will turn two cups from left to right. Just misses the birdie. He marks his ball. Seven inches to make par. Yes. One under after sixteen.

Hole 17—357-yard par-4 uphill narrow fairway. Can't wait till this is over. Can't believe what I have seen Jack do today. Holding his lead against these big top players. Murders his drive. A 340-yard drive. Miles past everyone. His coach just spun by. I told him he's under par through sixteen. "He's shown guts and character today," he said. "Real guts in his first D1 tournament. He can go as far in this game as he wants." Two holes left, and why am I scared to death right now? He's got only 120 left. Oh God, what a shot. High cut, and landing like a moth. He's ten feet from his fourth birdie this round. Just short. He's got par. One under to the last hole.

Hole 18—357-yard par-4. Holding a two-stroke lead in his group. One more par and he will have posted one of the best rounds in this, his first D1 tournament. Darkness is falling. "Close the deal, Jack," I tell him as he walks past. Cold and the sun has set. He massacres the drive. I am utterly amazed that he can play like this in his first tournament. He drives the fucking green! I swear. Here he is on the green! A 357-yard drive with a two-stroke lead on the last hole. Well, I have seen everything now. And water down the left side. He has an eagle putt on the par-4 last hole. Here comes his putt. Two feet short. He picked up on it. Here comes the birdie. Misses. A three-putt par on the 357 par-4. Jack finishes one under in his first Division I college tournament.

As he comes off the last hole, he tosses me his ball. "This is for you, Daddy," he says. It is one of those moments that we live for. And as I drive away from Greensboro, I am certain for the first time that Jack can play golf anywhere and hold his own against anyone.

Five months later. Money is very tight now with Erin heading to grad school, Nell in her third year of college, Cara starting her freshman year in the autumn, and Jack in his sophomore year. We are living the way we did when I was in grad school, only not quite so well without our youth, wrapped up in blankets on the couch in the evenings rather than turning up the heat. Dear Colleen found an exercise bike for me at the Cape Elizabeth dump so that I can keep in shape all winter for another season caddying in Scotland. I've been riding it every day since Thanksgiving, and I was churning through my ten-mile session this morning, staring out the window at the first buds on the maple tree in the backyard, when Jack called. I thought about climbing off the bike and answering the phone, but I decided that I would call him back, so I let the machine pick it up, and soon I heard my son's voice saying, "Call me back when you get this, Daddy. I've got some bad news."

Since North Carolina in October, we could afford to bring Jack home only once for a few days at Christmas, but each time he's called, he has been well and full of excitement. His new golf season is about to begin. He's in love with his girlfriend, Jenna. But there was something in his voice this time, a heaviness, I suppose. I played the message again after I finished riding, then one more time as I got down on the floor and did my forty push-ups. Each time my Saint Christopher medallion clinked against the floor, I imagined a different kind of bad news . . . His old car died. He lost his job at Inverness.

I didn't get him on the phone until tonight; he was busy working all day. And before he could deliver the bad news, I told him that I was flying over to Scotland on the fifteenth and that I had decided to set aside the money I made from my first ten loops to bring him across for a week.

"How's that sound?" I asked him.

"I'm through with golf," he said. "I got thrown off the team."

I listened to him explain that his grades had fallen so low that the university would not allow him to play any more golf. I was only on the telephone with him a few minutes. The whole time I kept thinking in one chamber of my mind, Well, it's small potatoes when you consider how bad things can go for your kids. It's nothing really. What does golf mean in the wider scheme of things? But the top of my head felt as if it were on fire. I walked into Jack's old bedroom and stood there for a while feeling as if a cold wind were blowing through me. I sat down on his bed and began reading through the entries I made in my diary last summer at Kingsbarns. That whole season, whenever I got discouraged or missed home, I reassured myself that even though Jack and I were on our separate roads, they were running parallel toward the same destination.

The first stars were out when I sat at my desk and uploaded the diary entries from my BlackBerry to my laptop. I've been meaning to do this for months, and when I finished, I walked out the back door of the house, across the yard, and down the hill to the marsh, where I threw the BlackBerry up against the side of a tree trunk as hard as I could and watched with some satisfaction as it shattered.

I have just written to Davy at Kingsbarns, telling him that I will not be able to return this summer.

CHRISTMAS MORNING, 2009

This is my first diary entry in nine months. I haven't felt like writing anything since Jack was thrown off the golf team, and now that he is home, I am sticking to the plan I made before he arrived—never to be alone with him in a room so that we won't have to talk about him pissing away his chance to earn a golf scholarship by not going to class and by letting his grades drop so low that the coach had no choice but to cut him from the team. With his three sisters in school now at the same time, I needed him to win a scholarship. And I told him last summer that he was on his own from here on. He is taking the loans in his name and he will be repaying them until his hair turns gray.

FEBRUARY 3, 2010

I've had plenty of time to drive to Pennsylvania to have that conversation about forgiveness with my father that Jack talked to me about three years ago in Scotland, but somehow I never did. My father got strong enough to leave the skilled-care wing of the assisted-living facility, back to his apartment, where he resumed watching his beloved Penn State football games with the old men who had been boys with him in the 1940s, but only for a little while before his decline began in earnest. Two months ago he made the short journey once again down the carpeted corridor into the skilled-care wing, where he was expected to die as quickly as possible and with little fuss.

Always the optimist, my father thought he was there to get stronger so he could return again to his apartment. But after several months when no one took him for a single walk down the hallway to see the people he missed, he began to understand what was happening, and he lashed out at everyone trying to care for him.

By the time I made the trip to see him on Sunday, I had four empty bedrooms in my house in Maine and another five in my house in Canada, and I was determined to get my father out of the warehouse, where the staff now kept him so drugged that he could barely lift his head up. I arrived at lunchtime. He sat strapped in a wheelchair at a round table with six others also in wheelchairs. They were all drooling and lost in their own misery while nurses' aides shoveled food into their mouths.

I held his hand and told him who I was, but he didn't acknowledge me. After half an hour I could barely breathe, and I got up to go outside and have a cigarette. I had just turned away when he called to me. "Donnie, you can do anything. Take me with you."

I told him that I would. "Someday soon I'll drive down here from Maine and take you back with me," I said as I lay beside him on his bed later that day. Then after he fell asleep, I left him there and drove home.

MARCH 7, 2010

I got to spend the whole night with my dad before he died. From midnight until 6:00, it was just me and the hospice nurse in the room with him, and I talked to him hour after hour, recalling every good memory I had from the start, from the time I was his little boy. I read him the eulogy that I had written for him, and I held his hand and told him that he had been a good father. For the sixty years I knew my dad, he was always a little lost. A little confused and uncertain. But all that seemed to end shortly after one o'clock in the afternoon, when the bugler from the U.S. Army Color Guard played taps and I laid his body down beside Peggy's in the Lutheran cemetery, in the rectangle of earth that has been waiting for him since she was buried there in August 1950, under the headstone they have shared and that was engraved with his name beside hers when he lost her sixty years ago. She was his nineteen-year-old bride when he lost her, sixteen days after she gave him twin boys, just nine months after their wedding. And he was just a kid. Now he was an old man being carried back to her by her twin boys, who would soon turn sixty.

He was no longer lost in the wide world.

I stood there once again recalling the stories people had told me, about how my dad had slept on Peggy's grave in the autumn of 1950, beneath his army blanket, and how his buddies who lived in the little towns around Hatfield and who had served in the Pacific with him during the war used to swing by the cemetery in the morning to pick him up and take him out for coffee.

They didn't believe that he would get over Peggy's death. And in many ways he never did.

Later in the day, after everyone had gone home, I went back to the cemetery. There had been a lot of melting snow, and the grass was drowning in all the standing water. I thought of my mother's body at age nineteen, her breasts swollen with milk for her babies just a few blocks away. A stranger at the funeral parlor turning her naked arms and legs to dress her for the wake. Her beautiful young body without a mark, laid in the ground alongside the young boys from her high school whose bodies had been torn apart in the war and then sent back home from Europe and the Pacific to be buried here with her. I wondered again if my young mother ever came to this cemetery during the war and stood at the graves of those boys in the summers before her own death.

My dad's two sisters had stood on either side of him when they buried Peggy on August 30, 1950. They were just young girls then. They had never been back to the grave until they returned as elderly women to bury their brother.

What I will remember most from the cemetery is the way that Jack could not look at me. There was a shadow across his eyes, and I saw in one glance that he was losing his belief in himself. Golf is just a game, this is true; but for Jack, it was a way of helping me get my four children through college, and it was a way for the two of us to fulfill an old dream, a pledge we had made to each other. A lot more than a game was at stake.

At a Citgo station near the entrance to the Pennsylvania Turnpike, I filled his tank with gas and bought him a coffee and a sandwich for the road. We shook hands and said good-bye without smiles or embraces. Then I watched him turn onto the highway into the procession of cars moving off into the distance before he disappeared among the other sons who had left their fathers' worlds and were making their own way through the bright March afternoon.

MARCH 9, 2010

I took my eight-iron and four golf balls to the Prouts Neck course this morning with Teddy and hit them around until I lost them in the snowbanks. I was standing on the 14th green when I called Glen up in Canada. I told him that this green always reminded Jack and me of the 11th on the Old Course with its steep back-to-front slope, and the two deep front bunkers, right and left, guarding the approach, and the tidal channel behind the back rushing past like the Eden Estuary.

The sun was breaking through the low gray clouds while Glen and I talked about fathers and sons. Two years ago I got Glen his caddie job at the Castle Course so he could try to walk off the death of his father. He had fallen in love with Scotland and was heading back over in late April for his third season. I told him that I felt like taking a long walk myself. "How long?" he asked. "Maybe another thousand miles," I said.

MARCH 18, 2010

St. Andrews, Scotland. It is 2010 and I am back in Scotland. How can this be true? What happened to the two years since I first came here to work as a caddie? This was on my mind when I was awakened just before 3:00 a.m. by the wind or by someone banging my door with a fistful of nails. A strange clanging noise kept repeating itself and seemed to grow louder as I lay in my bed trying one moment to remember where I was and to understand where the noise was coming from and what it might be, and the next moment to persuade myself that it would stop soon enough and I would be asleep again.

Whoever was there has to be a stranger because no one knows I am here, in this second-floor flat of three rooms nailed together, one with a double bed, one with a toilet and shower, and one with everything else—sink, stove, washing machine, table, two straight chairs, microwave oven, and two stuffed chairs—at the narrow end of Market Street three blocks from the center of St. Andrews.

This is my first night back in Scotland, my first night in these rooms that I found on the Internet. I flew across the Atlantic twelve hours ago with one travel bag that held my golf clubs, one book, and all the clothes I will need for the next half year, landing in Amsterdam, where I killed six hours before continuing on to Edinburgh, and then riding a bus from there to St. Andrews with enough of the day left before the shops closed to buy apples, pasta, butter, coffee, bread, peanut butter, jam, orange juice, a duvet, and two pillows. I have unplugged myself from the real world and no longer have a car, telephone, television, Internet, or radio. The walls of the rooms are bare except for a mirror that I stood in front of with my three-iron, preparing to go down the stairs and confront whoever the hell was standing out there in the storm making all the noise. In the light my reflection was a shock to me. Two summers ago, when I was here in Scotland working as a caddie, my hair was turning gray. Now it is white. Whoever was downstairs outside the door, banging to be let in, would see at once that I am a fifty-nine-year-old man who has wandered too far from home and is lost and afraid and shivering from the cold because I cannot figure out how to turn the damned heat on.

I have been in Scotland only ten hours, and already I am losing my resolve. Already I am finding it difficult to believe what I had been telling myself for the last few days as I prepared for this journey, that I was leaving home once again, leaving behind everything that made life good, including a loving wife who still opened her arms to me and a dog who slept beside me in bed, to work as a caddie in St. Andrews, Scotland, because I wanted my son to see that I had not given up on him and on our dream that one day he would make a professional tour and I would caddie for him.

But now that I am here, I feel as if I'm going to fade away.

One of our great weaknesses as people is that we almost never see ourselves the way other people see us. It requires a kind of hon-

esty that is painful. And I felt trapped inside a hollow space standing before a man in the mirror who looked too old to be a caddie,
even though I had been doing my forty push-ups every morning for
twenty-five years. I was worried that everyone in Scotland would see
me the way I saw myself. My little potbelly. My shoulders pitched
forward. My thin white legs like out-of-bounds stakes.

The secret is to look the part of a caddie, I know this. I told myself
this back home and told myself again as I leaned my three-iron
against the wall and got dressed in my fine black waterproof trousers from Callaway with the matching black-and-white jacket and
the black FootJoy shoes and the black wool cap with the Carnoustie
emblem pulled rakishly to one side of my head. I dressed quickly and
took one last look in the mirror, trying to believe that Colleen had
not been exaggerating when she told me I looked ten years younger
in this outfit.

The thought calmed me by the time I reached the tiny foyer at the
bottom of the stairs and saw the hinged metal door on the mail slot
blowing open and clanging shut—the cause of all the racket.

What did you expect? I said. Then I lit a cigarette and stepped out
into the storm.

It is morning now and there is gold light outside my windows and the
cobblestones in the street are beginning to dry out from the storm, a
low mist baking off them. I have a job here now as a caddie for the
Links Trust because the caddie master who refused to hire me two
summers ago is gone, and because Glen recommended me to the new
fellow in charge. Glen and I will be working side by side this season.
Last night I timed my walk from the flat to the caddie pavilion at the
1st tee of the Old Course so that I would know how long it was going
to take me to walk back in a few hours to present myself for my first
day of work. Eleven minutes that begins with a right turn outside
my door onto Market Street, seventy yards past the little park on the
left with the arched iron gate and the handsome three-story stone

houses with the bright orange chimney pots and the slate-shingled roofs, joined together at the shoulders. Past the fish-and-chips shop at the corner, right another hundred yards to North Street, across the intersection through the narrow lane beside the university courtyard with its majestic stone buildings set in a square around a magnificent bright green lawn. Left onto Scores Road, where the edge of the North Sea is bordered by granite mansions that step gracefully down the hill to the long strand of beach and the green fairways of the Old Course.

I stood under the overhanging roof of the caddie pavilion last night watching the sleet blow across the golf course, acknowledging that I began to make my way here two weeks ago after I buried my father, when Jack and I met up at the cemetery for the first time in a year. I told him that one of the last things my father and I had talked about before he died was me being Jack's caddie someday. "I had my chance at golf," Jack said, "and I pissed it away. You only get one chance."

"Who told you that?" I asked.

"It's true," he said.

"Not if there's still one person left who believes in you," I told him.

A few hours later I had said good-bye to him and to my daughters at airports and train stations and at the entrance to the Pennsylvania Turnpike. I watched each of them walk away from me, and all I wanted in the world was to have my children be small again so I could carry them on my shoulders and tell them the things about life and love that I never managed to say in all the years they were living beneath my roof, when there was so much time that it seemed we had time to lose.

After they all had left, it was dusk when I drove alone to the neighborhood where I was my father's little boy over half a century ago in the early 1950s, waiting inside the front door each day just after five o'clock with my face against the glass for him to come home from work so I could follow him around and sometimes walk beside him when he mowed the lawn. At a time when he wore khaki trousers and white T-shirts and listened to Tommy Dorsey records and was young, much too young ever to grow old.

I was walking up the 1st fairway of the Old Course as the sleet turned to rain around 4:00 in the morning, still thinking about my dad. Here I was in Scotland with its hard-packed ground beneath my feet, but what seemed more real to me was the neighborhood where I was a little boy. Those early evenings when all the fathers would be returning home from work. I remembered exactly how the lights went on in the little houses at the end of the day and there was a descending stillness, almost like innocence, that fell over the neighborhood. Out on the Old Course, with the names of the pothole bunkers running through my mind, there were also the names of the people from my childhood: Eddie Pincus and Terry Burke and the Moyer sisters, who lived on one side of us, and Tommy Grant, who lived on the other. Those people whom I had known there were all lost and gone, and I suppose most of the fathers were in the ground like my father, but as I walked out toward the Eden Estuary, with the lights of St. Andrews growing faint and then disappearing behind me, I could still see those people in the days when they filled their houses with children and with enough joy and sorrow to account for a lifetime. I stood on the 11th tee with the rain running down my face and pictured them all again, young and strong, kids racing up the hill toward the water tower on their bicycles, husbands in crew cuts, wives in lipstick and nylon stockings, their arms around each other, and their eyes bright with passion as if they almost believed that they could go on forever that way so that at the end of their lives they would have no regrets, they would not have to wish that they had loved each other better when they had the chance.

Soon enough the rain stopped, and the wind fell off to a gentle breeze. Here I am, I thought. I'm going to be a caddie someday with Jack walking beside me. I watched the sunrise from the 14th tee. Out ahead of me was the famous Hell bunker. I recalled telling Jack how

Arnold Palmer was the only person ever to drive into it in competition. Three hundred and ninety yards. Just up ahead of me was the place where we had buried his golf ball. My legs felt heavy from the short walk.

MARCH 19, 2010

I now have a caddie bib with my license in the little clear plastic pocket over my heart showing a picture of me in my wool cap. And if you stand back a little ways and don't look too carefully, I think Colleen is right. I pass for a man in his late forties. I am a caddie licensed for this 2010 season by the Links Trust, the organization that manages the seven courses for the people of St. Andrews. They are public courses, owned by the people. The first caddies worked here 222 years ago.

The rain has returned, and the wind is howling again tonight. An hour ago the sky was clear, and I saw the North Star pierced with light. From where I am sitting in the Chariots pub, forty paces from the 18th green of the Old Course, I can see the caddie pavilion, where I met the caddie master and promised him I would never say no to a loop if he needed me. "I'll be here as early as you want me in the morning, and I'll work until dark," I told him. I also told him that if I couldn't keep up with the younger boys, I would be honest enough to step aside. I looked him right in the eye when I told him this, and I believe he understood exactly what I was saying. Maybe he saw that I was a little afraid, because just before he turned away he said to me, "You'll be all right."

I will be starting out up on the cliff, joining a group of twenty-five caddies that includes Glen at the Castle Course, on April 1, which means I have ten days or so to get my legs working and to familiarize myself with the ground up there.

MARCH 20, 2010

Not a good start at the Castle Course. I was out walking late this afternoon, planning to catch the bus back into town before it got dark. I was pacing off the distances to the bunkers and studying the slopes in the greens, writing everything down in my yardage book with a mounting confidence. Somehow I made the wrong turn coming off the 12th tee, and before I knew it, I was lost out there, as the green hills vanished in the fog. No matter which direction I turned, it seemed that the North Sea was still in front of me washing rhythmically onto the shore.

By the time I found my way to the main road, it was dark, and I could see the red taillights of the bus off in the distance heading the wrong way, and another sleet storm was on top of me with freezing-cold wind off the sea. I stood by the side of the road for maybe half an hour waiting for the next bus. I couldn't feel my face or hands when I dropped down behind a rock wall to block out the wind. Lying there beside the road, I thought about my father and the screenplay of his love story that I was writing here two summers ago and of the thousand new pages I have written since then that are still not good enough. I have written the hundred-page script over and over so many times that I can now recite each scene from memory. That is what I was doing as I rode the bus into town. I bought two macaroni and cheese dinners for £2 at Tesco and ate them sitting on the floor, shivering, while I tried to figure out how to turn on the heater in my flat. I pushed every button on the panel five or six times in different combinations until it finally kicked on. I've got heat now to dry out my clothes, which are draped over my chairs, but somehow I disengaged the hot water. Tomorrow I'll try to figure that out.

APRIL 20, 2010

I just lost a month of my life to unrelenting storms of the mind that weakened me to the point where each night as a cerulean darkness settled over the tall stone spires of this town and gathered along the narrow streets, I carefully considered walking into the North Sea with my mouth open. Either it was going to be that quick death by drowning, or I was going to take a swim and then lie down in the dunes soaking wet and perish from hypothermia before morning. In either case I planned to wear my Links Trust caddie bib so that when my body was discovered, it would just be assumed that I had gotten drunk and made a wrong turn. No harm, no foul.

The truth is I made a bad mistake coming back here. In the first place there's the bloody volcano in Iceland that has emptied the golf courses and left all of us sitting around the caddie room staring at the floor like great idiots. A procession of dull, empty hours turning into more empty hours like cells dividing. And I can't fill the emptiness with my old dream the way I could two summers ago. And the math doesn't work for me unless I do at least one loop a day for £60, 7 days a week, for 187 days so that I can send home at least $11,000. So, there's the money, which is even more complicated now that there isn't enough work to go around. What am I doing here taking work from the local lads? I worried about this two summers ago, but I had a story then: I was working as a caddie to prepare to one day caddie for my son, blah, blah, blah. I don't have that story anymore to believe in. I have this new story: I'm working as a caddie again to show my son that I haven't given up on him. But I can't believe in that story enough to tell it to anyone here except Glen. And each time I tell him, he winces, and I see a flash of sorrow in his eyes. And there's also my right knee, which is swollen and feels as if someone were driving a nail under the kneecap ever since I stepped into a hole just below the bunker on the right side of number 12 while staggering beneath the weight of an exceedingly heavy golf bag owned by a Russian mafia pig who treated me like a dog. Not having my Black-Berry this season means that I can't get e-mails from Colleen and the girls, so I am completely cut off unless I walk to the pub at night with my laptop. And then there's the cherry pie at Tesco. I discovered that at 9:00 p.m. they mark it down to £1, and for the last three nights that's what I've eaten for my supper. A whole cherry pie each night. Everything has felt wrong here from the start when I did my first loop at the Castle Course with big Kenny, who grew up caddying at Turnberry, and Alan, who spent five seasons at Seminole. These guys are at the top of their game, polished and professional; if they had decided to become college professors instead of caddies, they would be deans by now sitting in leather chairs with their feet up on their desks in some ivy tower. On the 3rd hole I watched my golfer's ball fly into a bunker, and then I spent five minutes searching for it in the *wrong bunker*, cursing myself under my breath, before Kenny very discreetly waved to me and pointed. A rookie mistake caused by a lack of concentration. Since I arrived, I have not been able to drop through to the deep down world, where individual blades of grass and the lettering on a golf ball have meaning. The trouble is nothing seems to mean anything anymore.

And I must write to Jack. He was the last person I talked to from Logan Airport before I flew across. I was going to let his mother tell him—she understood why I was returning to Scotland—but I decided to call him just before I boarded the plane. "I'm heading back to Scotland to caddie," I said. There was a pause. Then he asked, "Are you ready for that?" Before I could answer him, my phone conked out.

Am I ready for this? I guess we'll find out soon enough. For now let me fall asleep dreaming that I can feel Colleen beside me as I listen to her heart beating like Morse code.

APRIL 27, 2010
_____

A small, good thing happened today. I was out with Malcolm, a caddie with nineteen years' experience at Gleneagles before he came to the Castle Course. He introduced himself to me with a strong handshake. "There are four Malcolms here," he said. "Think of me as Malcolm X." In his early forties with a wife and two daughters, he's got the rugged good looks of a movie star in a 1950s Western and a mischievous sparkle in his eyes. We were on the 1st tee when his golfer drove his first ball out of play. Then he teed up a second and nailed it right up the center of the fairway. He turned to Malcolm, handed him his driver, and said, "Same guy." To which Malcolm replied: "But more experienced."

I was suddenly laughing along with everyone else. Laughing for the first time since I got here.

MAY 1, 2010
_____

Glen is the elder statesman in the crew at the Castle Course, and completely at ease regaling the boys with stories from his days on the Canadian Tour and the Nationwide Tour, while he deals hands of poker like a riverboat gambler. The eternal optimist, whenever the chatter turns back to the subject of twenty caddies sitting around with no work and people start grumbling, Glen lights up the room with another story about one of his forty-two trips to Las Vegas. "It's too early in the season to be discouraged, boys," he said at one point. "We sound like a bunch of poltroons. There's a word for you, Donnie," he exclaimed. "What's a poltroon?"

I was staring out the window at the guy delivering rolls to the back door of the pro shop, thinking I could do that job. "An utter coward," I replied.

"That's right!" Glen said merrily.

We were all sent home after five hours, and Glen rode the bus into St. Andrews with me to see my flat. He's going to need to move out of his place and bunk in with me for two weeks during the Open in July so his landlord can rent the flat for top dollar. We moved around the chairs to get an idea of how he would fit on the floor. "I'll be fine right in the corner there," he said. "In the old days when you were out on the tour with your golfer and you could only afford one bed at the motel, the golfer got the mattress and the caddie got the box spring. I'll find an air mattress somewhere."

We were poking around the golf shop on Market Street, looking at the waterproofs the way caddies always do, and trying to kill what was left of the afternoon, when his phone rang. I heard him say, "I'm in St. Andrews with Don. Yes. When?" He closed his phone and said, "We've got ten minutes to get to the 1st tee of the Old Course."

We were already out of the store. Turn right and we were five minutes from my flat, where we had our bibs and towels and clothes and my hole-by-hole notes of the course. We started that way but then realized there wasn't time. We ran through the streets of St. Andrews, straight for the caddie pavilion. As we were charging down the road beside the R&A, the caddie master saw us from his window and held up two bibs. My God, I thought, I'm about to caddie on the Old Course. At last I felt myself dropping to the deep down world. On the 1st tee I took photographs of our four men from Norway as if it were something I did every day of my life. They couldn't speak a word of English, and it took us a while to explain that with the wind blowing twenty knots from straight behind us, driver could end up in the river at the front edge of the green.

Glen and I walked ahead of them, side by side, talking our way up the fairway. "I did a couple spins here last summer," Glen said, "but I don't really know my way around."

"We'll be fine," I told him. "This is home to me." I pointed up at the third-floor window of the Rusacks Hotel, where I had spent the winter writing my novel. "When I brought Jack here, I reserved the same room," I said. "I'll tell you this, Glen, if anyone had ever told me then that one day I would be caddying here, I would have thought they were crazy."

"Well, Donnie," he said, "you never know, do you?"

We had some rain of course, and without our waterproofs we got soaked to the skin. And we couldn't really speak with our golfers. But we made our way around in fine shape, converting all the yardages into meters and leading them to the good ground. We each looked after two of them and ran a silent competition on the greens, where I had the chance to confirm my theory that you could avoid three-putts on the Old Course by treating all long putts as essentially straight and concentrating only on pace and by never leaving yourself a downhill second putt.

Standing off to the side of the 14th tee, I glanced at the place at the base of the stone pillar where Jack and I had buried his golf ball. The sun was breaking through the clouds, and the ground ahead of us—running all the way back to the center of town to the stone shops and pubs and hotels bordering the 18th green—was painted with gold light. "It doesn't get much better than this, my friend," Glen said to me.

"Maybe we should celebrate," I said. "Buy a steak and cook it at my place."

"I like that idea," he said. "A few pints in the pub first. And I'll make my pear salad."

"Everyone plays their second shots to the left into the Elysian fields," I said. "But there's a passageway up the right side of Hell bunker that I like better." I pointed up along the stone wall on our right.

"Why don't we take two of them left and two right and see which works out better?" he suggested.

It turned out that one man in both groups made par and the other made hash of the hole, proving nothing at all. We just shook our heads. "I still favor the right," I told Glen.

We took pictures of our golfers on the Swilcan Bridge, then walked out ahead of them up the 18th fairway, where I glanced at the third-floor window of the hotel again. I didn't say anything, but when I turned back, I saw that Glen was looking at me.

We finally talked about it outside the Chariots pub, where we sat at a picnic table with our pints of ice-cold Tennent's. I began by saying that there was a symmetry to life after all. Two years ago, when the two of us walked this course for the first time the day Glen arrived in Scotland, he had just buried his father, and he had told me the story of their long-running battle that began when he lost his basketball scholarship in college. "Now we're back here," I said. "I've just buried my old man, and Jack has lost his chance."

"Well," he said, "you have to move on. You know that."

I told him that it was going to be hard. "It's not just that he lost his chance for a scholarship," I reminded him. "We were going to be on a tour together someday."

"I know," he said.

Of course he knew; of all the people I'd ever talked with about this dream of ours, Glen was the one who understood best exactly what it meant to me.

"You have to rise above it," he said. "And you will. You'll get up every morning and go to work here every day, all season long. We'll be standing here watching the Open in two months. Life goes on, Donnie. It just goes on."

MAY 9, 2010

The secret to growing old, I have decided, is to be calm. Calm enough to be grateful for all the chances that you had in your life. That is what I have been telling myself lately. But I fell off the wagon after today's round, and though I told myself again when I got into bed at 8:00, I was still telling myself at 3:00 a.m., when I finally gave up. I'm sitting on my back stoop under the stars writing this now to try to get beyond what happened today. I was out alone, caddying for two R&A fellows in their seventies. All caddies live in dread of these R&A members because they tend to be arrogant assholes. When I walked up to the 1st tee to meet my gentlemen today, the one with big ears said to the one with bushy white eyebrows, "Well, at least he's presentable." It never got much better. They treated me as if I were invisible except each time when ears handed me his ball and said, "Wash this." And when eyebrows asked me how long I had been caddying, I told him that I was the new guy at the Castle Course. "You look a little too old to be new," he said. I took a lot of crap from both of them. It was one of those rounds where you just say "yes, sir," "no, sir" for five hours and keep your head down.

I was walking to the bus when Malcolm sped up behind me and hollered out his window, "Get in, Big D."

Before we turned out onto the main road, he rolled a cigarette. "You don't smoke out on the course," he said.

I told him I was trying to stay alive long enough to see my four kids' weddings. Then I noticed he used two filters. "Two filters?" I said.

"You die slower this way," he said with a big smile. He sped right past the bus stop and said he would drive me into town. He was going to do some shopping for his wife and daughters at the second-hand shops.

There is a code honored by most caddies that you never talk about what you are paid and you never complain, so I was disappointed with myself for complaining about my R&A wankers.

"Ah, don't be bothered," Malcolm said as he pulled into the lane of onrushing cars, floored it, and then power jammed us back into our lane between two trucks. "We're out there every day, Big D, with billionaires, millionaires, and sometimes the scum of the earth," he reminded me with another big smile. He told me that in his twenty years he had never walked off the course for being mistreated. He'd had his share of assholes, but he had learned how to treat them. "You work like a dog for them, and that's okay. But you never let anyone treat you like a dog."

When he dropped me at my place, he said, "I've been watching you out there. You're a good caddie." He raised a finger to one eye. "Eyes of a hawk. And they say you know your way around the Old Course."

"I do."

"We'll be out there together someday," he said. "I'll follow you around."

I don't know why, but for the last seven hours, lying in bed, I've been thinking about my father and how modest his life was compared with the R&A guys I was with today. These people who own the world always make me feel kind of temporary about myself. And about my father, and guys like him. Simple people like my Nana, who did the neighborhood's laundry for a living and who always said to me, "It's not honest money if you don't earn it with your hands."

A couple of days ago Glen took me aside at the Castle Course and told me that he's been worried about me. "You've been really negative lately," he said.

I think that I am going to have to let go of my father now, and of my son as well. For a while anyway. I am going to try to live these days here in St. Andrews and to be grateful for them.

MAY 23, 2010

Here is the new deal. I now have two jobs, which means that I am the beneficiary of a simple but elegant equation that goes like this: In order to be grateful, you must be calm. And if you are too exhausted at the end of the day to even get undressed or eat a bowl of soup before you get into bed, it is easier to be calm.

It began a week ago when I finished my loop at the Castle Course at three o'clock one afternoon, and instead of walking home after the bus dropped me in the middle of St. Andrews, I strolled down to the Old Course, where I saw something I couldn't quite believe. Golfers were lined up at the caddie pavilion asking for caddies, and there weren't any. Actually, I saw half a dozen caddies turn down jobs because going out so late in the afternoon means you'll miss your supper and you won't finish until around nine o'clock. I presented myself to the caddie master, and I was on the 1st tee immediately. And so I've been coming down every afternoon after I finish my loop at the

Castle Course, and most days because I'm the only caddie on board, I end up taking around a foursome by myself. I carry each man's bag for four holes, give all the lines, read all the putts, search for all the balls in the rough, and get paid a ton of money. The best part about this night job is the feeling I have when I'm out there working by myself, the last caddie on the Old Course as the wind falls off and the sun goes down with its final burst of gold light, like light through stained glass. There is such a peaceful stillness out there. Walking up 17, you can hear the clinking of dinner plates in the Old Course Hotel. And guests of the Rusacks Hotel are often standing along the white rail fence that borders the 18th fairway, drinking cocktails like passengers on a cruise ship. When the course is busy, it's like a carnival with the shared greens and fairways, and the caddie's main responsibility is to keep the traffic moving smoothly and try to see that no one gets hit by a ball. But when you are out there alone at the end of the day, the last person to finish and to swing the door to the museum closed behind you as you walk off the 18th green, you feel the deep sense of privilege, and you know that this is something you will remember at the end of your time when you look back.

If you do enough loops as a caddie at the Old Course, you are going to meet up with an astonishing and varied cast of characters. I've been out with a prince and a princess in matching monogrammed shirts with ruffles on the cuffs. (Yes, on his cuffs too.) A corn farmer from Illinois who spoke to me for eighteen holes about the virtues of John Deere tractors as if he were describing old lovers. And the fellow who once trained the royal family's hunting dogs. It goes on and on. The job is like waiting tables in a Beverly Hills restaurant where the stars eat their meals.

MAY 29, 2010

Every day here now I am trying to become Cyrus Dallin's statue of the Indian *Appeal to the Great Spirit*. That fine Indian on horseback, his arms outstretched, his brave face turned to the heavens. Each morning after I step from the bus and walk across the fairways of the golf course to work, I try to let go of everything that I am afraid of and to surrender to the light and shadows, to the wind, to the scent of the sea, and to the game of golf. I am trying to find peace here in this new world of dreams while I become the best caddie I can be. I treat every golfer with dignity and respect. Most of them are decent people, finally making the trip they have dreamed of making for years, to the home of golf. Fathers with their sons. Old friends. Men trying to get through the death of their wives. I hear it all. And here I am to greet them and to help them play their very best. It is a job that requires such deep concentration that for the hours I am with them I never think of anything else. If your mind wanders even for a moment, you can make a mistake. It begins right on the 1st tee. Which position are the pins today? (They change every day.) What kind of ball is my man playing? What is his name? What are his three mates' names? What is the yardage from my ball to the front edge of the green? How much room is there behind the pin? Is there trouble off the back of the green? What club should I hit in this wind? From which direction should I approach the green? Are there bunkers left or right? How does the green slope? How far from where we are standing to the bunkers we cannot see? Remember that the wee burn is 54 yards in front of this green, but with the downhill slope of the land it comes into play at 92 yards. On and on it goes. Clean his ball when he reaches the green. Make sure your shadow isn't over his ball. I made a list; there are 103 things you can fuck up as a caddie. And at my age I could fuck up at any moment if I don't concentrate fully. Why do I keep blocking the ball off the tee? How can I hit a wedge off this hard-packed ground with almost no grass? Put your wedges away and I'll show you how to hit a bump and run with your seven-iron. How do I get out of these pothole bunkers? Do you have any tees? Do you have a pencil? Can you dry my grips in the pouring rain? Do you have a lighter? What ocean is that? It's the North Sea, sir. Straight over there, you see that long white blur just beyond the shoreline? That's the big hotel on the 18th green at Carnoustie. Will the wind blow hard today? No, whenever you see the small, open boats out on the North Sea in the early morning, you know the forecast is for only light winds. You say there is wind at the green, but I can see the flag and it's hanging straight down. Well, sir, that's because it's wet from the dew this morning. It goes on and on.

JUNE 19, 2010

After the universe folds back into itself in an explosion like the one that created it, I wonder how long it will take for someone to invent golf again. Or for a writer to compose an ode to the game. If I were to write the ode myself at the end of this day, I would make it an ode to gratitude, and it would begin with the four grandmothers from Finland whom I took around the Old Course. They couldn't play the game at all, and yet they laughed their way from start to finish, hugging each other and needling each other with such warmth and generosity. Whenever one of them had to pee, she just marched off into the rough and pulled down her knickers. How badly did they play golf? Well, let's just say you weren't safe even standing *behind* them when they hit the ball. But it didn't matter to them. They loved the game. They were just four old friends taking a long walk together over lovely ground and straight through the paradox that exists in golf: that you can love a game you play so poorly. You can even love the failing once you have lived long enough to learn not to take yourself too seriously. It rained on us and the wind blew hard again and we spent as much time in the rough and bunkers as we did on the fairways, but for five hours while I escorted these ladies around, there was no world except the world we inhabited together. Climbing up the 11th green, I lent my wool cap to the woman nearest me, whose ears had turned bright red from the cold. We stood for a moment looking off into the distance where the wind moved across the estuary and there was a pale moon rising in an opening of pink sky. When I turned to the lady to say something about the next shot, I saw that she was a million miles away, deep in thought, and so I kept silent. We were standing on a hillside in Scotland. She knew nothing about me and I knew nothing about her, and we had no common language, but something passed between us, and I felt privileged to be out there beside her in one moment of time, standing close enough to see the wrinkles at the corners of her eyes and the gray in her hair and then to catch an unexpected glimpse of her as a much younger woman and to wonder what she had been like and who she had been before she became a wife and mother and grandmother, and who my own three daughters would become in the world. I think that I was seeing them in her as her beauty became as real to me as the beauty of the place where we were standing. I thought of the great distances we had both traveled in our lives, in every possible direction, on paths separated by continents and oceans and years, to reach this one moment where I was bearing witness to her beauty and her gratitude.

I believe that I turned a corner today. By my count I have now walked just under two hundred miles on a knee with no cartilage. I have taught myself to walk a different way, to throw all my weight onto my good, left knee, and to come down on my heel so that the spark of pain with each step is dulled. I'm going to make it all the way to the end of the season, I can tell. And while I'm no longer taking the pain in my knee seriously, I'm going to start *not taking myself* so seriously. I'm going to bear witness to the beauty instead.

JULY 3, 2010

I may never be able to convey to anyone exactly what it is like to work a succession of doubles—ten hours of caddying—day after day after day, to walk off the 18th green exhausted, and before you can even sit down and have a cigarette, you are sent straight to the 1st tee to begin again, to walk for another five hours before you finally catch the 9:30 bus home and fall asleep in all your clothes and then wake up and do it again. There is no Saturday or Monday here. No June or April. Time has no edges or borders. Each day is the day before and the next day.

I think about Colleen every morning in the wee park where I sit, waiting for the bus, and I feed the same little family of sparrows, crusts from my peanut butter sandwiches. There are five of them and they seem so eager to see me each morning and I love watching them and talking to them. I have become an old man who feeds the birds. And I have also become a caddie, which means that from day to day I get to disappear from my own story and become a part of someone else's. It was about a week ago now or a month when I caddied for a father and son from California. The golf trip to Scotland was a graduation present for the son, who had just finished grad school, earning his MBA. In a month he would be leaving his father behind in California and moving to New York City to work for an investment bank. They were close, best friends. And the father had been knocked down by multiple sclerosis, so he could barely walk. I had to drive him in a buggy around the course, and he had to hold my arm to steady himself as we walked onto the greens. The disease was progressing. He was losing the control of his right hand and could barely hit the ball, though he had once been a college golfer himself and had played a fine game with a plus-two handicap. On the 4th hole he told me that he didn't know how he was going to get through each day after his son moved away. His son could hit the ball a mile like Jack, and he and I were cheering him on all the way around the course. At one point the father said to me: "I just love seeing my son play the game so well. It was different with my old man; he taught me to play, but once I began beating him, he would never play with me again."

When we finished, the two of them stood on the 18th green while I took their photograph. I was standing maybe twenty paces from them, and I was looking at them through the lens of the camera when I saw the son lift his hand to his father's face. It took me a moment to realize that his father had begun to cry and that he was wiping away his tears.

JULY 24, 2010

Being away from Colleen for so long often leaves me feeling as if I am falling down inside. She knows what this means to me to try for all I am worth to fulfill my pledge to our son, and she has told me again and again not to worry about anything and just to learn as much as I can, and to be calm about things. We can't talk by telephone because of the cost, but her encouragement in letters and by e-mail is constant.

But now I will get to remember Colleen here in her striped skirt and her ruffled blouse. She surprised me and flew over a few days ago, and she and I and Glen are now sharing the flat since the Open is in town. He and I are looping doubles every day in the rain up at Castle Course, leaving the flat at 5:30 in the morning and hitchhiking up the hill in the darkness. When we return home in the evening, Colleen puts supper on the table while we hang up our soaking-wet clothes. Life for caddies can't get much better than this, though I have only two hours a day when I'm not working or sleeping to spend with Colleen. I don't want to even think how lonely this flat will feel when I'm alone here again.

I have not written many e-mails this season, since it involves me walking to the pub at night, but yesterday I wrote to Jack and his sisters and sent them a photograph of their mother with the PGA Tour player Ricky Barnes. I was out in the morning caddying at the Castle Course for a friend of Ricky's, who told me that he had gotten into the field for the open as the last alternate and he was looking for someone who knew the Old Course and would walk it with his caddie. I spent the evening with Ray Farnell, a brilliant young caddie from Australia who had never set foot on the Old Course. Ray was caddying in his first major, and he wasn't willing to leave anything to chance. When I told him that the wind can turn 180 degrees when the tide changes, he looked right in my eyes and said, "Where can I get a tide chart in town, mate?"

"Hey, Jack," I wrote in my e-mail. "Here's your beautiful mother with a golfer you will recognize. Last evening I walked the Old Course with his caddie, showing him all the secrets of the place. Check the leaderboard tonight after the second round and you'll see that he is currently in second place."

I left it at that. When I told Colleen about it that night lying in bed, she knew exactly what I had been hoping. "You still think you'll be Jack's caddie someday?" she asked.

"It doesn't seem very likely," I told her. "But I don't give up easily, I guess."

"I'm glad you don't," she said.

I pulled her close and told her that I was going to miss her after she left. "I already counted the days I'll have to get through without you," I said. "Once I get home, I'm never leaving you again."

"We'll see," she said.

SEPTEMBER 8, 2010

The days have gone faster than I ever imagined they would. Working late loops at the Old Course, I have not had time to write anything in this diary since Colleen left over a month ago. Now I am at the end of my time. Things are slowing down. Of all the memories I have of all the days, yesterday I will remember. A real gale blew in overnight, and by the time I was out on the course in the morning, the winds were at thirty knots from off the North Sea and there was lashing rain. The kind of rain where you are soaked to your skin, right through your Gore-Tex waterproofs, in half an hour, and you can't feel your feet or your hands. When I finished at the Castle Course, I went to my flat and took a hot shower, drank a cup of coffee, smoked a cigarette, and then walked to the Old Course. For the record, of all the Links Trust caddies in St. Andrews, I was the only one who volunteered to do a second loop in the gale, and for the last three hours of light I was the only caddie working on the Old Course. The storm was nothing short of epic—a test of wills—and there I was, leading four crazy Irishmen from county Armagh through the gale. It was beautiful.

I've done my work here. I have walked nearly a thousand miles, and my body is very tired. Right knee. Left hip. Two toes that look as if they should be amputated. Right shoulder that wakes me through the night. It is a strange thing to feel your physical strength disappearing. Every loop here from the first day of April feels like a world of dreams I inhabited. I will miss the boys I marched beside, and I will honor each of them in my memories. There were dozens and dozens, men young and old with nicknames we had earned like Pots and Pans, the Butler, Donuts, the Beast, and No Chance. Mine was Gunslinger, because of the gait I adopted to lessen the pain in my right knee. Today in the shed we said the caddies' farewell, and it was a little rough. A handshake that turns into a quick, awkward embrace, and then these words, "Maybe I'll see you out there again."

I was walking up the hill alone, thinking how I knew many of their stories and that to know someone's story is to possess a part of that person. I'll miss big Malcolm. Once out in a sleet storm he saw me struggling with my glasses; I had nothing dry to wipe them on. He came over and untucked his shirt and wiped them off for me. It was a simple gesture, yet to me, one of great benevolence. I'll never forget it. Just as I will never forget Malcolm of Stirling saying to me on my sixtieth birthday as we headed for the 1st tee, "Well, Gunslinger, let's take a nice walk together on your sixtieth birthday." Or Loppy, the assistant caddie master, calling to me as I headed out on my second loop in the gale: "I'll say this for you, Don, you are some boy!" These little things that I have fought for and earned here this season mean more to me than anyone will ever understand. I fought for these things for Jack. Each loop I walked here with strangers from all over the world, I was really walking beside him.

And somewhere in the heavens it must have been written that my last loop as a caddie here in St. Andrews would place me on the 1st tee of the Old Course with a wonderful fellow in his fifties who had recently lost his father, a man from whom he had been estranged for many years. We talked about fathers and sons for the first two hours, and when we reached the 9th tee, he told me the story of his autistic son, now aged thirty, whom he and his wife had been caring for since the beginning. He had never been able to walk a golf course with the son because of the loud sounds the boy makes and the way he waves his arms uncontrollably. The father confided to me that in truth he was embarrassed.

We got to the 10th green, and I asked if he had made the trip to Scotland by himself. He said, "No, my wife and our son are here in the hotel." It was around 6:00 p.m. by then. When we made the turn for the homeward holes, I realized that there were only four groups behind us left on the Old Course. I told the man that if he wanted to sit for a while and let everyone play through, we could then be the final group, and we could call his wife and tell her to bring the son to the 14th tee so he and his father could walk a few holes together, side by side on the Old Course.

It all worked out perfectly. The son was making his loud noises and swinging his arms like some crazy helicopter that would never fly, but it was beautiful to witness the two of them. It was something I'll never forget.

I wonder what it must have been like for this father never to be able to fix what was so terribly broken in his son. What I did today I did for him of course, but also for myself, and for fathers everywhere, I think. And for my own father, whose presence I felt today out on the golf course. I think he was looking down at us from wherever it is we go next.

Logan Airport, Boston. Jack and I had been e-mailing through the spring and summer, but the last time I'd heard his voice was half a year ago, on March 17, when I called him from this same airport, about to board my flight to Scotland. He asked me, "Are you ready for that?" And then my phone conked out before I could answer.

I answered that question a few minutes ago, and then Jack had something to tell me. I want to get it down here word for word, exactly what he said to me, so that I will always remember. "I didn't want to tell you this in an e-mail, Daddy. All summer I worked harder on my game than ever before. Three weeks ago I took my playing ability test and passed. I have my PGA card now, and I've turned pro. I'm going to work one more season here at Inverness. I've pulled up my grades, and I'm going to graduate on time. And then I want to do a pro tour."

My mind raced to keep up with Jack's words, especially this last question: "How would you feel about caddying for me?"

I tried hard to hold back my emotions. "Count on me," I told him.

BOOK THREE

More than a year has passed since I last wrote in this diary. I watched Jack graduate from the University of Toledo in May. We played a round together at Inverness and set our sights on his first professional tour, the Adams Golf Pro Tour, which runs through the winter in Houston, Texas. Whenever we spoke about joining this tour, I heard the conviction in Jack's voice, but he knew as well as I did that we would need anywhere from $15,000 to $20,000—money neither of us had. It wasn't until last night that it began to seem real to both of us after our old friend John Carr called Jack to say he was sending him a check to get us started. "I don't care if you win any money back for me," he had told Jack. "Just be sure to give it everything you have in you." John was Jack's only benefactor during his junior golf years, paying the tournament entry fees that I could never afford. He had also inspired Jack with his own story of how he had enlisted in the U.S. Army the day after September 11, much as my father had after Pearl Harbor. John left his fiancée and his safe job as a government lawyer in Illinois to serve his country in Iraq, and so it meant something to Jack when he wrote to him: "Sometimes we have to leave behind everything we care about in order to fulfill our lives."

I was thinking about John this morning when I took Teddy out to the golf course at Prouts Neck to walk through the woods looking for golf balls as we do every autumn at the end of the summer season there. I always fill a shoe box with Pro Vis before the leaves fall and then keep them in my room to put under the Christmas tree for Jack. But this year it looks as if I will be taking them to Houston. I inherited an old cell phone from one of my kids when they upgraded to iPhones and I took it with me this morning and zipped it inside the pocket of my jacket as Teddy and I started out in the soft rain that was falling over the marshlands where the golf course is cut beneath tall pine trees. We had only just begun when the phone rang. It was my daughter Cara, a junior in college, calling me from her dorm at the University of New Hampshire and crying so hard I could not at first understand what she was saying. This thought goes tearing through a father's brain: A car crash! But she has survived! She is on the phone talking with me!

All she could say through her tears was "Buddy. Buddy."

He was her first boyfriend. She would have been sixteen when they were going steady. I suppose it was two years ago when they broke up.

"Cara," I said, "tell me what's happened to Buddy." Before she could stop crying long enough to tell me, I already knew that I would never see Buddy again.

Last night Buddy died. This is what Cara finally told me. She got a call from a friend early this morning. She didn't believe it of course, not for any reason other than that she holds in her heart an extraordinary measure of hope. She has her mother's generous heart and never gives up on anyone. It was just like her to keep hoping for Buddy even as she was dialing the number to his parents' house, right until the moment when his father told her it was true. And now I wonder if my daughter will ever have the same extraordinary hope again.

SEPTEMBER 24, 2011

It came down to me writing and delivering the eulogy for Buddy today. Cara asked me to do this for her. The whole town is in mourning, it seems. There wasn't an empty seat in the church, and I stood in front feeling as if something were being torn from me as I watched Cara help push Buddy's casket up the center aisle. I will remember that as the hardest part. But it was also difficult to look out and see so many of the boys from Buddy's soccer team crying for him. Some of them were friends of Jack's who had spent a lot of time at our house. I told them that someday they would be old men, leaning on their canes, and they should never be afraid to bore some stranger by talking about their state championship season, even though it would be ancient history by then, because they would be bringing Buddy back to life in all his glory.

It was a rough day. I was so proud of Cara for the way she had filled two years of Buddy's life with joy. The way she made him smile. The way she gave him her best and held nothing back.

When it was over, I felt so damned weary that I thought I might tell Jack that I just couldn't keep our appointment in Houston this winter. When I called his phone, he didn't answer. Then a text came through: "I'm golfing. Will call you later from the putting green."

That night I found the stirring passage in Mark Frost's outstanding book, *The Greatest Game Ever Played*. And I rewrote some of the internal thoughts of the young golfer Francis Ouimet for Jack:

Jack, you might know this story of young Francis Ouimet,
America's first great golfer who grew up with nothing on
the poor side of Clyde Street in Brookline, Massachusetts,

gazing through the trees at the Country Club, a place where he would work as a caddie as he began to dream of being a champion golfer. He gave up everything for golf and he was failing, missing every cut by one or two strokes. Then he was twenty years old, down to his last chance, playing for the Massachusetts Amateur title on June 19, 1913. Match play. He is three down with five holes to play, and what carries him through to victory this time is "an intensity of seeing." So that everything in the world disappeared except the connection between his mind, his hands, and his club. That was the turning point in his career. Maybe while we are driving to Houston in five weeks, we will talk about Ouimet. We will try to figure out precisely what he saw in those moments when he became a champion golfer. Maybe it is no more complicated than what I see when I drop to the deep down world so I can see the words. Maybe it is nothing more than intense concentration. But I believe it is more than that. Maybe for Ouimet it was the moment he finally believed in his worthiness. Growing up poor, across the street from the exalted world of the Country Club, knowing he did not belong there, knowing because his father would never stop reminding him that he was unworthy. He passed the feeling of unworthiness on to his son. The worst legacy of all. And the one sure way to doom a golfer because, though the game of golf is played on magnificent ground, it is *perfected* inside the mind. Maybe when Ouimet was *seeing* the game in a new way, he was finally seeing through everything that had blinded him to his own worthiness. He was seeing that he deserved to become great.

SEPTEMBER 30, 2011

Of all things, my friend Charlie Woodworth invited me to play golf at the Country Club today. It was a summer day in Brookline. We had spoken for a couple of years about meeting up there, but one thing or another had always derailed our plans. He'd called me almost every day since I told him about Buddy's death, and I knew that he had reserved this round of golf in his busy schedule to try to lift my spirits.

I don't remember the drive down at all. I just kept thinking that a week had already passed since the wake, when I'd held Cara at the casket.

On the practice range we met the two fellows whom we would compete against in match play. John, from England, and Rob, from Houston, who couldn't have been more welcoming. Charlie had told Rob that Jack and I would be there all winter on the tour, and he didn't hesitate to offer up the names of some people in the city who might help us. I didn't hear the names. I just stood there nodding like an idiot and thanking him.

Then I was alone with my clubs, which I had used twice in the past year. I took out my pitching wedge and dropped two balls at my feet. As I went through a few swings to loosen up, I glanced past the starter's hut, across the lawn, to the caddie shed, painted that dark green of summer cottages, where a few boys drowsed in the warm sunlight, their morning newspapers in their laps, like well-heeled pensioners rather than refugees from the economy that had most certainly left them behind long ago. The thought ran through my mind that I would give almost anything to be caddying this morning instead of playing.

I stepped up to the first ball, locked the wedge across the palm of my left hand, took aim at the hundred-yard flag, and swung. The ball sailed high, then dropped out of the sky, hitting the stick squarely on the way down with a dull clank. A few of the other golfers to my right looked up. My second shot sailed off on an identical flight path, landed about five feet in front of the pin, then rattled it solidly on one bounce, with roughly the same clank. It was enough to make me think that Charlie was right, a round of golf was just what I needed.

But it was not meant to be of course. I played like an orphaned dog, struggling to find my way right from the first hooked tee shot. Characteristic of most people who play when their heart is not in the game, I missed all the easy shots and then somehow pulled off a couple of miraculous ones.

Charlie was standing beside me on the 11th tee, an endless par-5 carved like a dream through a valley of towering shade trees and rock outcroppings. I was trying to remember something that had transpired since those two wedge shots on the range, but all I could think of was Cara and her Buddy. "It could have been my son, or yours, Charlie," I whispered to him.

"I know," he said. "I know."

On the 16th tee, he pointed through the trees to where Francis Ouimet lived on Clyde Street and reminded me that in his nearly flawless second round of the U.S. Open in 1913, Francis had seen his father through the trees from this tee box—a man who plagued his young life—and took a double bogey on the course's only easy hole. I asked him if he thought I was right about encouraging Jack to play the tour to try to help him believe in himself again. "Absolutely," Charlie said. "That's our job. Whenever they start doubting themselves, we need to step in." I thanked him before I pushed my nine-iron just enough to miss the green and catch the fringe, the first mistake in a series of three that squandered another par.

Almost every round of golf gives you something to remember. What I will take with me from today is the sight of Charlie walking the fairways with a jug of grass seed in his right hand, filling divots all the way around. It's been part of his daily walk for years, an expression of his affection for the land. He fills about a hundred divots per round, going through two or three jugs of seed, and still manages to finish eighteen holes in two and a half hours if he's first off the tee with fleet Marlon on his bag and the greenkeepers let him play through. After all the misery and slaughter I've seen on golf courses, particularly at the Castle Course, where so often the golfers resembled mourners in search of the funeral procession to the cemetery, I am going to hold on to the picture in my mind of Charlie at the Country Club, merrily shooting another round just off par while seeding the Brookline fairways of his boyhood like a farmer tending his fields.

The evening stars were bright outside the bedroom window, and Colleen was falling asleep while I sat on our bed booking a room for Jack and me at the Studio Plus hotel, in a part of Houston called Greenspoint. I leaned over and whispered, "It's got cable TV for Jack. A queen bed for him. A pullout couch for me. Caddies have slept on much worse. A full kitchen so we can save money on food. Both of us in one room. We'll be together there. We'll be okay."

"You told me in Scotland that you were never going to leave me again," she said. I kissed her and tried to say I was sorry.

"How will he do?" she asked.

"He hasn't played in competition in almost three years. We'll get our asses hauled for a while, I suppose."

"You have to promise me that you'll bring him home for Christmas," she said. And so I did.

OCTOBER 29, 2011

I boarded the 6:00 a.m. bus to Boston in darkness, remembering how this journey in golf began five years ago when Jack and I rode this bus to Logan Airport to fly to Carnoustie. There was no way I ever could have known then that I would return to Scotland to work as a caddie. That I would work one season there because of an old dream of one day caddying for Jack, and then return for a second season to show him that I had not given up on that dream. How could I ever have known that he and I would one day be heading to Texas? It all feels like scenes from a dream. Except for the things that I am worried about. First, I am not going to say anything about my right knee or the injection I had to try to relieve some of the pain. I won't let on that I'm really scared his old truck might break down somewhere along the highway between Toledo and Houston. Thirteen hundred miles. But really I am worried about his truck. I wanted to lease us a new car for four months, but the cost was prohibitive. I don't want to trouble him with my worries about money either. He has raised $8,100 from friends of our family and members at Inverness. And I have $6,000 left from my second season caddying in Scotland. We should make it if we are careful.

In Chicago, at gate B1 everyone was gathered around a computer monitor watching a massive snowstorm move up the East Coast. I got the last flight out of Boston before the storm moved in. A good sign, I think.

Motel 6, outside Cincinnati. Jack greeted me outside the Southwest terminal in Cleveland with a quick bear hug and these words: "Are you ready, man?"

A caddie must show no fear, only absolute confidence, and so I replied: "You bet I am. Let's hit the road."

We drove until eight, then stopped at this Motel 6 just south of Cincinnati to watch the Stanford football game. First we ate a steak dinner at a mom-and-pop restaurant that was staffed by four young women who were all overweight by at least seventy pounds. We both noticed. "They live in this town, I'm betting," I said. "They have dreams."

"Yeah," Jack said. "Whenever I'm just passing through some place, I realize that some people live their whole lives there. Amazing, really. Maybe working at this place their whole lives. What do you think they dream about becoming?"

"Our waitress? Maybe she dreamed of being a ballerina before she got so heavy. That changed the dream."

"Maybe not. Maybe she dreams of losing all that fat and becoming a ballerina after all."

"Good thought," I said.

She served us beer in these immense glasses. Must have been thirty ounces, which took me forever to finish, and while we sat there, we talked for the first time in my life about my own dream, which was to become a big-league baseball player. Over the years, I'd told Jack a few things, but never the real version. Tonight he pushed me for the facts. "You never told me why you walked away," he said.

So I laid it out as accurately as I could recall. "I was at the end of my sophomore season in college. Nineteen years old. I led the ECAC in batting all season long. I was playing a doubleheader at Boston College. After the game a scout for the Pirates walked up to me with my coach. I'd had scouts at most of my games. I remember this man saying, 'That catch you made in the third inning. I only know three center fielders who could have run that down. All of them are in the big leagues.' It didn't even faze me. I was really cocky then. I knew I was going to make it to the majors. I'd never doubted it since I was a kid. My grandmother used to listen to the Phillies games with me on her little radio, and she'd tell me over and over, 'Someday, Donnie, I'm going to be listening to you play.'

"Anyway, when the bus got back to campus from Boston, there was a group of students protesting on the football field. A big group. A couple hundred of them. This was May 1970. I got off the bus and wandered over with one of my teammates, and someone told us that students had just been shot at Kent State. I'd never paid any attention to politics of any kind before. I was just a jock, period, struggling through an English lit major and barely holding on. But this really got to me. I remember feeling like there was a whole world out there that I knew nothing about and that I had to start educating myself. Our season ended when the student strikes began. I never played baseball again. I started writing poetry instead. Lousy poetry. I remember my father calling me at college one night and telling me that if I walked away from baseball, I would regret it the rest of my life."

I stopped there and said, "I'm never going to finish this beer."

"Was Granddad right?" Jack asked.

"You mean, did I regret it?"

"Yeah."

"Yes. All my life," I said.

Before I fell asleep halfway through the second quarter, missing a Stanford victory in triple overtime, we talked about the tour. Jack brought all the clothes he owns in two big duffel bags. "Thirty-two golf shirts," he said.

"That should be plenty," I said.

"Maybe I'll do well and head straight to another tour from Houston," he said.

His optimism encouraged me. "Yeah," I said immediately. "That sounds like a great plan."

OCTOBER 30, 2011

We crawled out of the Motel 6 at dawn like fugitives, scraped the ice off the windshield of the truck, and hit the highway. I was up an hour earlier trying to walk the stiffness out of my knee in the dark parking lot, remembering when I stepped into the hole just below the bunker up the right side of the 12th fairway at the Castle Course almost eighteen months ago. A million miles from Little Rock, Arkansas, where we are now so we can watch the Eagles tonight. The truck is running well. Jack won't let me drive, but that's okay. I'm the old guy along for the ride, I guess.

We have only 440 miles to go, and I am finally more relaxed about the drive. We talked about maybe stopping here on our way back in late February to see a University of Arkansas basketball game. Then we'll drive the second day to Louisville and watch another game there. At the end of February, just before March Madness begins. I suggested this because I need to think of us on the other end of this journey. I don't know why. Maybe I just don't like being so far from Colleen and Teddy anymore. I am a little homesick. When you drive instead of fly, you watch a strange landscape sailing past you for twenty hours, and you know in your soul that you have ventured far from home.

Ten hours today hammering through Kentucky, Tennessee, and into Arkansas, we passed an unrelenting procession of tractor-trailer trucks blasting exhaust into the air in order to deliver all the stuff we're buying on the Internet. And so many people moving everything they own in beat-up trucks. Like the Joad family in *The Grapes of Wrath.* At the steering wheel the same man with a face as beat-up as his truck. Father. Husband. Maybe heading somewhere to look for work. Chasing a new dream perhaps.

OCTOBER 31, 2011

Houston, Texas. We crossed into Texas at 11:00 a.m. with another three hundred miles to go to Houston. This part of the state is brown from a long, punishing drought, which means the rough on the golf courses will not be thick. U2 was blasting from Jack's iPhone through the radio speakers as we rolled past boarded-up businesses and rusting mobile homes and shotgun shacks and car wrecks that need to be hauled away, and Walmarts that stay open twenty-four hours a day, and sheet-metal churches that offer the only hope, with buzzards circling the big sky overhead. I kept thinking, Thank God I never had to move my family here.

The Studio Plus, our new home until the end of February, will be fine, I think. Jack said, "Cool, this will work," as we entered the room for the first time. One room about thirty by thirty, divided into a kitchen and bath and sitting area, where the couch pulls out into my bed, just across from Jack's double bed. The first thing Jack did was check the water pressure in the shower, recalling how bad it was in our B&B in Carnoustie, where we stood, frozen after each round, under a weary trickle. I walked outside to see if there was any grass, and I found a nice patch of Bermuda rough at the far end of the parking lot where Jack can practice his wedges.

We put our stuff in the drawers and closet and then found our way to Walmart, where we bought two weeks of groceries for $184 and loaded everything into the back of the truck except for the beer and eggs, which I held on my lap.

NOVEMBER 1, 2011

I am up at 4:00 a.m. writing in this diary while Jack sleeps across the room. He looks comfortable. We sat up watching the Monday night game until around eleven. Before last night I had not watched a single sporting event on television from start to finish in maybe six years. I had fallen asleep during every World Series game this fall. Living in Scotland with no TV for so long, I lost my appetite for it, but now the TV is the center of our room here, and when we are not out on the golf course, we will be watching sports. And that is comforting to me because it reminds me of all the happy hours Jack and I spent watching sports on TV when he was little. Just listening to him breathe in his sleep feels like a privilege to me. The same kind of privilege I used to feel as the last caddie out on the Old Course at the end of a day. It has something to do with time, and history, but I'm not sure what it is. Maybe it's just the feeling you get when you realize you are standing in a moment that you are always going to remember.

I miss Colleen and poor Teddy, who will spend the next four months waiting for me to come home to take him for his run on the golf course. I'm feeling the dull ache I felt in Scotland when I first arrived for the season, knowing that half a year would pass before I returned home. Usually at this hour before dawn, the background noise is the dull percussion of waves breaking onto the shore across the cove like thunder. Here the thunder is the freeway traffic. But that's okay for now; we are going to be all right here. Just as soon as we get to the golf course today and I start concentrating on being Jack's caddie instead of his father, everything will fall into place, and it will all make sense to me, just as it did in Scotland each day when I stepped onto the 1st tee. But right now, this first morning, I can feel the fear in my hands. A slight tremor. This time it is not just about me. I am not the only one who has wandered so far from home. This time it is my son. Even though he is the one who will play the golf here and he is the one who drove us here in his truck, he has followed me to Texas. I know that we have spoken about this since Jack was ten years old, but in truth this journey was mostly my idea. I've been the one telling him all along that he deserved this chance to play on a pro tour, to see how far the game will take him in his life. I've encouraged him to chase his old dream, and if this turns out to be an experience that flattens him, I will be responsible for that. And to be honest, there were dozens of moments in the last three months while we prepared for this trip when I thought about backing out. I could have simply told him that my knee was not up to it or that I couldn't leave Colleen again to fend for herself through another Maine winter. I had any number of acceptable excuses. Yesterday on the road, when we crossed into Texas, I told him that he was now in the land of the great Byron Nelson and Ben Hogan, both Texans who began as caddies. I talked again about the business of dreams and whether it is more difficult to walk away from a dream you cannot reach or to keep holding on. I explained that Hogan never had a choice. Golf was it for him. Here was a kid who at age six or seven witnessed his father shooting himself in the living room. Golf became Hogan's cure. There was no other road. But the game was both the cure and the illness because for a long time he failed at the game. Nelson was winning on the tour, and he was getting nowhere. He was cursed by that damned hook. "I think he was on the tour for three years before he had any success at all," I said to Jack. "But if anyone had ever gone up to Hogan when he was struggling and said, 'That's it, walk away, you're never going to make it,' I think he would have said, 'What the hell do you want me to do? This is it for me. I don't have a choice.'"

Jack didn't say anything. He was steering with one hand and holding his iPhone with the other, trying to follow the path. I let it go.

This morning I am sure he knows that every time I bring up the subject of dreams, I am talking about his dream with golf and I am trying to prepare him for failure here. I am trying to tell him that sometimes you have to walk away. And he wants no part of that, and I don't blame him. It's just that I have seen so much misery on golf courses, and it is usually inflicted worse upon those who try to play the game with any degree of perfection. The punishment and the humiliation are out there waiting for Jack. It will come down to the same thing it always came down to on almost every round I caddied in Scotland. Limiting the damage from mistakes. Recovering quickly before the damage ruins you. Everyone in the tournaments will make mistakes on every round; that is a given in this game when you play it competitively. But if you can recover from the mistakes instead of being crushed by them, then you walk on unscarred. The only thing that you can't recover from is despair, as the great Harry Vardon said. I must remember that this is a serious business for Jack. He will have his game face on this morning as we make our way through our first practice round. He will stop talking with me as his way of claiming some space. In two days, when the real show begins, he will be even more distant. And I must grant him this space.

NOVEMBER 1, 2011, TUESDAY NIGHT

We went to work today after packing our peanut butter and jam sandwiches for lunch. By habit, I had my waterproofs with me when Jack stopped me as we were leaving our room. "It hasn't rained here in a year, man," he said, a little impatient with me. I knew this of course, and he'd already assured me that his iPhone called for another day of cloudless skies with temperatures in the eighties. "It's just that I never went to work in Scotland without them," I said as I threw them through the threshold while he held the door open.

"You're not in Scotland anymore," he said.

I told him about the five-day gale in Scotland when the wind never fell off. You couldn't escape the sound, and after a while it seemed as if it were blowing inside your mind, so I began taking my iPod and headphones with me everywhere just to drown out the noise with music. Here in Houston it's not the wind; it's the hammering of the freeways. As soon as I stepped outside into this new day, it was there again. "Where the fuck is everybody going?" I said miserably as I gazed across ten lanes of north- and southbound cars.

"Relax," Jack said.

Easier said than done when your heart is racing. For my sake he agreed to a compromise: he drove eighty miles an hour along with everyone else, but with two hands, while I held his iPhone and shouted out the directions to him. I have never in my life been on ten-lane freeways that narrow with astonishing suddenness into one-lane exit ramps that soar straight up into the sky and are held there by what appears to be a rather haphazard collection of cantilevers, flying buttresses, and hundred-foot-tall concrete stilts and then bend like a roller-coaster track at breathtaking angles so you feel as if you were going to be catapulted to a terrifying death. I used to be able to relax on the way to work in St. Andrews as my bus crept along the North Sea, stopping on the way to pick up pensioners with their folded grocery carts. I should have spent the last two months at home borrowing my daughter's iPhone and learning how to use it as a navigational tool. Too late now.

It began with my asking Jack a caddie question standing on the practice range at Hearthstone Country Club: "Okay, Jack, so if you were thrown off a train in the middle of nowhere with one club that you had to hit 220 yards, straight, every time, what club would it be?"

"Six-iron," he said as he stretched.

"All right," I said, pointing to a flag in the distance. "That flag is about 200 yards." He took his electronic scope out of his bag, and I cringed. "You don't need that thing. I know 200 yards when I see it, don't you trust me?" I said.

He scoped it anyway and nodded. I asked him to drop ten balls and hit them all 20 yards past the flag. "Don't you trust me?" he asked.

It hit me then. We had known and trusted each other for years as father and son, but the trust we would need between us now as golfer and caddie had to be earned.

"It's not that I don't believe you," I said. "It's just that I was lied to so much as a caddie."

It turned out he was telling the truth. We worked through all his clubs while I took notes in my book. In all my rounds in Scotland, with all the golfers I saw there, I never saw a single shot with the trajectory of Jack's. Miles high. Each ball sizzling off the ground with a small explosion as it took flight—as if it had been fired from a gun. I thought to myself, my Lord, I am into a whole new ball game here.

This Hearthstone course that winds through a subdivision with houses lining the fairways is probably what we are going to get down here all winter. It offered its own menu of distractions you don't find on any course I ever worked, which includes babies crying in their cribs, dogs barking, kids playing in their swimming pools, and women in short-shorts bent over their flower gardens. "Hit her and we're both heading home," I said to Jack on the 1st tee when I noticed he was looking at the lady too.

After the long drought, the fairways were baked hard with almost no grass, exactly like those on the Old Course when the Royal & Ancient stopped watering them in the weeks leading up to the Open when I was caddying there. They wanted the fairways to be hard so that balls would roll forever and reach pothole bunkers that were normally not in play. This made me feel at home until we reached the 1st green. Neither Jack nor I had ever played greens with Bermuda grass. They were as hard as rock, and we expected the ball to release and roll forever, and we held to that understanding with mounting confusion until we walked onto the 220-yard par-3 after hitting a six-iron downwind and discovered that the ball had stopped inside ten inches from where it landed. "All right," Jack said, "we get the message. We can go at every pin."

There is a lot to learn about reading putts on Bermuda grass, and we were really grinding away all afternoon. Unlike bent grass or the fescue grass in Scotland, which grows up and down, Bermuda grass grows along the ground, meaning you have to know which way the grain is going in order to putt well. And you can't always see the grain. Experienced caddies will take a look at the sun in the sky when they begin a round because they know that the grain will always run toward the west, where the sun sets. I've even heard of caddies carrying a compass for that purpose. The other way of determining the direction of the grain is by looking carefully at the hole itself. When the hole is cut in the morning, the edges are fresh. But as the day goes along, the edge of the cup that is worn is the direction the grain is growing. When you line up a putt, it is basically going to turn with the grain, even more than with the slope. On two greens today we had putts break *uphill* with the grain. And we were astonished how hard you had to roll the ball when you were against the grain. This is going to take a lot of practice, but we gained a little confidence when we sank a fifteen-footer for a birdie on 12. Officially, we weren't keeping score today in this first practice round. Meaning that Jack wasn't, but I was. We hit sixteen greens in regulation and then made hash of the putting. I had us at seven over par after eighteen.

I was beginning to feel comfortable when we finished, but I realized today that caddying for Jack on the tour is going to be completely different from caddying for tourists in Scotland. I'm going to have to quickly learn to be a silent observer rather than a chamber of commerce booster. This isn't vacation golf. It's work, and that is how Jack approaches it.

We had a moment today at the turn when we walked inside the clubhouse for a cold drink, and on the TV above the bar the Golf Channel was playing a rerun of the Dunhill Links Championship from St. Andrews. The moment I spotted the 2nd hole of the Old Course from across the room, it was as if someone had called my name. I wandered over to the bar, where I fell into a dream until Jack joined me there after a few minutes. "Your old track," he said. I was remembering playing that hole with him when he hit a nine-iron from Cheape's bunker that carried straight through a thirty-knot wind and landed two feet from the flag over 150 yards away.

When we finished up, I sat off to the side of the practice green while Jack rolled some more putts. I was worrying about the ride back to our place in the rush-hour traffic, something I am going to have to stop worrying about. While I watched Jack, it struck me that if I keep my head up here, I am going to discover some new truth about life almost every day this winter. Here is something that I never knew before today. If you are fortunate enough to have a little boy in your life for those few years when all he wants is to be with you and when he stands before you in his footed pajamas, begging you to play knee football with him before he gets into bed at night just because he wants you to tackle him softly so he can feel your arms around him, if you get that in your life, then you are going to spend the rest of your life looking everywhere for that little boy. I realized today that in the last four years since Jack left home for college, whenever I've seen him, I've had this gnawing disappointment that I couldn't explain. Now I know its point of origin; I've been looking for the little boy he once was.

There must be no more of that this winter. My son is now a young man who is trying to become a professional golfer, and I must get to know him on his terms. This is one of the new rules I must abide. On the range today, from the moment he took his first practice swing, I felt myself dropping to the deep down world that always served me so well when I worked as a caddie. We both have a job to do here, I told myself. We have to make shots. One shot and then the next shot, one hole and then the next hole, for two rounds in twelve tournaments, 432 holes across the next four months while Colleen keeps the woodstove going through the winter. And I must learn to stop talking so damned much.

Back in our room tonight after we ate microwaved lasagna while watching Toledo play Northern Illinois on ESPN, Jack disappeared as I was reading what the experts had to say about Bermuda greens online and writing SOS e-mails to Glen in Canada and to Ray, who was at the moment caddying for Ricky Barnes at a PGA event somewhere in Malaysia. When Jack hadn't returned in half an hour, I was concerned. Our part of Houston is called Greenspoint on the maps and Gunpoint by the locals.

I walked down the long corridor outside our room, and when I got to the window at the far end, I looked down and saw him sitting by the pool with his laptop, Skyping his girl. I could see Jenna's face on the screen.

I smiled to myself, walked back to the room, and fell asleep on the couch.

NOVEMBER 2, 2011

When I awoke at 4:00 a.m., I was already wondering if Jack's iPhone has a compass I can use to find west at every green so we know which way the grain is running. There was thick fog when I walked outside at 7:00 a.m. My first thought was if we have an early tee time tomorrow in round one, we are going to have to give ourselves an extra hour to get to Hearthstone. Maybe two hours. Something else to worry about, I thought as I was telling myself to stop worrying about everything.

We discovered last night that with Southwest Airlines offering $89 flights from here to Boston and Detroit, it is cheaper for us to check out of our room and fly home for the Thanksgiving and Christmas breaks in Toledo and Maine, just as the golfers do on the big tours. So we can now divide this journey into three parts. The first three events, then Thanksgiving break. The next three events, then Christmas break. Then the long stretch of six events through January and February. Jack feels good about this, and it will give me a chance to try to shoot a goose out on the marsh for our Thanksgiving dinner now that I have my first hunting license. It will also make it a lot easier for Teddy. And I am going to try to persuade Jack to spend a few days in Maine over Christmas so I can meet the promise I made to his mother.

The Adams Tour flags were flying at the course today, and all the slots at the range were filled with studs. Among them the son of the great PGA golfer Bob Tway. I watched and no one hit the ball any better than Jack with his compact, homemade swing. In eighteen warm-up holes today he mis-hit only two shots, and with his compressed swing, even when he's off line, he doesn't miss by much. We made a bunch of birdies (five by my count), reached two of the par-5s in two, and felt a little less tentative on the greens. They are big greens, and our main task tomorrow in round one will be to go right at the pins and get as close as we can. It is still amazing to both of us how the ball sticks on these greens that have been baking in the hot sun, with no rain for ten months. Even little wedges, twenty feet from the hole, can stop ten feet short if the ball is rolling against the grain. We agreed that rather than picking a landing area short of the hole, we would use the hole as our target. Try this on the Old Course and you'll run every shot 40 yards past the hole. Not here.

While Jack was on the range, hitting through his irons, I was walking around the practice putting green with his iPhone, experimenting with the compass. It seems to work; you find west and you know that the grain is running in that direction. I never could have imagined that Jack's iPhone would be so vital to us here. Without it we are blind men on the concrete freeways and on the Bermuda greens.

For the first nine holes today I was writing down the direction of the grains in my notebook for tomorrow so we would know how the ball will roll on our approach shots. But after Jack and I discussed this, we decided that it was unnecessarily overcomplicating things. We're just going right at the pins, period. If the ball rolls forward, so be it. Today we had only two approaches release and roll forward, and we were only ten feet beyond the hole on both.

At noon Jack got an e-mail on his iPhone from the tour, notifying us that we have the last tee time tomorrow at 9:40. We lucked out. We won't have to vary our schedule too much. We can leave the hotel at 8:00 and have plenty of time for traffic and a little practice. Jack is not a big range golfer. He warms up quickly. I saw no sign of nerves in him today. He lopes his way around the course like a big, tall Texan. He takes everything in stride. Coming into the par-5 number

9 today, he pulled his second shot from 230 into the water hazard, left of the green. It was a red-staked hazard. He dropped a ball, stuck it to five feet, and drained the putt to save par. "No worries," he said as I put the flag back into the hole.

No worries. It made me wonder if he was trying to give me a message. Maybe I look nervous. I prided myself on always keeping a calm and composed countenance in Scotland. I remember being out one day with Glen and one of the real veteran caddies at the Old Course. After the round he told Glen that I was the most relaxed caddie he'd ever worked with. I admit I don't feel calm now. I feel a disconcerting weariness. But all that matters right now is that Jack not see this. We never know how much our children see in us. Maybe we delude ourselves about this because when they are small it is so easy to trick them. Today, when I walked onto the 4th tee box, I saw a woman reading a book on her porch, and my mind went off the rails. I lost sight of Jack's drive because I was thinking about my new novel, which has just been published, knowing that it isn't going to do well enough on Amazon or in the wider marketplace to keep us from losing our health insurance. I can't tell Jack that in another two weeks he won't have health insurance, and if either one of us gets sick out here, we're going to be at the mercy of the system, driving up and down the freeways following the refugees from Hurricane Katrina to a free clinic. Just thinking about this paralyzed me all the way to the green. I was there beside Jack, but really I just wanted some way to hide my fear from him.

I need to find my defiance somehow. Only defiance can banish the fear. Two weeks ago I was sailing my small boat through a storm. Black skies, wind whistling through the shrouds, every wave breaking into the cockpit, and even though there were eleven ways I could have fucked up, I was calm. Tomorrow in round one of our first event, I need to find that same calm.

Jack is across the room as I write this. I just told him that as far as I'm concerned, he's a solid enough ball striker to hold his own here. "We'll soon find out," he said.

NOVEMBER 3, 2011

Game Day. Jack is sleeping like a bear at 4:00 a.m. I remember when he was little and we would stay at hotels, there always had to be a swimming pool, and he would wake me holding his blue blanket, his swimming trunks always on backward.

At 5:00 a.m., I went downstairs and rode the exercise bike a few miles to get the stiffness out of my knee. Condi Rice was on the TV news trying to justify the Iraq war. I thought of all the dreams that had been shattered there. And the dreams that had turned out to be only lies. I thought of the fathers who had lost sons and daughters there. For what, I do not know.

I woke Jack at his requested hour, 6:45, with news that somehow overnight some good, cold weather had moved in on racing winds. "It will be like Scotland out there today," I told him. I couldn't have been happier.

"Sounds good," he said.

While he took his shower, I counted the clubs in his bag again to be sure that he had taken out the extra putter and the five-wood to meet the fourteen-club limit and that we had plenty of balls. Since awaking, I'd been thinking about what I could say this morning to get us both in the right frame of mind for our first event. I thought back to Scotland during the week of the Open, when I did four days of doubles in a row, most of that time in freezing-cold rain, starting each day by hitchhiking to the Castle Course before dawn with Glen, then marching for ten hours with rainwater sloshing in my shoes. Whenever I felt as if I couldn't take another five minutes of it, I would say to myself, "It ain't Normandy." That might work here, it might place things into perspective, but I feel as if I owe Jack something more personal. Since making my coffee this morning, I have been running through my memory of our recent history, and I can't remember the last time I praised him for anything. I wonder if it is possible that I am still disappointed in him for failing to win a scholarship. For fathers, it always comes down to fear, I suppose. You're alone in the world and doing fine, and then before you know it, you've got a wife, and kids, and a mortgage, and the fear mounts silently like falling snow. I walked almost a thousand miles that second season in Scotland to get the anger and the fear out of my system, and it was in the past now. But why hadn't I found some way of telling my son that it was in the past?

And this morning I began to wonder if Jack had put it in *his past* or if it was going to be waiting for him at the Hearthstone Country Club, on the 1st tee this morning. We bring children into this world, and from time to time they disappoint us, and we have to forgive them and bear no grudges. It has been this way since the beginning of time, and if you can't accept these terms, you shouldn't have children. Until this morning it had not occurred to me that our children have to strike terms of their own to get out from underneath the ways they have let us down. And maybe they need our help to do this.

Considering all that, I didn't think that a reference to Normandy would cut it today. It wasn't until we were walking onto the practice range to take our place among the other young men lined up there inside their solitary worlds of dreams and doubts, worlds their fathers could no longer inhabit with them, that it came to me. "No matter what happens out here today, Jack," I said as I stood beside him cleaning the grooves on his irons, "thanks for bringing me along. Of all the cool things I've had the chance to do in my life, this is the coolest by far."

"Okay" was all he said.

I watched him take his place on the range, and though he looked as if he belonged there and he seemed at peace with himself, I was thinking about what Colleen had said to me a hundred times across the years: "Why didn't you encourage him to play a team sport? He was so good at baseball." Yeah, I thought, baseball would be nice today. A dugout filled with teammates to console him.

I walked off to the men's room to soak my towel. We had forty minutes. I could picture the first three holes clearly in my mind and the shots we were going to have to execute in order to get off to a solid start. One shot at a time, I said to myself. Driver on number 1 straight into this thirty-knot wind. We'll be taking a seven-iron to the green instead of the wedges we'd hit in our practice rounds. The change in weather had made it a new game today. On number 2 we had hit three-woods in our practice rounds to the narrow landing area with another 40 yards to spare before the ground fell into a ravine that would be death. Now the wind was going to be behind us on that tee, and I made a note to tell Jack that a three-wood would be far too much club. No more than a five-iron this morning, I wrote in my notebook. On the 3rd hole, a 210-yard par-3, we had hit rescue clubs into the wind in both practice rounds. Today a six-iron would be plenty.

On the putting green Jack looked handsome in his black banker's trousers he had worn since his sophomore year in high school and royal-blue jacket, the biggest guy out there and a dead ringer for Jack Nicklaus when he first broke onto the tour. I told myself that these other boys, no matter how good they were, would not be our opponents today. In golf, you have no teammates to console you, but you also have no opponents; it's just you against the golf course. A perfect equation. I closed my eyes for a moment and pictured Jack in his first NCAA tournament in North Carolina, when he was up against many of the top Division I players in the country and he had shot one under par. That was his high point, and as I watched him on the practice green, I was hoping he could remember that. And not that his first tournament had turned out to be his last.

On the 1st tee, the Adams Golf tent was in a heap on the ground, battered by the wind. "Nice and smooth," I said to Jack as I handed him his driver. He striped it up the middle, a mile out there, but when we got to his ball, we discovered that it had kicked left off a mound and was lying directly behind a tree. "That sucks a little," he said with a short laugh. We were only 140 yards to the front of the green, but the best we could do was punch a five-iron below the branches of the tree, into the green-side bunker, blast out with a wedge, and two-putt for a bogey. I gave him my standard Scotland line—"We'll get that stroke back"—and we walked on to the next tee box. Jack played the tee shot on number 2 perfectly, riding the wind 253 yards with a five-iron straight up the middle. He made a solid par there and another solid par on 3, then, as we were walking to the 4th tee box, he said, "This has to be a birdie hole today; with all the wind behind us, we'll get there in two."

"It is a birdie hole," I said. I handed him his driver and watched him hit it dead center, sawing 327 yards off the 502-yard hole. With the wind still right behind us, he knocked an eight-iron the rest of the way, and we were lying four feet off the right side of the green, seventeen feet from the hole in two. The perfect birdie chance we were both hoping for.

Everyone who has ever tried to play golf with some degree of perfection knows that there is a point in every match where you have the chance to set the tone for the round. This was our point. Make a birdie here, and we will be on our way, I thought.

Jack took a couple of practice swings, then settled into the shot. He looked relaxed and confident with his knees flexed, but just before his club struck the ball, he raised his head, and this prevented him from accelerating through the swing, and the club face stuck in the Bermuda grass. The ball moved forward only two feet. I watched his shoulders slump, and then he hurried the next shot and bladed the ball, sending it twenty-five feet past the pin. From there he made a bad putt and then a good one that should have fallen in. Instead of a birdie, we made double bogey.

As we walked to the next tee, he muttered to himself, "So stupid. So stupid."

Maybe I should have played the optimist here as I always did with my golfers in Scotland. I almost said something upbeat, but Jack was angry at himself and I felt as if he needed to be angry just then, so I let it go.

On the next hole, a 192-yard par-3, Jack hit a terrific six-iron to twelve feet right of the flag. "We're all right, Jackie boy," I said. He was silent all the way to the green. And then he three-putted. I got only a quick look at his eyes, but it was enough for me to see that he was no longer angry. He was scared now. He could feel the despair that Vardon feared, and there was nothing I could do for him. Which really pissed me off. Four years ago a college in Maine invited me to donate all my manuscripts to its library. I turned in forty thousand pages from thirty-four years of writing. Since then maybe another five thousand pages. All those pages, all those words, and there I was standing right beside my son without even a handful of words to make him feel better about what was happening. I heard a dog barking across the fairway, and all I wanted was to be at home with Teddy. How are we going to get through the winter? I thought.

The essence of competitive golf rides on a very narrow rail inside your mind. Either you see each hole as an opportunity to make a birdie and get one hole closer to perfection, or you see each hole as another chance to screw up and fall further behind. We were there after six holes. Jack was buried in a silent, upside-down world for the rest of the round. I stayed beside him and gave him the best I had, but I was no help to him as a caddie or a father.

He hit some wonderful golf shots before we were finished, and on the 16th tee box I finally found these words: "Here's my take on it, Jack. You look like a professional golfer out here. You have all the shots. And if we learn how to fight, you'll be fine this winter."

He listened to me, but he had no reaction.

Fathers whom I know well who had talked with me about this journey told me that no matter what happens on the tour this winter, Jack will always look back fondly on this experience that he and I shared. I hope this is true. I really hope this is true. And that is what I was thinking about when I told Jack that tomorrow in our second round we were going to make five birdies and start fighting our way back. I carried his clubs to the truck while he went to the scorer's table to sign his card.

I stood by the truck looking up into an empty blue sky, telling myself that we were at the bottom now and that on the ride back to our hotel, or tonight watching sports, I would find some words that would make things better for Jack. A few minutes later, when I watched him walk across the parking lot, there was something wrong with the way he moved. He seemed to be struggling just to walk a straight line to where I was waiting. I called out my father's words to him: "Tomorrow's another day, Jackie boy."

"There is no tomorrow," he said as he approached.

"What do you mean?"

"We missed the cut."

"There is no cut," I said. "Did you know there was a cut?"

"No," he said. "But when you shoot over 86, you're cut from the second round. The guy just told me."

"What did we shoot, Jack?" I asked.

"I shot a 90," he said, almost yelling at me. "I haven't shot a 90 since high school. If you play the way I played, you don't deserve to make the cut. It's embarrassing, man."

So we're not coming back to this place tomorrow, I said to myself as we sped out of the parking lot. Then what the hell are we going to do tomorrow?

I think the only thing that saved us on the ride back to our hotel was Springsteen at full volume singing, "Good night, it's all right, Jane . . ."

"I'm going to sit out in the sun and warm up a little," I said when we got out of the truck, the first words to break our silence. "Are you okay?" I asked him.

"It is what it is," he said as he walked away.

It is what it is. Those had been his words after his graduation when I tried to start a meaningful conversation with him about his four years of college. *It is what it is.*

I sat on the curb by the truck, thinking about this and saying to myself: Maybe it is what it is, but we are going to have to find better words than those because saying it is what it is, is not much better than saying, look, I don't talk with you about important things, okay? We stopped doing that before I was kicked off my golf team. Remember?

No, I thought, we are going to talk. Maybe not now, and maybe not tonight, but sooner or later we're going to talk. I rolled a cigarette, then sent Colleen a text: "I was prepared to get our asses hauled down here for a while. But today we got our hearts torn out. Sorry. I love you."

It was all swirling through my head, and when I stood up, I had to lean against the truck to catch my balance. I was talking to myself then, telling myself that Jack has to understand that he hasn't played golf competitively in three years. He is going to have to learn all over again how to do that. And fast. Because this is misery for both of us. He's going to end up being haunted by it just as I've been haunted by my failures and by never letting my father inside my life when we still had the chance.

I closed my eyes for a moment, and before I opened them, I heard an ambulance racing by on the freeway. I turned and watched the flashing lights. The real world. Someone's life being ripped apart. I walked on, but when I was climbing the stairs to the second floor, my mind was going all the way back to the days when Colleen was pregnant with our first child. It struck me that when we start out and are waiting for our children to be born, all we ask is please, God, just give us a healthy baby, with all the parts in working order. And then later, when they begin to grow up and start to leave the house, we just pray that the siren in the dead of night will not be for us. But then, as the years pass, we raise the ante. We start asking our children to work hard, to get into good colleges, and to make their lives amount to something that makes sense to us. It goes on and on. But maybe in the end, the only thing that will matter is that we treated our time together as a gift.

When I got to the room, Jack was talking with Jenna on his phone. His voice was low and solemn. I made a call on my phone, talking loudly enough for him to hear, as I spoke with the pro at Cypress Lakes Golf Club, where our next event is being played in three days. "Can we get a practice round in tomorrow?" I asked. "Noon is great. Thanks."

Midnight. My thoughts at the end of this long day are about something I wrote in my new novel: "When we lose the people we love best in this life, most of the time it is our own fault."

We are so close to our children when they are small. They tell us everything. We hold them and kiss them whenever we want to, and we cannot imagine that this will ever end. But somehow a space opens between us, and it grows wider each time they turn on the television when we enter the room, or plug themselves into their iPods, or send us a three-word text instead of answering the cell phone we bought for them when we call. It just happens. And after a while, we are grateful when they give us an excuse *not* to talk because it is easier to fill the silence with music or television or another trip to the mall than to try to find the words.

Tonight Jack broke the silence for both of us after he took a walk just before dark. We hadn't eaten anything and had just filled two tense hours staring at the talking heads on ESPN as if we were waiting for them to tell us something meaningful.

When I heard Jack opening the door, I was thinking that I would just pretend I was asleep, but as soon as he entered the room, he said, "I'm sorry for being so negative today."

I sat up straight on the couch. I wanted to jump into his arms and thank him as I had never thanked anyone for anything before in my life. But I was afraid that might scare him away. Instead, I said as calmly as I could, "That's all right, Jack. But could you sit here and talk with me for a few minutes?"

He looked surprised by this, and when I clicked off the TV, that space of silence between us felt even more intimidating. For some reason, I thought it best to begin with a confession. "I've made a lot of mistakes in my life," I said. Then I got up and opened a couple of beers and handed him one while I said that our tendency is to believe that our lives are shaped by our achievements and that this is how we will be remembered. But it's not true. It's the mistakes that really determine the shape of our lives. The mistakes we make and then how we recover from those mistakes, exactly like a round of golf. There will be mistakes, that is given. The great unknown in a round of golf is whether you will be crushed into despair by your mistakes or whether you will recover. "So we could say that Jack Snyder's story is how he left home three days after his high school graduation to chase his dream of playing Division I golf and he made the team at the University of Toledo as a walk-on. Or should we say that he was kicked off the team? Both are part of his story. We are here now because of both parts, right? Or maybe not. Maybe we are here because of the mistake you made. You are trying to recover from it. What do you think?"

He considered this for a moment, then said, "I don't know, man. It is what it is, I guess."

Not what I was hoping he would say.

"Okay. Look at me and my life," I said. "There is something I never told you. The greatest mistake of my life. In order to make it clear for you, I have to go back to the beginning when I first met your mother. We fell in love. And when you fall in love, you make a silent pledge that you will do everything possible to help that person reach her dream. Colleen's dream was to have a family. A big family. Four or five kids. And I was on this path to try to become a writer, to write books that matter in some way and that deprive the world of some of its indifference. That was my battle cry through the ten years I had been writing before I met your mom. She was twenty-one years old; I was already thirty-one. I'd written three novels no one would publish. Dozens of stories. I had no prospects really. In golf terms I was shooting rounds in the upper 80s and telling myself that I was going to make the big tour. Nothing less. In those days there was the Iowa Writers' Workshop, where a new writer could earn an MFA degree and land a college teaching job, a good job for life. The chance to work with young students. I decided I had to go there. It took nine years for me to write something good enough to get in, but eventually there we were in Iowa City. Erin was born my third semester there. Iowa got me my big break, the chance to teach at Colgate University. We had Nell by then, and you were born three weeks before I went there for my interview. Anyway, there we were and it was paradise. I loved my students. We loved the town. We bought our first house on Maple Avenue, five blocks from campus. That first semester I would look out my office window and see your mother with the three of you, playing in the leaves. We spent the winter sledding down the big hill on campus.

"So it's spring of my first year, and an old friend of mine from Iowa had become an editor at *Harper's Magazine*, and he was willing to come to campus and talk with my students. It was great. We had a class where he went over my students' work, and then we all had dinner together. The next day I was heading down the hallway in Lawrence Hall to my office when the head of the writing department, the fellow who had hired me, stopped me and said, 'I hear you had an editor from *Harper's Magazine* here.'

"I began telling him how much it had meant to my students, and he stopped me and said, 'You brought an editor from *Harper's Magazine* to campus and you didn't introduce him to me? What are you trying to do, cut me out of an important contact in New York?'

"He said it and then just turned and walked away. I remember standing in my office at the window, lighting a cigarette, and trying to figure out what the hell had just happened. Then I went to his office. I knocked on his door, and when I opened it, he looked up at me from behind his desk, and he said, 'As hard as I worked to bring you here, I will now work to send you on your way.'

"I still remember those exact words. I tried to reason with him, but he dismissed me. 'Why are you still standing there?' he said. 'Don't you have any work to do?'

"So I started walking back to my office to try to think. Only I didn't get all the way back. I couldn't even breathe. I was thinking, Okay, just let it go. It will all disappear in time, and everything will be all right. But I had been listening to a lot of Springsteen in those days, and there was this one song with the lyric about how we grow up and we keep our silence and hope that it passes for honor. I turned around and went back to his office and threw open the door and I said, 'From now on, I'm going to think of you as nothing more than a fat asshole.' I slammed the door and that was it.

"He was my boss. He was the big deal in the English department. I had three more years on my contract, but when my vote for tenure came up, he killed me. And during the last year, when I was applying for teaching jobs at other colleges, he blackballed me. I remember we were out in the parking lot one afternoon and he smiled at me and said, 'I heard from Cornell today. I'm telling them everything I know about you.'

"'Fuck you,' I said.

"I never told your mother about this when it happened that spring. We had just moved into our first house, and she was pregnant with Cara. When summer came around, we were back in Maine, and my closest friend at Colgate came to visit with his family. John Hubbard was the photographer there. You don't remember him, but he was a really great guy who took all the pictures of the university. He only saw what was beautiful about the place. The students, and the magnificent campus. He and I were out in my sailboat, just the two of us, and when I told him the story about what had happened—I'll always remember this—he just bowed his head. I said, 'John, will I be able to survive this?' He shook his head and said no.

"So I knew. It was tough. You were almost four years old when we left Colgate. I applied to over a hundred jobs and never even got invited for an interview. They were jobs teaching writing, and there was no way they weren't going to call Colgate and speak with the head of the writing department. I was cooked and I knew it.

"So then we were broke. Worse than broke. We had you and your three sisters, and I couldn't pay for our heating oil. It was winter, and I took the only job I could find, working as a laborer at a construction site down the shore where they were building a mansion house. I kept a journal and wrote a book about it."

"*The Cliff Walk*," he said.

"Yep. It was your mother who came up with the title. The next thing I know, the book is under contract with Little, Brown and we're all going to New York to celebrate. You remember?"

"Of course. I got my Yankees hat."

"Then I'm on *Oprah*. Then Disney buys the film rights, and we're off to Ireland for the summer. That book opened the doors for me to live a writing life. I wrote five books and a movie in the next seven years. The movie enabled me to help your grandfather get into the assisted-living place, which was great for a while. You know, before he got too sick. But the reason I'm telling you this is that for the last twenty years I've regretted that I didn't keep my mouth shut at Colgate, because when I turned around in the hallway and walked back to that asshole's office and told him what I thought of him, I placed in jeopardy your mother's dream and the life we were building together. I always thought that she and I would get to grow old on a college campus. You know, shuffling through the leaves with Colleen to go see a football game on a Saturday afternoon. It would have been a wonderful life for us. But now I see that this great mistake also gave me something I never could have even dreamed of in those days. It gave me the chance to be here with you. I let you down today. In the first place, as your caddie, I should have known that there was a cut line. That was inexcusable. And when you gave up on yourself after we pissed away our first chance for birdie, I should have found some way to keep you in the game."

Somehow all those words opened a paved highway through the silence, and Jack seemed very relaxed now when he began telling me his take on what had happened. "I was really pissed off," he said. "There was nothing you could have said."

"Well," I told him, "it's okay to be pissed off out there. And I wasn't going to try to sugarcoat what had just happened."

"I needed that birdie. I mean, hell, I started off with a stupid bogey, then fought back for two pars. And here's the first par-5, and I busted the drive and hit the second shot to twenty feet."

"Seventeen feet."

"Whatever, man. And I've hit all my wedges in both practice rounds, and then I chunk it."

"It happens."

"But it shouldn't have happened."

"You picked up your head."

"I know that."

"So, you made a mistake, and it cost us the birdie that we needed."

"It was a swing of three strokes. I should have made birdie and pulled back to even par there."

"Yeah, I know that, but why did you give up?"

"Because it was over. I'm realistic about golf. I knew it was over."

"We were three over par, Jack. Three over par after four holes. If we fight like hell and make pars on the rest of the holes, we finish the round at the top of the leaderboard. Right where we want to be."

"I guess so. I guess you're right."

"No, me being right doesn't mean anything. It's just like you saying, 'It is what it is.' We have to figure out how to work together out here, or it's going to be pure misery for both of us. Tell me what you expected when you stepped onto the 1st tee this morning."

"I expect to shoot par or better."

"Okay. And I believe you have the skill to shoot par or better. And if I didn't believe that, I wouldn't tell you. I'll never lie to you. So we're on the same page. That's good. So, how do you want to proceed?"

He was still looking right at me and thinking now, I could tell.

"I need to be pissed off out there when I do something stupid," he said.

"Okay, you can be," I said. "That's fine by me."

He thought a little longer and then said, "I don't know, man."

I heard the discouragement in his voice, and at that moment I didn't want him to be discouraged. Hell, we were talking with each other again for the first time in so long. "Let's watch the football game, and we'll figure it out tomorrow," I said. "Is that okay?"

"Yeah, sure," he said.

When the game was over and the lights were out, I found a few last words, which I spoke to Jack through the darkness. "I've always thought that you are going to make a great coach someday when your playing career is over," I began. "And it would be nice to be able to say to your players, 'I played on a pro tour one winter in Texas and I was terrific.' But it will be more meaningful to your players if you say, 'I played on a pro tour one winter in Texas, and even when I got slaughtered on the golf course, I never gave up. I kept fighting back, right to the last shot.' And, Jack, when I think of your college golf career, all I ever think about is you down in North Carolina, playing in your first big tournament against the best players in the country from all the universities that wouldn't give you a chance. You were playing so well, then you had one bad hole and lost the first round. You remember. You walked past me on your way to the 1st tee to start the second round, and you said, 'I don't have a shot left, Daddy.' But somehow you fought back. You shot one under par in that round."

"I was lucky," he said.

"No, it wasn't luck. You fought back hard that day. And from that moment until right now, I have believed that you can fight back from anywhere. That is all I will ever be thinking here this winter, no matter what happens. Okay?"

"Okay," he said.

"Good night, Jack."

"Thanks."

NOVEMBER 4, 2011

No sleep really last night. But progress has been made with the father-son stuff. I feel so relieved that we were able to talk. The space between us didn't feel so wide this morning. And the ride to Cypress Lakes Golf Club was different too. Jack still drove way too fast like everyone else, and I couldn't bear to look up from the blinking blue dot on his iPhone showing us where we were, but we were talking for a change. Not about golf, but about other things. His old high school buddies back home. His sisters. Colleen. It was nice. I think we were both relaxed in each other's company for the first time since he left home after high school. It made me wonder if all we really need to close the space between us is time together.

I watched him on the range going rhythmically through his practice like a wheel rolling on its track, using his electronic scope to check his distances so he knew exactly how far he hit each club when he swung smooth, and then when he really went after it. I had already written these distances down in my notebook the first day we practiced together, and I would keep those numbers fixed inside my mind unless he told me he wanted to amend them.

All along the courses in St. Andrews you find these tiny white flowers, like miniature daisies, each petal tinged with pink, and whenever I was really missing Colleen, I would pick them and mail them home to her in matchboxes. When I wandered over to the practice green to roll a few balls to judge the speed, to my surprise I found the same daisies growing here, only tinged with purple. I knelt down and picked some and put them in my pocket while I thought through our game plan for this round. We had agreed to play the course today as if we were in competition, keeping track of every shot, and I was hoping we would make hash of one hole early, take a triple bogey or worse, and then fight our way back from there. I believed that our battle existed only inside Jack's mind, in those five inches between his ears that the immortal Bobby Jones had spoken about so often. But I was wrong. Today we also have a golf course to battle. This was a real golf course that made Hearthstone look like a picnic. Here we had water lining both sides of the fairways, narrow landing areas from the tee boxes, deep bunkers and trees, blind shots over tall mounds, and 460-yard par-4s, all set on an open plain where, if the wind came up, there was nothing to knock it down. Okay, I said to myself, we're going to have to hit golf shots today, and when we finish our round, I'm going to work Jack like Rocky Balboa on his short wedges and putts.

We had a tall order ahead of us, I thought, a true test of golf. But right from the first drive, which Jack ripped 330 yards up the middle, it was easy for him. He played an almost flawless round, landing fifteen greens in regulation and hitting three perfect wedge shots to inside four feet on the other three. And not a single three-putt green. We were in trouble only twice, and after making bogey both times, he came back and birdied the next hole. And it was easy for him. I watched closely. He putted like a pro and finished the practice round in one under par.

It struck me all afternoon that maybe Jack was being handicapped by his natural talent at this game. Maybe when you have so much natural talent, you feel as if you shouldn't have to fight, that every round should be a stroll in Elysium. Let the less talented golfers get their trousers muddy while they scrap and fight their way around a golf course. I had known writers like this from the beginning of my career, writers so talented and brilliant that they could not even begin to endure the rejection and humiliation and so they gave up and walked away.

NOVEMBER 6, 2011

I am doing laundry now while Jack is off at the range, and I am wondering if anyone who is at least forty years old can ever walk into a Laundromat without finding part of his history waiting there. There was a long stretch of time in my twenties, eight years in fact, when no one would publish a word I wrote and I would carry my wash into the Laundromat and think that maybe I would know I had achieved some success as a writer and as a man when I was finally no longer doing my wash in a stranger's machines.

And I remember after our first baby was born when I loved going to the Laundromat and then hanging out everything on the line and measuring my daughter's growth by the size of the undershirts and socks. Those were the days when Colleen believed in me so profoundly that she would have followed me anywhere in the world with her babies. When we lived five miles outside the village of Rathdrum in Ireland and I walked those miles into town with the dirty laundry and then back with everything clean and neatly folded, I always felt that I had accomplished something meaningful and that my life was amounting to something.

Today, the whole time I watched the clothes turning in the big dryer, I thought about Jack out at the practice range alone. His first time alone since we arrived. Fear rose through me as I worried about him driving around Houston without me. And then a gradual calm as I folded his clothes, realizing that these are the clothes that fit a man.

NOVEMBER 7, 2011

Game Day. Awake at 3:00 a.m., I suppose the most difficult thing we ever face as parents is seeing our children in pain and not being able to make the pain go away as we were always able to do when they were small. We are not prepared for this. I don't want Jack to be in pain again today out on the golf course. I don't want him to feel embarrassed the way he was in our first tournament. What can I say to him after he makes his first poor shot today? How can I help him *not* feel embarrassed by that poor shot? How can I help him believe deep inside that he has the skill to follow that poor shot with a good shot? How can I help him believe that he has just as much right to be playing here on this tour as the other players from the celebrated golf schools who may finish at the top of the leaderboard in these events week after week?

What is the battle here, the real battle at the center of this thing?

In a real battle the thing is not just to stay alive. The thing is not to be a coward. These are the questions I am taking with me to the golf course.

I need to find some way to persuade Jack that his only battle today is to fight as hard as he can for each individual shot, one shot after another, no matter what occurs, and never to give up, even for a moment. If he does this, then he cannot lose.

We arrived at Cypress Lakes at 9:00 for our 10:10 tee time. While Jack went up to the range, I went into the men's room to wet my towel. I was just inside the door when I got hit at both ends. Throwing up and diarrhea. I was honestly sick enough to bow out of this round. In Scotland in two seasons, no matter how I felt, I never called in sick a single day. It was a point of honor among all the caddies there. You show up. Period. This is supposed to be fun, people have told me. But I cannot help thinking that we came down here to play our first professional tour and we shot a 90 in our first event and didn't make the cut. That was four days ago. If we do this again, it is going to be very difficult to keep going. We just have to get over the hump by shooting a respectable round today. I am secretly hoping for a round in the 70s. Seven over par.

Here we go.

Hole 1. A 368-yard par-4.

A great drive with the three-wood. Wind behind us. Three hundred and thirty yards. We have only 70 yards left to the hole. Fifty-six-degree wedge, comes up forty feet short. Three putts. Bogey. Jack is pissed off at himself already.

One over after one.

Hole 2. A big 557-yard par-5.

The wind behind us. Jack hits three-wood, 345 yards. Two hundred and twelve left. He wants to go for it with his four-iron, over water. I am scared to death. I would like to lay up and take our chances for a birdie from our third shot. I say nothing except "Finish the stroke." He nails it. We have a thirty-foot putt for eagle. Missed. Made birdie.

Even after two holes.

Hole 3. A 422-yard par-4.

Into the twenty-knot wind. I hand him three-wood. Why no driver? Because the fairway narrows to only 30 yards way out there, remember? He nails the three-wood. We have an eight-iron uphill into a lot of wind. Wind pushes the shot into a bunker. He hits a great bunker that falls straight into the hole, then bounces out to three inches. Par save.

Even after three holes.

Jack is still pissed. I am now talking with him about Ronnie Kovic and Bruce Springsteen, how Bruce met him after he read his auto-biography, *Born on the Fourth of July*, and then wrote the song "Shut Out the Light." This seems to be relaxing him.

Hole 4. A 204-yard par-3.

Wind behind us now. I say to Jack, "You deserve to be here, man. Let's go to work now." He doesn't finish his swing and pushes it into a bunker. Hits a fine bunker shot to five feet. I miss the read. The ball breaks along the slope as I thought it would, but the grain pushes against it. I tell him I'm sorry that I missed the read. No comment. Bogey.

One over after four.

Hole 5. A 426-yard par-4.

Great drive with the driver here. A hundred and eight yards left to the hole. Fifty-six-degree wedge. Fourteen-foot uphill putt. Somehow even rolling uphill and against the grain, the ball rolls ten feet past. We're in trouble here. Three-putt bogey.

Two over after five.

Hole 6. A 382-yard short-hole par-4.

Great drive, but it rolls to a stop in a damned divot. A decent wedge from here, but we're forty feet from the hole. Three-putt bogey.

Three over after six.

Hole 7. A 212-yard par.

Across the wind. Water on the left. Out of bounds on the right. A tough shot. He pushes a seven-iron to ten feet off the green on the right. A bad shot. He is pissed at himself, and now we face one of those tricky wedge shots that killed him in round one. All I say when I hand him the wedge is "We are across the grain here, so run it up hard and make sure you get onto the green. Finish the shot." He nails it to one foot. Saves par.

Three over after seven.

Hole 8. A 545-yard par-5.

Into the wind now with water all the way up the left side and out of bounds right. I say nothing but hand him his three-wood. He wants driver instead. I don't like this call at all. He pushes it right and it looks as if it will be in a fairway bunker, but when we get there, we find his ball has skipped through the bunker onto decent ground. Okay, we have a chance now to get there in two. "I'm going for it, man," he says. He wants the three-wood. We have 240 left straight uphill into the wind, which is gusting to fifteen knots now. Maybe twenty. "Finish the swing," I say. He nails it. We have a forty-foot eagle putt. We miss the eagle and the birdie. Make par.

Three over after eight.

Jack is really pissed now. "I can't miss these damned birdies," he says.

Hole 9. A 410-yard par-4.

Out of bounds up the left side. When I hand him the three-wood, I tell him that we are out here playing golf because of Ronnie Kovic and all the other soldiers who made the sacrifice. He hits another great three-wood. We have 138 left, uphill into the wind. I want a nine-iron here because there is big trouble off the back of the green. He wants a soft eight. A decent shot. Another three putts from forty feet. Damn. Bogey.

Four over after nine.

Hole 10. A 587-yard par-5.

Downwind. I want a three-wood here because if he pushes a driver left at all, it's going to kick into the water. He wants driver. A great drive right up the center 345 yards. An easy four-iron to the green. It catches a bunker just right of the flag. A good bunker shot to seven feet. We missed the birdie putt. Made par.

Four over after ten holes.

———

Hole 11. A 193-yard par-3.

Wind behind us. He hits a terrible seven-iron. His first really bad shot. Leaves it 50 yards from the green. We need another good wedge here. He leaves it six feet short. Bogey.

Five over after eleven holes.

Hole 12. A 404-yard par-4.

We need to stop the bleeding here. Jack is still pissed about missing the birdie putt on number 10. I start talking about Springsteen again. A great drive up the highway. A hundred yards left into the wind. He flies a wedge to the bunker on the right. "Fucking pathetic, man," he says. "You can't hit shots like that." I say nothing. He makes a great bunker shot to two feet. Saves par. "God, I'm playing with my head up my ass," he says. I start telling him another Springsteen story.

Five over after twelve.

Hole 13. A 354-yard par-4.

Into a hard wind. He nails a low three-wood 300 yards right into the mayor's office. A fifty-six-degree wedge short. Leaves his twenty-two-foot putt six feet short. Drains it to save par.

Why is Jack so damned angry right now? This is something we are going to have to talk about after the round is over.

Five over after thirteen.

Hole 14. A 564-yard par-5.

Across the wind. I have a sick feeling about this drive with the wind blowing hard left to right, which is out of bounds. "I like a three-wood here," I say.

"No," he says with some anger. "Driver." He murders it. Three hundred and sixty yards right up the center. We have 204 left. Five-iron, pushed right again. He's not finishing his swing. He is steaming now. "Let's make a birdie here anyway," I say. "We're in a green-side bunker in two on a par-5." A strong bunker shot to four feet. He drains the putt to make birdie.

Four over after fourteen.

Hole 15. A 470-yard par-4 into the wind. A big par-4.

He nails the driver again. Three hundred and thirty yards right into the teeth of the wind. He's got a tough lie, ball below his feet for this five-iron. "I need to hit a fucking green in regulation," he complains. "I can't keep missing these greens." Thirty-foot putt for birdie. Missed by two feet. Saves par.

Four over after fifteen.

Hole 16. A 397-yard par-4.

I am fighting myself not to want this round to be finished right now. I have to keep my mind on one hole at a time. But I want this to be over now. With the wind behind us, we are going to have it in our faces on 17 and 18. He fans his driver for the first time. We need a break here among the trees. My heart is in my throat. We missed the trees, but the ball is in a hole. Only 125 yards left. The ball flies too low. It is off the back of the green. We need another good wedge here. "You're against the grain, Jack," I tell him. "Run it up there hard. Finish the swing." Bad shot. Forty feet left. Three putts. Bogey.

Five over after sixteen.

Hole 17. A 175-yard par-3.

I'm nervous about this shot. Water right. Trees left. A big wind in our faces.

Our playing partners, both seasoned veterans on the tours, miss the green.

Jack is up last after that bogey on 16. He nails it to fourteen feet. Two putts for par.

Five over after seventeen.

Hole 18. A 462-yard par-4.

Dead into the wind over water on the left. I want Jack to go up the right side obviously. But he nails his driver right over the short line, across the water into the center of the fairway. A hundred and fifty-six yards left. Amazing really into this wind.

He hits a nice knockdown nine-iron to twenty feet. Two putts for par.

Five over after eighteen.

I feel like collapsing. Jack is not at all happy with his round. On the drive home, I just close my eyes and tell him, "Look, man, I'm proud of you. I know you wanted to play better."

He cuts me off. "I gave away six shots out there, man. I putted like an idiot. I only hit like eight greens in regulation."

"I know that. But here's my take on it, okay. We came down here and shot a 90 in our first tournament and missed the cut. Today in our second tournament we shot five over par, 77, and made the cut. I say we should be proud and thankful. We had no disaster hole to fight back from. We might tomorrow. One drive out of bounds and we're going to have to find out what we're made of. You played with some big boys today, and you held your own. They beat you by two strokes. So can we just take it easy now for tonight? Watch the Eagles play, and be thankful."

"Yeah, I guess so. But I need to play better, man."

"And you will. Okay? You will. Tomorrow."

It's a day.

NOVEMBER 8, 2011

Up at 4:00 for our 8:40 tee time in round two at Cypress Lakes. Outside the humidity seems to have fallen a bit from yesterday.

Last night during the Eagles game I asked Jack if he had seen the fellow with the necktie. "A throwback to old Harry Vardon. Which reminds me, I might tell you my Vardon stories all the way around tomorrow."

"Good by me," he said.

"And let's be thankful for something tonight."

"What's that?"

"When your mother called, she was very happy. Whenever you do something that makes your mother happy, that's a good thing. Good night. Sleep tight."

He said good night and turned down the volume on the game.

"Oh, and one more thing," I said. "Let's keep it simple tomorrow. All we have to do is hit more greens in regulation and get closer on our first putts."

"Okay, go to sleep."

"Oh, and one more thing, Jackie. That putt we ran fourteen feet past the hole, uphill, and against the grain—what green was that?"

"Five."

"Are you sure? I thought it was 3."

"It was 5. I'm going to watch the second half now."

At the range this morning I was thinking about what Charlie Woodworth had written to me last night after our round yesterday. "Golf is not a straight line." Meaning I must expect setbacks today. Maybe a hooked drive on the 1st tee and a triple bogey that tests us right out of the blocks and forces us to bear down hard and make birdies. I didn't want that. Or maybe I did.

Of course it didn't matter one way or the other what I wanted. It was up to Jack. And from the 1st hole, where he tapped in for par after a deep drive and a perfectly struck sand wedge, he was in his own world, playing with the calm confidence of someone who believed he had as much right to be on this tour as anyone. He birdied the first par-5 after hitting a gorgeous six-iron second shot that carried 224 yards over water, to a narrow green, and then ran off a string of easy pars while I talked with him about Teddy, recalling the time I had accidentally nailed the poor dog in his chest with a golf ball on the first swing I took with a rescue club that Jack had given me for Christmas. And how Jack had once jumped into a pond to save his life after he had fallen through the ice. The more we talked about Teddy, the more relaxed Jack became. It was a picnic, and the one under par he recorded for the front nine included a forty-five-foot, downhill, double-breaking putt for an eagle on the par-5 8th. He rolled the ball into the center of the cup fifteen seconds after I asked him if he would please sink the eagle for his mother. I wish Colleen had been here to see that. And how handsome he looked in the black jacket I'd bought him at Carnoustie when he put it on as rain moved in. I was thrilled to see him marching beside me in that jacket with the Carnoustie emblem over his heart that marked the place where this journey of ours began.

The only disagreement we had today was on the 10th hole, a 572-yard par-5 with a narrow fairway that sloped severely left to water. Instead of taking the drive up the right side, he hit it dead center of the fairway, and when we both saw the ball kick hard to the left, we were certain it was in the water. It was a red-staked hazard, meaning if we were in the water, we would take a drop and lose that one stroke. When we got to his ball, we found that it had come to rest in the weeds just short of the water. Jack wanted to punch it out. I tried to persuade him to take a drop and the stroke penalty and then hit our third shot toward the green. He overruled me and knocked an awkward wedge out of the weeds but still short of the fairway. From there we faced an impossible shot to the green—257 yards, uphill, over towering trees with more water running up the left side. I urged him in the strongest possible terms not to try to reach the green from where we were. I was pretty sure that we were standing at the point in our round where the wrong decision would prove ruinous, and I wanted to run a low four-iron harmlessly up the hill in the direction of the green. Jack overruled me again, and then somehow he hit one of the most marvelous golf shots I have ever witnessed. The ball flew up straight over the treetops, all the way to the green, where it landed softly. Both our playing partners called to Jack, "Great shot. Great shot, man."

After remaining at even par through sixteen holes, we collapsed at the end with a three-putt bogey on 17 and a double bogey on 18 after hooking a drive into the water.

When we shook hands at the end of the round, there was no smile from Jack. He was steaming mad at himself. We just shot three over par against a tough field of players on a tough course, and in pouring rain for a few hours, and he was not satisfied at all. Maybe this is good. Because we threw away three strokes on the last two holes and you should never be satisfied with that kind of play. Tomorrow on to the Houston National Golf Club for a noon practice round. Thursday we start our next event there.

NOVEMBER 9, 2011

Somewhere off the Frontage Road, about three miles from our Studio Plus here in Gunpoint, there is a driving range straight out of the movie *Tin Cup* with an open field of weeds and a guy who calls himself a pro dispensing lessons from his lawn chair with a cat curled on his shoulder. My theory is that he was once a good player because every time you drive past, he's got another client, and these clients are always driving very expensive automobiles. He could be a drug dealer, I suppose, but I prefer to believe that he was once a fine player with professional prospects who is now living in reduced circumstances and trying to squeeze a meager living from the game he loved and devoted himself to before the game wrecked him with despair. As a favor to me, Jack agreed to stop here this morning and hit a few balls before we drove to the Houston National for our practice round. I thought this would be the perfect place to speak with him about being grateful, and I told him the script for the pro's life while he tried to nail the armadillos racing across the field with knocked-down nine-irons. "He chased the dream," I said. "He could hit fifteen greens in regulation every time out because of his natural ball-striking ability, and so he believed that he should be shooting in the red numbers. And he believed the game should be easy because when you're hitting almost every fairway from the tee and every green, it is an easy game. Sound like anyone you know, Jack?"

"Maybe," he said.

"It was easy out there for you yesterday for a stretch of about two hours. And on number 10 you made a shot that very few people in this game could ever make. The truth is very few people would ever even attempt to set up a birdie from a third shot 257 yards uphill over tall trees. You went for that shot because you want to be great, I know that."

"I could have shot seven under par yesterday," he said.

"Sure," I said. "Or that shot on 10 could have clipped a branch at the top of a tree and we're in a world of trouble. Maybe we end up shooting another 90, and we're embarrassed again. That's golf."

Instead of answering me, he put some music on his iPhone. But he didn't plug in his headphones; instead, he dropped the iPhone into the grass so we could share the music. U2. Music that had been the sound track of our years together before he left home. I stood beside him for a while, hitting soft eight-irons, sliding into the rhythm. From time to time he would stop and glance over at the old pro giving his lesson from the lawn chair. For the last few days I had been thinking that all I wanted Jack to learn here in Texas was how to fight hard in his life for the things that matter to him. But now that didn't seem to be so important to me. It was something deeper. "You know," I said, "if I hadn't been named a First Team All-State wide receiver when I was a senior in high school, I would have gone to Vietnam like a lot of the guys I graduated with instead of college. And I've never been grateful enough for that."

I paused and hit a couple more balls before I went on. "I was teaching at Colby College back in the day, as you say, before you were born. Nell was born there and she was perfect in every way. She was born in the same hospital where one of my students was being treated for cancer. A beautiful girl, a sophomore, I think. It was throat cancer, and the first thing they had to do to her before they began radiation was pull out all her teeth. It tore my heart out. And I told myself that I had so much to be thankful for and that I would always be grateful. But I wasn't content teaching at Colby. I wanted to be at Harvard, you know? I think that's what I want you to learn here, Jack. If you can go through your life being grateful instead of always asking for more, you'll be in good shape. And tomorrow if we miss a birdie putt, maybe you give yourself ten seconds to be angry, and then you'll feel some gratitude just for the chance. Because when you're grateful, you're calm. And if you're calm in this game, with your skills, you can go as far as you want. End of sermon."

He looked right at me and said, "I hear you, man."

"One thing is for certain," I said to Jack as we sped along 290 West. "If you can't drive the ball into the fairway, you can't play on a pro tour."

"Agreed," he said.

Then Dylan came on, singing that great song "Forever Young." "Maybe I'm wrong," I said. "There's Dylan, who distinctly could not sing, and yet he became a legend."

"Dylan had a great short game," Jack said.

I laughed and thought, good line.

Game Day. Houston National Golf Club. David McLay Kidd earned an international reputation as a golf course designer after he created his masterpiece at Bandon Dunes in Oregon. Soon he was building golf courses all over the world and looking forward to the day when he would finally be commissioned to build a course in Scotland, his home country. Finally, he got the call when the Links Trust hired him to build the first new championship course in St. Andrews in one hundred years. He held nothing back and created what has to be one of the most difficult courses in the world. From the moment I first laid eyes on the Castle Course, I called it a magnificent battlefield. All the summer I spent caddying there and at the Old Course, golfers who were about to play the Castle would ask me just how difficult a track it was. I always told them the same story about how on a Wednesday afternoon I caddied at the Old Course for a young man from New Jersey, a fine and fastidious golfer, and took him around at two over par. He was delighted and asked me if I would caddie for him the next morning at the Castle. He was one of those golfers who had a little temper tantrum after each shot that disappointed him, and frankly I didn't feature watching him torn apart by the Castle Course, so I lied and told him that I already had another tee time. Playing in the same weather the next day, he shot 116. And to make matters worse, he blamed his caddie and paid him poorly.

After walking once around Houston National, I pictured it in my mind as a version of the Castle Course because of the greens that are placed on top of hills with steeply sloping sides. Only a little worse because the grass on the sides and at the bottom of the hills died during the drought here, leaving only hard-packed dirt. In order to have any chance today, we are going to have to land these greens and hold them on our approach shots. And that is going to be very difficult if the wind is up as it was yesterday because we will be coming at six of the greens with five- and six-irons instead of wedges. And what worries me most is that there is out of bounds left and right off almost every tee. At the Castle Course there is only one out of bounds on the whole course. Nothing destroys a round faster than a penalty for out of bounds.

I had an e-mail just before five this morning from a fine golfer in Scotland who reminded me that when Tiger Woods won the Open at the Old Course in 2000, he never hit a single bunker in four rounds. He thought his way around the course, using only irons off the tees. This is the way I would like to play Houston National. Unfortunately, the holes are much longer than those at the Old Course, and if the wind is up today, we're going to need all the club we've got to get to five of the greens in regulation. And I don't think I can scale Jack back at this point. He's got some confidence now, and he wants to really tear the roof off the place today. However, if we have a couple of drives out of bounds early, we will have to quickly change our game plan if we want to have any chance at all.

We await our turn on the 1st tee. The wind is blowing hard in our faces. And it's a cold wind for some reason. All the players are in jackets and wind pants. And I should have worn my wool hat.

Hole 1. A 410-yard par-4.

From here there looks to be no safe place to land our first drive of the day. A road runs up the left side, and out of bounds is right. I take the three-wood from the bag. In this kind of wind, I want to keep the shot low so it won't be blown off line. And whatever distance we might sacrifice by not using driver, we can make up rolling along the hard-baked fairway. "What do you think, Jack?" I say hopefully. "A nice little stinger under the wind. Get it rolling through those hills out there somewhere?" He nods and takes the three-wood. He drills it straight through the wind, right up the middle to hard-packed dirt, a terrible lie. I think we both know that we will never reach this green in two, into this wind from this lie. Jack stripes a four-iron 230 yards. The ball hits the left side of the green and goes bounding down the side of a steep hill. We have no idea what we will be facing when we get to the ball. Now we're forty feet from the hole and hitting a wedge off ground like concrete. He gets it up there, twenty feet from the hole. A good putt shaves the right edge of the cup. A tap-in bogey. "I hate starting this way," he says when he hands me his putter. "We'll get that stroke back," I assure him. I'm not worried. He looks very confident.

One over after one.

Hole 2. A 575-yard par-5.

Right into the wind. "It's a three-shot hole, Jackie," I say, handing him his three-wood again. "Just hit another one the way you did at the first." He nails it up the middle. We are now on dirt again. He takes the three-wood and tops the ball. The first really bad swing he's made in days. It rolls maybe 150 yards. Now we are 247 to the green, into the wind, uphill, over water. I want to hit an iron to the only safe landing area, short of the green. "We can save a par from there, Jack," I tell him. "I want to get there," he says. "I'm not holding back." I've got a bad feeling about this. He tops another three-wood, and this one goes into the water. We drop four. That wasn't good, he says to himself. Then he settles in and hits a decent five-iron onto the green in five on this par-5. A bad three-putt, and we have an 8 here.

Four strokes over after two holes.

But Jack isn't looking discouraged at all. I know this is the moment where we are going to either record another 90 and miss the damned cut or learn to fight on after a miserable beginning. I think this is the test that we both need. On our way to the 3rd tee I start talking with him about the movie *Gettysburg*, which we used to watch over and over when he was little. There is a moment in the movie when Joshua Chamberlain is about to move his men onto Little Round Top. A colonel comes up to him and says, "Now we'll see how professors fight." Jack always loved that line because I was a professor for a while when he was little. I get a smile out of him, and then I say, "Four over par looks like a good score out here today, Jackie boy. Let's just make a ton of pars the rest of the way." He nods.

Hole 3. A 200-yard par-3.

Across the wind today to another green perched on top of a mound. He hits a brilliant seven-iron to twenty feet. Almost drains the birdie putt. Makes par.

Four over par after three.

Hole 4. A 453-yard par-4.

This is a tough tee shot with a severe dogleg right, into the wind again. The landing area is heavily bunkered. Jack nails his driver over all the bunkers right up the center. It is a drive of 367 yards. Amazing. Our player partners are 80 yards behind us. "I hammered that drive," he says happily. We are fighting well now. No complaining. No whining. Just plain digging in for the long fight ahead. He hits a perfect wedge to six feet and drains the putt for birdie. We get back one stroke. And I am feeling very good. So is Jack.

Three over after four holes.

Hole 5. A 440-yard par-4.

The wind is behind us, and Jack stripes his driver right up the left side. He nails his wedge to five feet and misses the birdie putt by one inch. Tap-in par.

Three over after five holes.

Hole 6. A 575-yard par-5.

Wind in our favor now. Our playing partners have already hit three drives out of bounds and lost one ball in the weeds. We have hit every fairway from the tee so far. Another great drive here, 300 yards. He wants the three-wood to try to cover the remaining 275 yards in one shot. He nails it, but the ball rolls down off the steep front of the green. We are thirty feet from the pin in two on this par-5. He tries to putt it up the steep slope because the ground is just dirt. We go sailing past the pin, then miss two putts. A lousy bogey. What a shame. "We deserved better," I tell him. "But we'll get it back." I break into more talk about Joshua Chamberlain. Jack is relaxed, not at all defeated. I think he knows that this is a brutal course and in this wind a tough test. He seems focused on each shot.

Four over after six holes.

Hole 7. A 210-yard par-3.

Downwind. A lovely seven-iron to twelve feet. And a good two putts for a tap-in par.

Four over after seven holes.

Hole 8. A 414-yard par-4.

He nails his three-wood up the middle again. I don't think I ever caddied for anyone in Scotland who hit so many fairways up the center. And in this wind, with out of bounds on both sides, it's impressive. A hundred and thirty-seven yards left. A wedge leaves us with a difficult downhill putt of twelve feet, breaking hard left to right. I want him to just cozy it up there close, but he goes for the birdie putt, and the ball rolls ten feet past the hole. We need to drain this putt somehow and make par here. This could be a turning point in the match. He makes it. Great par save.

Four over after eight holes.

Hole 9. A 400-yard par-4.

With the wind behind we can hit only a four-iron here because the ball can roll through the narrow fairway to water on the right. He mis-hits the four-iron. We have 180 yards left. He pushes a seven-iron left. Now we are thirty feet left of the green, and we must save a par. He leaves the first putt ten feet short. Damn. But now he drains the putt. Par save. So we lost four strokes on the first two holes but somehow manage to shoot even par the next seven holes. We hit every fairway. Our partners are discouraged, but we're holding our heads up.

Four over after nine holes.

On the back nine we lost four more strokes and finished with a round of 80, but we played so much better than the score. We battled back from a disastrous start—four over par after the first two holes—and finished the front nine with no more damage. We hit every fairway from the tee box, something I doubt many players did here today with these narrow landing areas and out of bounds on both sides.

"You fought back hard today, Jackie," I say as we are walking to the truck.

"I threw away five strokes," he says.

"Maybe six," I say. "But you putted and drove the ball like a pro. And now we know that we can fight back from any kind of start. We'll get another shot tomorrow. Right?"

"Yeah," he says.

"I'm proud of you, man. You played a tough course in a tough wind, and you held on."

"Thanks," he says.

"If you shoot three over par out here tomorrow, I'm buying you a steak dinner tomorrow night."

Early tee time tomorrow for round two.

A lot of fine players elected not to finish today rather than post a poor score. One of the guys who beat us in the last event was shooting 90 after the 17th hole, so he quit. We will never *not finish*. And for now we live to fight another day.

NOVEMBER 11, 2011

There is a reason why football games are not played at eight in the morning. It takes a while for big guys to wake up and get moving. We had our first early tee time, an 8:10 start, and this meant heading out on the interstate in the half-light while Jack drank a Diet Pepsi for his caffeine and played Springsteen at high volume to keep from falling asleep at the wheel.

"Let's say your granddad is looking down on all of this. Let's give him something to smile about this morning."

"I'll try," he said.

We arrived an hour before our 8:10 tee time only to find that the course was covered in frost. A one-hour delay. I went off in search of some bananas.

Two hours later at the 1st tee, I hand Jack his three-wood and say, "For your grandfather. He went to war at age eighteen. He had his older brother die. His twin brother die. His bride of nine months die. And he kept on fighting. And you know something, Jack, I never told him I was proud of him for not giving up. Never once."

Jack just looks at me.

Whenever I caddied with my pal Duncan at the Old Course, he used to say to me on our way to the 1st tee, "Set your sights low." Today I turned my back on that good counsel and began hoping for an easy round, or at least a smooth start. Instead, we were in trouble on the 1st hole. After nailing a three-wood right up the middle of the fairway, we had a simple 120-yard wedge left to the hole. But with the green still frozen as hard as concrete, Jack's second shot bounced high into the air, and we watched in a kind of stunned disbelief as the ball then ricocheted off a mound beyond the green, sailed across the cart path, and bounded over a sidewalk before it came to rest in a mud hole. We took a double bogey from there, and because I knew that it could have been much worse, I lost my patience with Jack when I heard him curse himself. For the next four holes while Jack was making pars, I was looking for a way out. I'd never left a golfer before, but on the 6th tee box I told Jack that I had to find a bathroom. Then I walked by myself for almost an hour composing out loud the lecture I was going to give my son at the end of the round. It was all about being grateful just for the chance to compete, no matter what happened.

I didn't catch up with him until the 12th hole, a 616-yard par-5, and when I climbed up onto the tee box, I heard him laughing and chatting up his playing partners. From there on in, I watched Jack make pars and birdies to finish strong for a score of four over par.

This was good. But he and I still had a private score to settle after this round. On the ride home I blasted him for his behavior after that 1st hole. He shrugged it off and said, "It's all good."

"Not to me," I said. "Here's what we're going to do, Jack. And I'm talking as your caddie now, not your old man. We have some time off now for practice rounds. Tomorrow or the next day, you pick the day, but you and I are going to play a match for five bucks a hole. You'll give me ten strokes anywhere I want them, and I'm going to beat your ass."

"Really?" he said sarcastically.

"Really."

That's enough for today.

NOVEMBER 15, 2011

The grudge match never materialized. Instead, it was a knock-down, drag-out shouting match in his truck that began with me telling myself not to say anything that I would later regret and then saying a lot that I regretted almost as soon as I said it about how I was down here in Texas trying to help him get back what he'd lost when he was kicked off his university golf team and the least he could do was act a little grateful out on the golf course instead of behaving like a bad apple. "When the Scottish caddies are stuck out on a golf course with a wanker," I yelled, "they don't put up with his bullshit."

At some point I stopped long enough to hear Jack yell back at me, "Why does it always have to be about you! This isn't about you, man!"

I was shaving the next morning and thinking that I would give almost anything to get back the days when Jack used to climb up onto the bathroom vanity with his make-believe razor made from Legos to shave beside me.

It took me another day to finally see that he was right. He was hitting wedges onto the practice green while it all went through my mind. We were here together on this journey, but we had different objectives. I was happy just to be here with him, walking through the fulfillment of an old dream we had shared. That is what mattered most to me. For him, this was the chance to see how good he could be. In all likelihood this would be his best chance, and his last chance, to find out. One of the things he had yelled at me during our shouting match was this: "I hit the middle of every fairway for two rounds, and the best I could do was twelve strokes over par. You don't get it! That's pathetic. I start off with a stupid double bogey, and while I'm trying to fight my way back into the match, I've got to worry about what you think of me?"

As parents, I think we cross a line where we start needing our kids more than they need us. While I watched him practice, I began to see what he meant. He didn't need a father to be worrying about out on the golf course. If he was going to play this game better than he had ever played it before and move up the leaderboard as the tour progressed through the winter, he needed me to be a caddie who lived up to the caddies' code to show up, keep up, and shut up.

I didn't admit to him that I was wrong until he was driving me to the airport for me to catch my plane to Maine for the Thanksgiving break. We stopped for gas and were waiting in line when a truck loaded with Christmas trees pulled in to the station. "It's coming on Christmas," I said.

"It's ninety degrees," he said.

I asked him if he remembered the Christmas when he gave money to the old man on the sidewalk.

"Yeah," he said.

And I saw him smile. We had a tradition in our family when the kids were little. No matter how poor we were, we always drove into Portland on Christmas Eve just before putting the kids to bed and gave a $100 bill to someone walking the streets who looked down on his luck. Jack had watched his older sisters get out of our car each year, and then, finally, it was his turn. There was an old man sitting on the sidewalk leaning against the corner of a building with his back to us. When Jack tapped him on the shoulder, he turned around, and we saw that he had a full white beard. Jack's hands flew up into the air. "Look, Daddy!" he exclaimed. "It's Santa Claus!"

When we pulled up to the Southwest terminal, I said, "I've been thinking about what you said to me, and I think you're right. This isn't about me. It's about you playing the best golf you can. So from here on out, you don't have to be my son on the golf course. You just play golf and I'll just be your caddie."

He nodded and said, "Okay, man."

We shook hands. "I'll see you in two weeks," I said. "Have a good Thanksgiving."

"You too," he said. "No snow in Toledo. I'll be playing at Inverness every day."

"Good," I said. "That's good. And thanks for bringing me along on this journey. I mean it."

"You bet," he said.

DECEMBER 6, 2011

Cypresswood is a handsome track, cut out of a thick forest. With no houses, cars, or strip malls, it has the feel of Maine. It is as quiet as a cathedral, and it's a big course of over 7,200 yards with muscular 464-yard par-4s like the ones Jack is used to at Inverness. It suits his game very well, and he waltzed through our first practice round without adversity except for a couple of tee shots that have me a little worried. Most of the holes are big swinging doglegs, and Jack is determined to take aggressive lines, trying to shave all the corners rather than settling for the middle of the fairways. Twice we nicked trees, and the balls ricocheted so deep into the woods that we didn't even bother looking for them. I am of the opinion that we forget about shaving the corners and take dead aim at the middle of the fairways; so what if we're left taking six- or seven-irons to the greens instead of wedges. But I must be careful not to do or say anything that might cause Jack to doubt himself. We have three events coming up in the next eleven days, the toughest stretch of the tour, and he is going to need to preserve all the self-confidence he earned in the last two events before our Thanksgiving break. I didn't express my opinion in our practice round yesterday, but one lost ball in the woods on Thursday, when it matters, and I will be trying to rein Jack in.

He spent the break in Toledo with Jenna. I returned to Maine, where I felt like an astronaut who had returned from Mars. Houston is a strange place, but we're both settling in again in Gunpoint, which isn't as bad as the name implies, though a couple of nights before we left for break, we woke up to the sound of glass breaking. Out our window looking over the parking lot, we watched two guys with baseball bats breaking the windows in every parked car, working their way methodically down the row while alarms went off. We keep Jack's truck in the front lot, right beside the entrance to the place, and so far we haven't had any problems.

We were talking about this as we played our way through a practice round today, talking about America, starting with the African American families in our hotel who are refugees from Hurricane Katrina. We've seen them walking the hallways with plates of fried chicken and sauce pans of gravy. The young mothers have their children polished and shined for school at six in the morning, when they walk them to the city bus. You can tell they are trying hard to build some kind of life here without a house to live in or a car to drive. "Not unlike your great-grandmother when she came to America from Ireland," I said at one point. "We've got a new wave of refugees here."

"Americans as refugees in their own country," Jack said just before he nailed a four-iron through the wind and watched it land softly on the green about 235 yards away. "That's a new concept, I guess."

I asked him if he remembered the time we were watching the news on TV and there was a story about immigrants coming to America. "I think you were twelve years old. Some politician was arguing that the new immigrants from Somalia should be sent home, and you said, 'Who are we to tell anyone they can't live here, Daddy? We stole all the land from the Indians.' Do you remember that?"

He did.

"You were quite a little philosopher," I said.

I've been careful not to bore him with stories from my seasons caddying in Scotland and to remember Colleen's admonition not to speak negatively about America, but while we played this afternoon, I told him about the round I caddied for two brothers who were grandsons of one of the wealthiest families in America. We were the last people out on the course as darkness fell, and I used the lit screen of one of their iPhones to line up the putts on the 18th green. When we were finished, they took me to a local pub for a late supper and a few pints. I walked almost two thousand miles as a caddie in St. Andrews, and I never accepted an invitation from a golfer except this one time because they were such great guys and I was hungry and it was late. We talked about America, the nation in ruins, that I had left behind. "Here is essentially what they said to me, a kid who grew up stupid and poor in a depressing city in Maine," I told Jack. "They said they were pretty sure that I had believed all my life that America is a meritocracy where if you work your ass off, you might get somewhere. 'Your father and grandfathers probably taught you that,' they said. 'Nothing is further from the truth, though we are thrilled to have you believe that shit. Get this, and tell all your friends about it: Rich people in America today are no longer content to have just their own wealth—much of which they simply inherited, like the two of us, and never earned themselves. We know that there is a worldwide economic apocalypse coming, and so now we want *all the money*. We want the welfare mother's fifty bucks a week. We want the retired teacher's $400-a-week pension. Give us more tax breaks and we won't create new jobs. We'll keep putting the money into our pockets. Trust me. And we don't even believe that guys like you are entitled to any dignity. You can starve to death for all we care.'"

Jack asked me if I believed that.

"No," I told him. "I still believe it's a meritocracy. Maybe I'm just a dummy from Maine, but I believe hard work can get you anywhere you want to go in America. But I do think we're headed for a civil war in this country. A class war between the people who belong to private golf clubs and the guys with dirt on their faces who carry their bags."

"The rich and the poor," he said.

"Yeah, it's coming. Once the average workingman looks in the mirror shaving in the morning and realizes that he no longer has a fighting chance, there will be a real war. Take a look at your great-grandfathers. They both worked forty hours a week at hard labor for the minimum wage, and they were able to own houses, their wives didn't have to go out and work, they had a new Ford in the driveway every three years. Today they would be beggars in America. So, yeah, there's a war coming. I probably won't live to see it, but you will. And you'll have to decide which side you're on. For now, though, look at us, chasing a dream. This is a country where you can still chase a dream, Jack."

"I guess so," he said.

We played a few more holes in relative silence before he said, "At least golf is a meritocracy. You work hard, you play well, you don't cheat, and you win."

"Perfect," I told him.

"Did you notice that all my irons were flying ten or fifteen yards farther in the clear air today?" Jack said. "All my distances were off."

"I know," I said. "Usually the air is thick and dead here. We'll have to take that into account."

"Maybe you should write it in your notebook."

I assured him that I would do that.

Outside our door one of the Katrina mothers was crying. I had heard someone crying the night before as well.

"Can you imagine trying to raise a family in this place?" Jack said.

I told him that I believed it was going to be these people, the people at the bottom, who would one day return America to its greatness. "I mean the people who are not spoiled. The people who don't have too much. The teachers in the ghettos, and nurses' aides who take care of the elderly." I told Jack that the driver of my shuttle the other night was one of them. He was working the graveyard shift, and he had his two little boys with him, a four-year-old and a five-year-old sleeping on the floor of the van because his wife worked at night cleaning offices, and together they didn't earn enough money to pay for a babysitter. Their beautiful little sons were spending the night sleeping on the floor of the van beneath their blankets. I almost stepped on one of them when I climbed into the middle seat. It was one in the morning, and America was sailing past me—the Bible seminaries and the "XTC" sex parlors, and gun shops and shopping malls—and every so often the highway lights would illuminate the boys' faces. I wanted to take them home with me. No, I wanted to persuade the father that he could leave this place and go to Scotland with his wife and their boys, and he could work as a caddie there, walking lovely ground every day, and they could live with a little dignity. "I didn't say anything," I told Jack. "But, you know, this man was filled with hope and enthusiasm. He talked on and on with me about the new planet that astronomers just discovered that resembles Earth. He was filled with wonder. I wish you could have met him."

Jack turned out the light and swung the TV in the direction of his bed so he could watch some college hoops while I fell asleep.

I closed my eyes and was soon sailing back across the years again, to the days when he was little and we would camp out in the family room watching sports for hours and hours, just the two of us lying on the couch together with Teddy sprawled across us, napping, and the girls wandering through from time to time with their dolls or hula hoops. I didn't know then that there would ever be things I would keep from my son. Fears, I mean. Fathers hide their fears from their sons. When you are a sixty-year-old caddie in St. Andrews, management keeps an eye on you to make sure you are not slowing things down, and I went to work there every day with the fear that I might be let go—"sent down the road," as they say when referring to a caddie who has been released. My first season after the recession hit us, when suddenly there wasn't enough work to go around and it became every man for himself, I was afraid each day that I might not be able to make my pay to send home. I never told Jack about those fears, or the new fear of mine back at home during the Thanksgiving break— the grinding motor of the heating-oil truck as it passed through our neighborhood. If it stopped at our house now, it was a mortgage payment to fill the tank. Enough to make me shudder.

My second morning home I shot a big fat Canadian goose that would serve as our Thanksgiving dinner. I'd never shot anything before. It was a single goose, flying alone, maybe seventy feet above my head, and it fell out of the sky and into the cove with a lovely little pirouette like a ballerina falling off her stage. Unfortunately, as soon as the gun went off, Teddy hightailed it straight home, scared to death. And with the tide exceptionally high, the bird was at least a football field from me across the open water. I decided to walk home and return after the tide had receded. Two hours later when I rounded the corner of the marsh and stepped out of the tree line, I saw a flock of crows tearing my Christmas goose apart. I lost that battle, but the next morning I rowed a dinghy out in the high tide and dragged it across the marsh to the shore, where I tied it to a tree so I would never again be caught without a way to retrieve a bird. Dragging the dinghy was difficult. Shocked at the strength I have lost since I turned sixty, I could make it only in ten-yard stretches before my legs burned and buckled and I had to rest. My heart felt as if it were scraping against my rib cage. I pretended each ten yards was another first down as I worked my way through the thick marsh grass, and the whole time I was seventeen years old again playing football for the chance to go to college instead of Vietnam. I had loved everything about football. I loved the sweat from the hard work. I loved getting knocked down and getting up again. I loved the way all the noise in the world fell off to a marvelous ground of silence so I could actually hear the ball spinning in its spiral the moment I took it out of the sky into my hands. And even though it had become a game of millionaires since then, played across a disillusioned and broken nation, it was still a meritocracy and I was grateful that my son loved the game.

I closed my eyes and waited for sleep to come. Outside the door to our room the Katrina mothers were rounding up their children to put them to bed. I thought about the missing fathers, and I wanted to believe that they were back in New Orleans busy rebuilding a life and they would summon their families someday. But maybe they had been defeated by the flood and by their fears, and they would spend the rest of their lives wondering what had become of the little children who had smiled at them, and the women they had taken into their arms with a certain measure of hope for what their future held. Hope that somehow gave way to fear. And what about the rest of us?

The vast army of fathers out there with our new fears of the next oil delivery, or the pink slip, or the hike in insurance premiums, or the doctor's bill, or the bottom falling out of the stock market, or tuition bills we might not be able to pay. I suppose we are afraid of disappointing the people who depend on us, or being cut loose from what protected us for so long and ending up as haunted, weary travelers on a night journey, bound for where we might never be certain again.

I was looking forward to morning, when all these thoughts would fade away and it would just be Jack and me and the eighteen holes in front of us. I pictured the first dogleg at Cypresswood. On Thursday, in round one, maybe I will ask Jack to just hammer his drive straight up the middle and forget about trying to shave the corner. Make a few early pars, and then take our chances.

I e-mailed old Glen that I was frozen the whole way around today, as cold as I'd ever been caddying with him in Scotland. He replied with one line: "A caddie goes nowhere without his long johns."

DECEMBER 8, 2011

At five this morning it was clear and cold as I took my walk around the hotel and went over the course in my head. I know we have decent birdie chances on the 1st and 2nd holes, but after that, if the wind is up again today, we'll be fighting to get on the greens in regulation. And I hope the battle doesn't come down to number 17, the 328-yard, drivable par-4, with ponds on the right, left, and behind the green and a creek running in front. The hole reminds me of number 12 on the Old Course. A 316-yard par-4 with a stroke index of 3, marking it as one of the toughest holes on the course because of all the hidden bunkers. But if you hit an eight-iron off the tee, and another eight-iron into the center of the green, you could take all the trouble out of play and be putting for a birdie. Yesterday when I asked Jack, "So, how do you play this hole if you have to make a par?" he didn't budge from his earlier position. "You take driver, and you drive the fucking green," he replied.

Not exactly music to a caddie's ears.

I had a terrible golf dream in the night. I had become one of those overbearing fathers; I guess they call them helicopter parents because they're constantly hovering over their kids' lives. Anyway, I was caddying for Jack, and we were within shouting distance of making it onto the big tour, and I began cheating secretly. Suddenly these two officials from the Royal and Ancient Golf Club showed up at our hotel room, formidable fellows in double-breasted blue blazers with brass buttons. They wanted to inspect my wardrobe. "Actually, we're only interested in seeing your trousers," one of the gentlemen said. I had seven pairs of pants hanging on the rack, and they discovered that I'd cut a hole in the right pocket of each pair so that I could drop new balls into play without being detected. Jack stood there mortified while they read me my rights and summoned the gendarmes. "What were you thinking?" he kept yelling at me. "Golf is a fucking meritocracy, man. We already agreed on that!"

We left the hotel at 9:15 for our 10:40 tee time. In the four hours since I'd been outside, the sky had cleared to a beautiful pale blue, and the wind had risen. On the radio in the truck there was news about a mother somewhere in Texas who, having been denied food stamps, shot both her children and then herself. "Jesus," Jack said.

It was as good a time as any, I thought, for me to follow the advice of a man I respected in Maine who had recently counseled me that if I was going to talk with my son about the civil war between the rich and the poor in America, I should be sure to present both sides equally. I began by telling Jack that plenty of the wealthy guys I'd caddied for in Scotland had done a lot to try to help the poor, just like this man in Maine who had worked his way from nothing to the top of his profession and had given millions of dollars to underprivileged kids and worthy college students along the way.

"The same with the people at Inverness," Jack said.

"So, what's the answer then?"

"What do you mean?"

"Well, how come every great civilization since the beginning of time fell apart for the same reason—when the divide between the poor and the privileged grew too wide?"

He thought about this while he tuned the radio to ESPN. Then he said, "It's like anything else, man. People blame each other for the problems instead of working together to solve them. You take the biggest problems in America right now, and if you could get a hundred smart poor people and a hundred smart wealthy people in the same room to talk to each other instead of blaming each other, you'd solve them. Maybe in a couple of hours."

From the mouths of babes, I thought.

I was still smiling about this when we made our way to the range, and I was thinking to myself, He's a good boy. No, he's a good man.

He struck the ball beautifully on the range and stepped onto the 1st tee and drove it 322 yards right up the left side. "We're in the mayor's office," I said.

So there we are, a simple soft eight-iron to the flag. He takes his smooth practice swing, steps up to the ball, takes the same smooth swing, and—what! The ball squirts right and barely flies 60 yards. He looks at me. "What was that?" he asks. I don't know. I don't know. Maybe I wasn't paying attention. I've grown so used to seeing all his iron shots fly straight to the pins. "I shanked that ball off the toe of the club," he says with a disgusted little laugh. "I can see shanking it off the hozzle, but off the toe? I almost missed the ball completely."

"Maybe you didn't settle into your swing" is all I can say.

From there we nearly saved par but took a bogey.

Up to the next tee and another bomb right up the middle, 80 yards past our playing partners. Now we're 90 yards from the hole, a simple wedge.

And bang, he pulls it into the bunker left. Trying to adjust from that last iron, I am thinking. The sand is as wet as concrete, and he leaves the first shot in the bunker. It's a double bogey. We're three over after two holes, another miserable start after two perfect drives. "I guess I just don't ever want to make it an easy start," he says to me with a shrug. He's not upset. I'm not worried.

But I should have been. The rest of the round is the same thing. One perfect drive after another, and every iron shot flies 40 or 50 yards off line. On the par-4 number 4, we've got 117 yards left to the hole after a monster drive. I hand him his wedge, and I'm already taking the putter out when—what! He shanks it straight into the woods. We take a triple bogey.

And we never figured it out the rest of the round. One terrible iron shot after another. I'm talking wedges, short irons, long irons. All just awful. We hit two greens in regulation, and by the 12th hole we both knew that without four birdies coming in, we weren't going to make the damned cut.

We kept our composure; we were talking about Jack's sister Cara, heading home from college tomorrow for Christmas break, cutting down a tree with Colleen. Jack looked perfectly relaxed. He just missed every iron shot. I thought for a while that it was something with his hands, not getting the club square and through at the bottom. But if that was the case, he would have been blocking drives all day long. At one point I thought maybe he was standing too far from the ball, an inch perhaps. But when he made that adjustment, he pulled the shot left by 50 yards.

So we missed the cut by four strokes. And just to add to the puzzle, on the one hole I had worried about, the drivable 328-yard par-4, 17, we made an easy birdie. Our only birdie of the day.

"I'm pissed," I said when we got back in the truck. "I fucking hate missing cuts."

"Crazy," he said. "I never hit irons like that before."

"Maybe you were tired."

"I wasn't tired."

"Yeah, I guess not. You couldn't have hit drives like those if you were tired. And you looked great on the range."

"What the hell," he said.

"We couldn't make the adjustment. Something was wrong and I couldn't see it. I think it was the long break."

"I played every day during the break."

"Yeah, but flying back here, you know, the traveling is rough."

"No excuses."

"You're right, no excuses."

"I should have been able to figure out what I was doing wrong."

"Yeah. I wish I could have helped. I guess I was just stunned. You know? I'm so used to your solid iron play. Usually, I'm watching the ball tracking right toward the flag, and I'm thinking after each swing, Just be as good as you look. I don't know."

We were both thinking the same thing by the time we got back to the hotel. We were going to have to start over again, just like after the first round of the first tournament.

"I'll hit a million irons tomorrow on the range," Jack said as he left the room to go ride the exercise bike.

"Okay," I said.

After the door swung closed, I threw my notebook across the room and cursed.

DECEMBER 10, 2011

Yesterday passed. And it passed miserably. If I'm honest, I'll have to tell Colleen that I wasn't really living that day here with our son. I was just stumbling through. I remember telling Jack that I was going to rest my knee the day after we missed the cut, and he said, "That's okay," as he headed out the door to hit balls at the range. The moment he left, an emptiness settled in the room, and I wished that I had gone with him. These were the last days I would ever get to spend with Jack, and he was at the range by himself while I pissed away a long afternoon feeling sorry for both of us. Sorry for him because he knew that everything he had fought for in the first three tournaments, he had lost in the fourth, and now he was going to have to start over from ground zero. Sorry for myself because I didn't know what to say to him to make missing the cut any easier to accept, and because I should have been able to do something *before* it happened, *to keep it from happening.* We had gone into that fourth tournament believing that we would play our best. Or if not our best, at least well enough to make the cut, which was thirteen strokes *over par.* We should have been able to do that with our eyes closed.

What made things even worse was that while Jack was at the range, I think I figured out what I could have done. I remembered one afternoon on the Old Course when one of the old Scottish caddies had rescued his golfer after the man had hit two miserable shots. He handed him back his club and said, "Sometimes the body abandons us in this game. Now go over there and take five good, hard practice swings, and you'll get back into your groove." It had worked. He had turned the man's game around.

I spent the afternoon on the couch in room 228, thinking that is what would have saved Jack and kicking myself, while he was off at the *Tin Cup* range hitting a million balls by himself.

It was getting dark when I stood outside for a few minutes watching the wind move through the tall brown grass, thinking about Scotland and what I would have given to go back and caddie there for one more season. It would be Christmas soon, and I would be home in Maine. And then back on the tour for January and February. And then Jack and I would be driving away from Texas in his truck, back to our separate lives, where what we had shared here would be divided into our separate memories of the time and the place. I would be in my house in Maine with four empty bedrooms, waiting for the next time my children came home to visit. Colleen would be busy each day with her little school. And I would be dreaming.

The last thing I did before I turned my couch into a bed was say to Jack, "We'll play a good practice round tomorrow."

"We'll see," he said.

We'll see, I thought. With golf that's about all you could say really. One of the guys we'd played with on our disastrous round was a tour veteran and a fine player. He told Jack that in the second event he was in the lead, standing on the 17th tee with two holes to play for the win. He made a triple bogey on 17 and then another triple on 18 to drop out of the money.

"What should we think about tomorrow?" I asked Jack after he turned out the light.

"One shot at a time, I guess," he said.

DECEMBER 11, 2011

This morning, without any warning, Jack asked me to tell him the story of my life while we played our practice round at the Island Course at Kingwood, a beautiful track with tree-lined fairways and ponds filled with ducks and herons.

"I don't want to talk about golf," he said. "I'll play and you tell me your life story."

"The whole deal?"

"Yup, in eighteen holes." He said that he thought he ought to know the story in case someone ever came to him wanting to write a book about me, and I started by telling him that they wrote books only about the great writers, not the good ones, even though the good writers have more failure and heartache and humiliation to tell about, which would make a better book. I told him, "I'll give you my whole life story in eighteen holes, and I won't leave out the bad stuff. Just the really bad stuff."

The 1st hole. A 545-yard par-5. If you drive the ball up the left side, you have a good chance to be on in two and putting for an eagle unless you pull that shot left of the green into a pond. Up the right is death behind trees—a struggle to just make par from there.

"Here's how it begins, Jack. I grew up poor and stupid with a father who could never really look at me. On my fourth birthday just before I was supposed to blow out the candles on the birthday cake with my twin brother, my grandmother who took over when our mother died sent me into the alley to look for him. I found him sitting inside his

Chevy, smoking. When I called to him through the windows, he just stared off into space."

The 2nd hole. A simple 414-yard par-4 if you drive up the left side and avoid the bunker. An open shot at the green from there.

"I graduated from high school in the thick of the draft to Vietnam, and because there was no money for me to go to college, I was preparing to go into the army until I made the First Team All-State in football. I suddenly had offers for scholarships from a dozen colleges. In the spring of my sophomore season there was the tragedy at Kent State. One of the students had been shot in the mouth. It made me so angry that I couldn't sleep. I just kept thinking about a grown man with a rifle, a member of the National Guard, taking aim at an unarmed kid that way. It made me feel something that I had never felt before. I never played another baseball or football game. Sports just didn't matter anymore. I began to apply myself to learning about the world. I was so far behind; I didn't have a day to lose. And I wanted to change the world. I believed with all my heart that writing books was the way to do that."

The 3rd hole. A 168-yard par-3. A simple hole if you land the left side of this green, where the ground is flat. The right half has a steep slope that will carry a ball off the green.

"I washed dishes in a hotel and worked construction and lived alone for five years after college while I wrote lousy poems. Then on a morning in the winter of 1977, I began writing my first novel. I can't remember what it was about, but I know that I wrote three pages of dialogue that first morning, and when I read it that night, it felt like the people speaking were not me, and their words belonged to them. It was intoxicating to me. They occupied a world that I did not inhabit, and yet the next morning when I got up to write, that world was waiting for me to enter it again. Living inside their world was like a drug to me. The way I've heard some people describe their introduction to cocaine."

The 4th hole. A 411-yard par-4. Water up the left side. You must keep the ball right off the tee, or you're in for big trouble. But if you're too far right, you'll be left with a blind shot over tall trees into a small narrow green, protected by four big bunkers.

"Then it was the winter of 1977, and I had moved to a small tourist town way up the coast of Maine. They had a weekly newspaper there, and the editor had quit. I begged for the job and got it. I was sitting at the editor's desk my second day on the job. There was a blizzard tearing through the town. Every summer store was boarded up. The little light on my desk was the only light on in town. I looked up from the black Royal typewriter, and there was a man walking through the storm, straight to my door. In that moment, I felt my life as a writer begin to turn.

"He was a big man with wide shoulders. He kicked the snow off his boots and asked me if I was the new editor. I said I was. He said he had a story to tell me. He had just sat down when the telephone rang. Someone wanted me to hurry to the dock to take a photograph of the storm tide ripping a restaurant off the pier and carrying it out of the harbor. I asked the man if he could come back and see me the next day. He said he would.

"The next morning on his way to see me he dropped dead of a heart attack. Just fell into the snow. And I ended up writing his obituary that week instead of his story.

"But I met his widow, and she told me he had been a young soldier in the army during the Korean War. They had just had their first baby when he left for the war. Six months after he got there, he was captured by the Chinese army. He was a POW for three years, held in a cave for most of that time. He lost over a hundred pounds and was very sick. For a while the POWs were in the hands of a sadistic Chinese commander who would pick one American soldier each night to tie to a pole in the freezing cold, torture, and execute. All through the night the man would howl with pain. So this soldier cut a deal with the commander; he said, 'If I get my men to sign germ-warfare confessions, will you stop this torture?' It worked, and no other prisoners were harmed.

"Three years later the soldier came home to America, and it was the McCarthy era. The United States Army accused the soldier of being a traitor. They court-martialed him. And all the men he kept alive in the cave testified against him. This was just a little man from Maine with no education. He loved the army so much that he told his wife: 'The army will know that what I did over there in Korea, I did to keep my men alive.'

"Well, the army sent him to prison on a life sentence. They held him for three years, then released him. All his life he claimed he was innocent, and his wife believed him. Now that he was dead, she asked me if I could find the truth. 'I need to know the truth,' she said to me.

"The story got its hooks in me. I quit my job and went after it full-time. I survived again by writing feature stories for newspapers while I did my research. I thought it might take me six months. It ended up taking me six years. I fought the army and the FBI, who lied to me that the soldier's file had been destroyed in a fire. I eventually found the file with some help from a journalist at the *Washington Post* named Bob Woodward. The truth was in the file. The army had pressured the soldier's men to testify against him. I tracked them all down—all the prosecution's witnesses—and they agreed to go on the record for me, to clear the soldier's name."

The 5th hole. A 407-yard par-4. A dangerous hole. You have to drive the ball over a lake—a carry of at least 230 yards. You miss this drive and the match is over.

"I spent another two years writing a book about that soldier, but no one wanted to publish it. Editors kept telling me that no one in America cared about the Korean War.

"During those years someone told me that all serious writers went on to study at a place called the Iowa Writers' Workshop where you spent two years working with some of the best writers in the country and earning a master of fine arts. I spent the next eight years trying to write something good enough to get in. I wrote three practice novels during that time and lived alone in one room like a monk where I made myself read all the classics. I found that I could read and absorb a five-hundred-page book every twenty-four hours if I really bore down on the words. And the words entered me. I fell in love there with the beautiful sentences of F. Scott Fitzgerald and became determined to write those kinds of sentences, no matter what it took, while I supported myself by writing feature stories for Sunday newspapers and for *Reader's Digest* and the *Saturday Evening Post*. One story in *Reader's Digest* was a check for almost $3,000, which was enough money to live for ten months easily. I was buying time to write my novels. That was the governing dynamic."

The 6th hole. A 573-yard par-5. A dangerous S-shaped hole with water winding its way up the left side all the way to the green. If you don't play smart and well here from tee to green, you could easily make a 10 on the hole.

"Nobody would publish my book about the soldier, but a great young editor at *Yankee* magazine named Mel Allen commissioned me to write a story, and then somehow Paramount Pictures found out about it and bought the rights. Suddenly I was living in the Beverly Wilshire hotel down the hallway from Warren Beatty working on the script. The producer rented me a red convertible to drive around Beverly Hills. A young director named Marty Brest was assigned to the project. He would later go on to make *Scent of a Woman*. Tom Cruise was in discussions with Paramount to play my role—the young reporter tracking down the truth about the dead soldier. It was wild."

The 7th hole. A 428-yard par-4. A straight-ahead hole, and a good chance for birdie here if you can land the tree-lined fairway from the tee.

"Finally Iowa accepted me. Your mother and I had met and fallen in love by then, and we drove out there in an old Volvo with no heater. I remember her mom crying when we left and saying, 'You don't even own a broom.' With the wind chill, it was fifty degrees below zero in Illinois, and the seats of the car were frozen as hard as granite. I drove, wrapped up in blankets with your mother pressed against me the whole way. I was writing a novel then, and when I submitted the first fifty pages to the people at Iowa, they loved it, and I was awarded a fellowship that allowed me to study there and earn my degree free. In fact, I made a little money there teaching extra courses in the undergraduate English department. I fell in love with teaching right from the first class. I remember the marvelous feeling when I walked into the classroom and looked at my students' faces and realized that for the next few hours I could finally forget about myself and my writing and my fears and my doubts and just concentrate on them and their work."

The 8th hole. A 198-yard par-3. Not an easy par-3. Water off the left side of the fairway and the green, and the right half of the green slopes to bad ground. You have to hit a golf shot here.

"Colleen and I eloped in England at the end of my first semester. We rode a train to Paris, which is where your sister Erin was conceived. We spent Christmas in a tiny village in Austria living like royalty on tips your mother had earned as a waitress while she was doing her student teaching. One morning in Austria I got up and began writing the first chapter of a baseball novel. A love story really between a local farm girl and a young pitcher playing on the minor-league team in her town. This was my fourth novel. The first three had been lost causes. And right then on that first morning, I had a feeling that this one was going to make it. And that morning, writing in bed beside your mom while she slept, began my routine. I've written in bed beside her now for twenty-seven years."

The 9th hole. A 453-yard par-4. A long and dangerous par-4. A tough drive with water down the left side and the hole swinging to the left. If you don't get the drive out far enough to the right, you have to go over the water to get to the green in regulation.

"I'm trying to keep this in order, Jack. And just hit the high points. Your sister was born in the autumn of my second year in Iowa. Five days later my agent called to tell me that my novel had been bought in New York. Mommy and I walked through the leaves to a pizza joint to celebrate with some friends. Erin slept right through it. That night I told Colleen that we could have as many babies as we wanted. Every door was going to swing open for me. I was thirty-four. I'd been writing every day, seven days a week, ten or twelve hours a day, since I was twenty-four. Now it was all paying off."

The 10th hole. A 444-yard par-4. All you have to do to make this a good hole is hit a perfect drive in the middle of the fairway. Anything right or left leaves a blind shot over tall trees to the green.

"With my first novel coming out in New York in the spring, and with my MFA degree from Iowa, I had five or six job offers. I mean professor jobs for life. But I wasn't interested in signing on anywhere for more than a one-year gig. I loved teaching, but I was afraid to settle into academic life. Frankly, I always found professors a little too pompous and difficult to bear. Plus, that cosseted life was too easy. It could kill a writer's dreams of writing important books. So I took a one-year job at Colby College, where I had gone as an undergrad. It was pretty cool to be back there, in an office just down the hallway from the guys who had been my professors twenty-five years earlier. We had a great winter. I loved my students. Got my first computer, a Mac. Until then, I'd used only my manual Royal typewriter. To get a four-hundred-page novel ready to send to New York with no mistakes would take three months of work, seven days a week. Now with my Mac, I could do the same amount of work in three days. Amazing. More time to spend with Mommy. And so Nell was born in March, the same month my first novel was published in New York. I remember taking her cross-country skiing when she was four days old. The novel got decent reviews but sold poorly. And, lo and behold, a small press published my book about the soldier—*A Soldier's Disgrace*. It sold pretty well, and the reviews were all outstanding. In fact, a man named C. Michael Curtis, an editor at the *Atlantic Monthly*, offered to write a blurb for the cover—and he said the book deserved to win a Pulitzer Prize. Big stuff for me."

The 11th hole. A 575-yard par-5. Wide-open driving hole. But terrible second shot. Water and trees blocking your path to the green. It's a three-shot hole. No chance for eagle.

"So as our year at Colby was ending, I was offered a job teaching at the University of Maine. I think the salary was $26,000, and there was the chance for tenure. I turned it down when I got an advance of $7,000 to write my third book, another novel. And off we went to Ireland because we knew that if we could find a cottage in the countryside, we could survive for a year on seven grand. Your mother and I were so crazy in love we got on the plane out of Boston on a Sunday night with two babies and we were asking the Irish stewardesses if they thought we should get off in Shannon or Dublin. We had no idea where we were even going to spend the first night. We took Dublin. I went for a walk the first morning, and I saw this little necklace in a store window that I knew Colleen would love.

I bought it and the clerk told me about a cottage in county Wicklow, and off we went for the winter. We lived on cabbage and potatoes. All we had for heat was a fireplace, where we burned coal. The cottage was down a country road, five miles from civilization. That's when I began getting up at four in the morning to write, because that was when the coal fire was dying and I needed to keep it going."

The 12th hole. A 189-yard par-3. A pretty straightforward hole. Water down the left side.

"After my third book was published, it became clear to me that I was never really going to be a popular writer in America. What I mean is all three books lost money for their publishers. The movie deal in L.A. had vanished. Colleen was pregnant with you, and it was time to settle down. I was thirty-eight. I think I was ready to settle into a life of teaching. I was hired at the University of Maine for one year, and while I was there and we were living in Bangor, I was hired into a tenure-track job at Colgate. We fell in love with the place. You took your first steps there. We were living in a dream until I got fired, and you already know that story. We moved home to Maine. I couldn't get another teaching job, and it had been five years since my last book was published. I was working hard on a new novel, but because my first three books had lost money in New York, no one there wanted to even read this new novel.

"We were broke when I was hired to work as a laborer building a mansion house on the shore through the winter. We worked ten-hour days outside in brutal weather. Some mornings it was twenty-five below zero when I walked down the beach to work. I began keeping a journal there, and eventually that led to a cover story in *Harper's Magazine* and a book contract with one of the best editors in New York at Little, Brown that paid me more than I would have earned as a day laborer in five years."

The 13th hole. A 426-yard par-4. A good hole for us if you can avoid the trees up the left side from the tee. It's a ninety-degree right-to-left dogleg.

"About two months before the book was published, Disney bought the film rights for a ton of money. That's when I took us all to Ireland to spend the summer there. You remember this part of the story. I think that taking you and your sisters to see where your great-grandmother had lived before she immigrated to America was one of the coolest things I ever did as a father.

"Over in Ireland I got an e-mail from the top literary agent in New York, Lynn Nesbit. She had read my book and she knew about the Disney deal and she wanted to take me on. This was 1997. I was forty-seven years old, and Lynn got me four book deals in the next six years, including a two-book deal with Alfred A. Knopf. We bought our first house in Maine. And I was about to step into the one story that I was probably put on this earth to write. My mother's story."

The 14th hole. A 420-yard par-4. Another hole that requires two good shots to have a chance for birdie. Must stay left of the bunker off the tee. At least there's no water on this hole.

"You know, from the time I was a kid, I knew there was something wrong with my father. As I said, he never was able to really look me in the eye. He was an old man now, and when he was diagnosed with a brain tumor, he told me about my mother, who had died sixteen days after giving birth to me and my brother. She was only nineteen years old. They had been married for only nine months. I decided to find out all that I could about her and to write their love story. It was a book I called *Of Time and Memory*, and it was a pretty big hit. I went all over the country giving readings. I was on the *Today* show.

The front page of *USA Today*. What I learned writing the book was that the only way my mother could have saved her life was by terminating her pregnancy. She made the choice to give up her life for us. When she did that, she was really choosing her babies over the boy who loved her, and my father barely survived. He worked at a print shop in those days; it was the job he took when he came back from the war. So he stood at the big Linotype press printing up the engagement announcement. Then the wedding invitations. Then the notice of the twin babies. Then the notice of the funeral."

The 15th hole. A 462-yard par-4. We must hit a three-wood here to avoid the creek that cuts across the fairway at 300 yards. From there it is a straight shot to a tricky green that slopes steeply off the back half to awful ground.

"The month after the book was published, Oprah Winfrey began a new enterprise of making book videos that she hoped would do for books what music videos had done for records. My book was the first she chose, and I was sent out to Hollywood, where the brilliant young director Mark Pellington had been hired to direct the project. He took a film crew to Pennsylvania and produced a haunting thirty-three-minute film.

"It was during the time I spent with Mark Pellington when I pledged myself to one day making a feature-length motion picture of my mother's story. I spent ten months reading all the great scripts and in 2002, when Hallmark Hall of Fame bought the film rights to my novel *Fallen Angel*, I fought for the chance to write the script. I was in northern Ontario on the set of the movie, telling the star, Gary Sinise, about my mother's story and the screenplay I planned to write about her life. And, Jack, those days on the set of the movie, with your mother, were the happiest days of my life. Beside our bed I have one photograph of Colleen sitting in Gary Sinise's chair. I look at it every day, and for the last eight years I've told myself every morning when I open my eyes and every night when I close my eyes that someday I'm going to see your mother on the set of my mother's movie."

The 16th hole. A 415-yard par-4. A good birdie chance for us if we can stay up the right side off the tee. We'll take a three-wood off the tee and then go for broke here.

"The summer before *Of Time and Memory* was published, I was up early with the radio on, National Public Radio. News of a bombing in Northern Ireland in the town of Omagh. The IRA had chosen that day to set off the bomb in the center of the town because that was the particular morning when mothers took their children into town to buy their back-to-school uniforms. Those innocent people slaughtered. Most of them were mothers and children. Hundreds wounded. We never think about the wounded. There are now several people in that town who had both feet blown off in the blast. And others who were so horribly disfigured that they wear masks over their faces. If you were to go to Omagh tomorrow, you would see the people in their wax masks.

"I heard that radio news, and I knew that I had to go there right away to bear witness to what had happened because I had been there with you and your sisters and Mommy and we had been so happy."

The 17th hole. A 228-yard par-3. A tough hole with water up the left side and bordering the green and bunkers up the right side. If you land in these bunkers, you risk flying the ball off the green into the water on your second shot.

"I wrote my next novel, *Winter Dreams*, living one winter in the Rusacks Hotel, on the 18th fairway of the Old Course. You were in love with golf, and I wanted to write a novel with a lot of golf in it. I fell in love with Scotland, and I poured myself into that novel.

screenplay of my mother's book. You know that story—3,628 pages of script and none of it has been good enough."

The 18th hole. A 578-yard par-5. Nightmare hole. *Golf Digest* has called this the roughest finishing hole in golf. If you take the direct route, it's a tee shot with a 240-yard carry over a lake onto a narrow landing area. And then a second shot of 230 yards over a pond to another small landing area. If you go up the right, there's another pond right in the middle of the fairway, and from there you'd need a perfect second shot. Impossible. We could easily make a 10 on this hole and miss the cut. There is a bailout area to the right off the tee, but it's miles from the green.

"So here we are at the end of my story, Jack. Down in Texas with you, chasing your dream. Back home my new novel has been published. My ninth book. Mommy is happy running her little preschool. You and your sisters are healthy."

"What's next then?" he asked me.

"I'm not sure," I said.

"What about writing?"

"When I was home over the break and out hunting on the marsh one morning, I had a new vision for my mother's movie. After we're finished in Texas, I'm going to write a new draft of the script. We'll see what happens."

"You need to get your mom's movie made," he said.

DECEMBER 12, 2011

Game Day. Colleen has been writing to me and telling me on the phone to please remember to give our son one hug each day and to tell him that I love him.

I have not done this. Somehow I feel it would be awkward for both of us.

But this morning as we walked to the practice range, I told him this: "Here's what I love about how you play golf, Jack. First, you never make excuses. I've heard other golfers out here complain about the course, the wind, the greens. Not you; when you play like a dog, you admit it. Second, you refuse to play scared. And third, you never quit. We've been in four events so far, and in each one we've had one of our playing partners walk off after blowing up the front nine."

"We've got twelve tournaments here this winter," he said. "This is our fifth. I'm just getting started, man."

"That's right," I said. "That's good."

Then he asked me if I remembered telling him the story of Bobby Jones ripping up his scorecard and walking off the Old Course the first time he played there. "What hole was that?" he asked.

"Number 11. The par-3," I said.

"We were walking past the bunker."

"Hill bunker. Front left."

"Yeah. You stopped at the bunker and told me the story."

"Of course I remember. And all the times I caddied there, I always told the same story to my golfers. He took three swings in that bunker and couldn't get out. So he quit."

"The next time he played there, he won the British Open, is that right?"

"Yep. Nineteen twenty-six. On his way to winning the Grand Slam. No one's ever done it again. But Jones grew up privileged; maybe he thought that just because he had this beautiful swing and he played so well, he shouldn't have to struggle on a golf course. He had to learn stuff that you already know."

Yesterday I surprised Jack and bowed out of our second practice round. I needed to rest my right knee. But most of all, I thought some time on his own out on the course would be a good break for him. He played his practice round well enough to win $45 from three other boys on the tour, and on the practice range this morning before round one began, it was nice to see him talking and joking around with the boys. I have to remember to step aside from time to time this winter.

The story of this first round of our fifth tournament is that after failing to make the cut last week, Jack had a mountain to climb, and he began the round by making five straight pars, which included dropping two putts from twenty feet. He then landed the 573-yard par-5 in two and missed the putt for eagle, the putt for birdie, and the putt for par. But instead of falling apart, he righted the ship and stood on the 18th tee at six over par. We would make the cut barring some disaster on the final hole. I wanted to play safe up the right side, but he bashed his driver 358 yards over the lake to the narrow island only 23 yards wide, then took a five-iron the remaining 223 yards over the second pond, leaving himself eighteen feet past the hole for another eagle putt, which stopped one inch from the hole. So with the birdie, he shot five over par and will probably be in the middle of the leaderboard after round one. A hell of a comeback from our last tournament.

The best thing that happened out there today was meeting Barry O'Neill, one of our playing partners, a brilliant young player from Waterford, Ireland, who finished with a 67 and has the lead going into tomorrow's final round. Barry and I talked about Ireland all the way around, and when we finished, I asked him if he would play some practice rounds with Jack after our Christmas break, heading into our final six events. "It would mean a lot to me," I said to him. "There's really nothing I can teach Jack out here."

"He hits the ball a fuckin' mile," he said when he shook my hand. Then he said, "Any father who goes to Scotland at age sixty to become a caddie for his boy is a hero to me. I'd be honored to help your son."

You've got to love the Irish!

DECEMBER 13, 2011

A skirmish in the hallway just after 4:30 this morning. A man's angry voice. A door slamming. Children crying from the bottoms of their hearts. I cracked open my door, and this is what I saw: The man lumbering down the hallway toward the exit. The woman, maybe twenty years old, in a polka-dot dress that was a foot too short and ripped open up one side. Her four children, all under age five, hanging on her arms and legs as if they were afraid of being washed away in another flood. Before I could close my door, the woman turned to me and asked if I could help her. I'm ashamed to admit this, but my first thought was: five years ago, four children ago, a hundred pounds ago, didn't she have a fine chance to make par, standing on the tee, the sun is shining, it's a straightforward par-4, and somehow you end up making a 10, and you're out of the match before it's scarcely begun. Life slips away so easily.

She asked me for $5 for bus fare. I gave her a little more than that.

Instead of driving up the left side of the fairway on the 1st hole, Jack pushed his drive right, which placed us among tall trees. I wanted him to punch out and go for the green in three on this opening par-5. But he went for it and hit a spectacular shot that cut around the trees and landed in a green-side bunker. His birdie putt lipped out. Then he lipped out a par putt on number 2, and then another par putt on number 3, and he hung his head and never picked it up again the whole round except on the par-5 6th hole. We were facing 268 yards over water and trees to reach the green in two after his drive. I started to hand him a five-iron to play safely right of all this. He took his hybrid instead. I was thinking, How stupid is this? The objective is to make a birdie on this hole, and we can be putting for a birdie if we play this second shot safely and take a wedge to the flag. His shot clipped a branch about a hundred feet high and fell into the water. Not our last stupid shot of the day. The killer was the harmless par-3 number 8. We were standing three off par on the tee and swinging pretty well. The pin was in the middle of the green. To me it was a sucker pin, because going for it and missing even slightly left meant the ball kicks off the green into the water. I said nothing. I just watched the ball fly straight for the pin, land slightly left, and skip off into the water.

We let this round slip away because of stupid decisions. And so what that he hit two amazing shots on number 18 to be putting for an eagle? I'm sick of amazing shots. I just want to play smart shots and make pars. And I said nothing, but I am growing tired of this now. I know that every father who ever played golf with his son would consider it a dream to be caddying for his kid on a pro tour. But I am beginning to think that I can do nothing as a caddie or a father to get through to Jack that if he isn't more patient out here, he's never going to turn a corner. He is killing himself now, I can see this clearly. And this isn't easy for me to admit, but the truth is we are not working together. We're miles apart. Today by the 7th hole I would have taken a year splitting rocks in a quarry rather than caddie another round for my son.

DECEMBER 13, 2011, TUESDAY NIGHT

Maybe there's a lesson here. If you can climb out from under your disappointment and take a six-pack of beer to a *Tin Cup* range and pound a million balls side by side under the stars while the armadillos race tumbleweed across a field lit up like a carnival, there are things between fathers and sons and golfers and caddies that get resolved. In the first place you can talk to each other without actually talking to each other because you're just hitting golf balls. And then there's the rhythm of the swing, which seems to carry the words. With the pressure off, I began by saying, "Can you imagine that we ever ended up in a place as strange as Texas?"

"Pretty strange," he said.

"Ten bucks, Jackie boy, that I get this one closer to the pin."

"Go for it, man."

It was not a bet that I could win. "I owe you ten bucks," I said. "Do you have your iPhone with you?"

"Yep."

"Can you do me a favor? Can you check and see if even par won money today?"

It took a minute. "Yeah. Thirteen hundred."

"Can you check all of the first five events please while I kill that armadillo with this five-iron."

He knew what I was getting at. And the proof was right in front of us. There were good players on this tour, some of them with full exemptions on the Nationwide Tour, and even par was still a good score. "Maybe we need a different strategy," I said.

"I'm not playing scared," he said.

"I know that. I respect you for that. So go for every par-5 in two, that's fine. That's your game. But on every other hole why don't we just go for the middle of the green with our approach shots. Take some pressure off and collect a few pars. See what happens."

The silence is easier to bear as well because it has no meaning, there's nothing riding on it—you're just out there hitting golf balls.

"Colleen e-mailed me," I said. "I wish she could come see you play in one tournament."

"We'll try it in our practice round tomorrow," he said.

He was too busy hitting balls to notice that I was smiling.

DECEMBER 15, 2011

The Forest Course at Kingwood is a spectacular layout with the kinds of golf holes that are as different as you can get from the open links land of Scotland. Until late last night, after playing a practice round there yesterday afternoon with three other guys on the tour, Jack and I were still marveling over it. I think it's the best ground I've ever walked, a splendid puzzle cut out of thick woods and marshlands, with mounded fairways and old-growth trees that frame every hole. There is no flatland to be found. Most of the landing areas are artistically placed, elevated plateaus. Even the greens are complexes of hills and valleys, hollows and ridges. On nine of the greens you could easily take four putts to find the hole. I think the par-5 5th captures the essence of the place. You climb onto an elevated tee box, and off in the distance there is the red flag—straight out there about 900 yards across a marsh that Lewis and Clark might have crossed in a canoe if they swung through Texas. Then you turn slightly right on the tee box, and 243 yards away, over the water, in the thick woods you spy a narrow tunnel of light, which is your target. If you hit that tunnel, the ball rolls forward to a fairway 30 yards wide that forms a path around the right that will eventually take you to that red flag you saw across the marsh. The whole course is an astonishingly beautiful labyrinth with each hole hidden in the trees so that you have the feeling you are the last golfers left in the world. Jack had his "A" game in the practice round and shot three over par with two birdies to beat the other fellows there and win another thirty bucks. But today, under pressure, without the "A" game we could be in trouble. It is going to take total control and concentration to hold it together well enough to make the cut. And Jack told me he wants to make the cut just for the chance to play the course again tomorrow. He loved it. If there had been any daylight left when we finished our practice round, he was determined to go back to the 1st tee and play it again.

My knee this morning is rubbish after climbing all the hills yesterday. I'm a little concerned that I might slow things down. I'm also concerned because in my mind I can't see the straight lines that will lead us to pars. There were too many blind shots, too many twisting fairways and doglegs for me to get a feel for the place after just one round. I've decided that while Jack is on the practice range this morning, I'm going to take a cart and drive the whole track, every hole from tee to green, looking for the simplest line of logic that we can impose on the course and follow through our round. I am thinking of my friend who played for the prestigious Eden Trophy in St. Andrews and wrote to me just the other day: "Don, remember what you sent me in an e-mail before I played the event? Here it is: Gordon, when you play the Eden Tournament, try something for me. It's a new caddie approach that I've used with spectacular results. Break the course into pieces. You are on the tee, and you see the white stake at 150. You play that shot. Don't try for more. Then you are at the 150 stake, and you know you can stick the nine-iron onto the center of the green from there. So you play that shot. Don't try for more. That's the way Mr. Watson played the third round of the Open in that cold rain. Everyone else was trying for everything and falling apart. But old Tom just played patiently and collected all pars and one of the best rounds of the day."

This is the way that I would like us to play today. If we can break the course into pieces and conquer each piece, we have a chance. But if it is us against the *whole* course, we will be swept away. Yesterday my mind was so engaged just trying to find our way around the Forest Course that I forgot it was my wedding anniversary. I finally called home around eight, and the moment I heard Colleen's voice, I remembered her standing in the train station in Winchester, England, twenty-seven years ago, an hour after we eloped there and were married before the justice of the peace. We rode the train into London late that afternoon, sneaking into the first-class compartment, then checked into a small hotel. I bought scalped tickets outside the Victoria Palace Theatre for *Cats*, the hottest new show in town. She asked me last night how Jack and I were doing. I said, "I wish we had a wide-open course tomorrow like the Old Course where you've got room to make a mistake."

She didn't mean about the golf, she said. "How are you and Jack doing?" she asked again.

"Fine," I said.

I didn't tell her what had been on my mind as I watched Jack hit his first drive that morning. We were almost halfway through the tour; it had taken me that long to understand that if a father spends enough time with his grown-up son, he sees what he's passed on to him. With us there was me believing all my life that I was never good enough, that as a writer I would never measure up no matter how hard I worked, no matter what sacrifices I made. Jack has inherited this. And in golf, without that deep, persistent belief in yourself, you always lose, because that last poor shot is proof once again that you're not good enough.

We are going to have to overcome this ten or twenty times today in order to play well.

Round one begins under low hanging fog and a black sky at 10:10.

Hole 1. A 371-yard par-4. Jack hits a three-wood on his first drive, dead center. Well done, I say. What I am thinking is, In the fog this puzzle of a golf course will be even more confusing today. And if we don't have our "A" game, we won't make the cut.

We have 117 yards left to an elevated green surrounded by deep bunkers.

He nails the wedge. We are left with a twelve-foot uphill putt. It looks as though it will break two cups left to right. His putt stops on the edge of the cup. It could fall in. But it doesn't. A tap-in par.

Even after one hole.

Hole 2. A 425-yard par-4. He stripes the drive. It has to be out there 320 yards. He hits his wedge to ten feet. "This putt will break a cup," I tell him.

I'm wrong. Another tap-in par. I hate missing reads. Just fucking hate it.

Even after two holes.

Hole 3. The short 522-yard par-5.

Another perfect drive. We're left with 220 yards uphill to a narrow green. Jack takes his four-iron and lands the green. We have an eagle putt about twenty-two feet.

The ball stops short four inches. A tap-in birdie.

One under after three holes.

———

Hole 4. A 202-yard par-3.

I am trying not to think about anything but the shot in front of us, but in my mind I am thinking this is the best start we've ever had on the tour.

Jack hits a seven-iron right at the flag. It looks perfect from where I am standing.

We are left with twenty-two feet uphill to the hole. "What do you think?" he asks me.

I am sure of this one. "Just lay it up on the right edge," I say, "and it might fall in." It does. Birdie. Our second birdie in four holes.

Two under after four holes.

Hole 5. A 530-yard par-5.

Now the rain is falling hard, and I am thinking, Good, this is very good for Jack. The only golf we could afford to play when I was teaching him the game was when we could sneak on the course, when the weather was bad enough to drive away all the members. But they call a rain delay. Apparently, they don't believe in fucking playing golf in the rain in Texas. We have to sit at least an hour. This could work against us. And here we are an hour later on this mysterious hole. You have to hit the narrow tunnel of light between the trees off to the right. Jack takes a three-wood and nails it, right up the slot into the mayor's office. We'll have a shot at reaching this par-5 in two. But there is water all along the left side of the green. And Jack takes a very aggressive line, starting his three-wood out over the marsh and counting on it to cut back and fall to a back-left pin. It does. We have another eagle putt, about a forty-footer. We get it up there short by five damned feet. Not a good putt.

"What do you see?" he asks me. I tell him I am sure of this one—inside the left half of the cup, Jack. He drains it. Another birdie. And for the first time since we started this tour two months ago, we are working together. Actually working together! I'm so excited that I'm scared I'm going to do or say the wrong thing. I've never been this nervous before out caddying. Never even close.

We are now three under par after five holes.

Hole 6. A 158-yard par-3.

Water up the left side and behind the green. No room for error. And the pin is up there back left. I just want to go for the middle of the green, but I say nothing. Jack goes right at the pin. He flies past the pin, and the ball disappears. I can't see it. It has to be in the water. "Too aggressive," Jack says. "We'll see when we get up there," I say. And the ball is sitting on the wood plank at the edge of the water. He makes a two-putt par from there. "We just dodged a bullet," I tell him.

Three under par after six holes.

Hole 7. A 478-yard par-4.

The big par-4. Another tree-lined, narrow fairway. He nails his drive to 141 yards. He takes his wedge and goes right at the pin. We have only five feet left for birdie. The putt sits on the edge. A tap-in par.

Three under after seven holes.

Hole 8. A 414-yard par-4.

Jack has a bounce in his step now, and as I watch him, I am thinking, At this moment my son is *not me*. He is not his father. He expects to be playing this way. He believes in himself. It is the first glimpse of this that I have had on the tour. And it makes me smile. Hell, I could cry.

Another monster drive up the center. A 138-yard wedge to eight feet.

We miss the birdie and tap in the par. Jack isn't happy. He says, "I should be five under right now. I'm missing all these birdie chances." "We'll have more," I tell him. So far we have hit every fairway and every green in regulation. We have three birdies and five tap-in pars. Golf doesn't get any easier, I am thinking.

Three under after eight holes.

Hole 9. A 426-yard par-4.

A 248-yard carry over water to safe ground. And it's a narrow chute from the tee through the trees. Jack nails it. He doesn't even look like the golfer I've been walking beside these past two months. He hits his wedge to twelve feet, and he drains the birdie putt.

Four under after nine holes.

Hole 10. A 510-yard par-5.

A good hole for us. The rain has stopped. The sun is breaking through now.

Jack is relaxed, talking with the other two players. One of them has won money in every event so far. We're beating him by four strokes. Jack hits a perfect drive. Another dead-center fairway. Not as far as usual. We have 234 left to the hole. Uphill, water left of the green. A worrisome shot. We are on the green with another eagle putt. About thirty-seven feet. We leave ourselves a tricky four-foot putt for our fifth birdie of the day. The ball stops on the lip again. These greens aren't breaking, Jack says. He's not happy.

And I am thinking that right now we are probably in first place. I want to call Colleen and tell her. And then I'm kicking myself for getting ahead of what is happening here. We have miles to go.

Four under after ten holes.

Hole 11. A 210-yard par-3.

He lands the green, twenty-two feet from the hole. And here's my punishment for allowing myself to step out of the moment. We make our first bogey. A stupid three-putt. What a dumb ass, Jack says to himself. Be careful, I am thinking. Stay in the moment.

Three under after eleven holes.

Hole 12. A 433-yard par-4.

"Hit a good one, Jackie boy," I say as I hand him his driver.

He nails it. His best drive of the day.

We have only 106 yards left but to a dangerous green that falls away to the left and the right. He hits his wedge a little left, and it kicks left and falls into a bunker. Our first missed green in twelve holes.

We're in a bunker that is filled with water and sand as heavy as concrete.

He looks worried. But he gets it up and out. We face a downhill putt, fifteen feet. I tell him, "This one will be fast." He hits it poorly, and we're six feet past the hole. Another bogey. Damn. Our second bogey in two holes.

Two under par now after twelve holes.

Hole 13. A 369-yard par-4.

A short but dangerous hole. He hits a bad three-wood. It goes right and lands behind trees. It feels like a stake right through my heart. Ever since I thought about calling Colleen to tell her that her little boy was leading this tournament, we have played like yellow dogs.

We make our third straight bogey. We've given away three of our four strokes in the last three holes. There is a point like this in every match under competition. I know this. We just have to play through it.

One under after thirteen holes.

Hole 14. A 150-yard par-3.

I say to Jack, "Fight hard, man. We'll get back in this."

He doesn't say anything. But he makes a good swing and lands eight feet from the hole. A missed birdie. A tap-in par. "Good par, Jackie," I tell him.

One under after fourteen holes.

Hole 15. A 473-yard par-4.

A wicked hole from the tee with water up the left, right in our landing area. I hand him his three-wood instead of his driver and remind him that we hit three-wood from this tee yesterday in our practice round. He takes the three-wood and nails it up the right side. Good. Good.

One hundred and fifty-four yards left to a green that slopes right to left, with big bunkers up the right. Jack takes a nine-iron and hits it straight at the flag. The ball never moves off the flag the whole way. I hear one of our playing partners yell, "Wow!" I run up the hill to have a look. It looks as if it's two feet from the hole. It's not. It's one foot. An easy birdie. We are back! "That's how you fight back, Jackie," I tell him.

Two under par after fifteen.

Hole 16. A 392-yard par-4.

And Jack is thinking now; he takes a four-iron on this short par-4. Right up the center. I want to calm him down, so I start talking about Teddy again. How since we canceled our telephone landline to save money, there's no longer an answering machine, and I always thought that when Teddy was left home alone, he must have loved hearing the voices on the answering machine—his beloved Cara saying, "We're not home right now to take your call . . ." Jack makes a solid par here. He looks good.

Two under par after sixteen.

Hole 17. A 602-yard par-5.

"We are going to get there in two," Jack says as he takes his driver. He nails it a mile. We have 237 left. I want him to hit a four-iron and let it run onto the green. But there's wind in our faces, and he wants the hybrid.

He hits it too far; it flies the green. A bad mistake. We don't even know what is over there behind the steep mounds and the bunkers.

It's not good. It's the worst ground we've been on today. Soaking wet. I hand him his wedge and say, "Just get it on the dance floor, Jackie."

He leaves it short. Then two bad putts and we throw away a stroke.

He is steaming mad at himself now. And I'm just trying to hold on. Hold on.

One under after seventeen holes.

Hole 18. A 455-yard par-4.

Into the wind, but I still hand him the three-wood. There's water left and woods right. He nails it right onto the plateau, the only flat good ground out there. Here we go. A simple 167-yard nine-iron to the last green. We have hit every fairway off the tee but one. And every green but two.

He flies a beautiful shot, but when it hits the green, it has too much juice on it and spins off thirty feet down a hill.

I feel the bogey coming. And it comes. We lose another stroke and our chance of shooting an under-par round.

Even par after eighteen holes.

I am thinking, Two months ago in our first tournament we shot a 90 in round one and didn't make the cut. Today for about an hour we were four under par through ten holes, and no one on this tour was playing any better.

But Jack is just miserable. "I can't believe I pissed away a great round like that," he says. And he doesn't say another word. I want to sit and have a beer with him at the bar outside the clubhouse where they shot the movie *Tin Cup*.

He wants to get out of here. So off we go. Speeding all the way back to the hotel. Bruce Springsteen at top volume. Not a word between us.

But here's the deal. Jack will no longer wonder if he belongs on this tour. I'm just going to let him figure out how to feel. I don't think I've ever felt so tired in my life. We might have a new lesson to learn now: how to play when you're on fire and leading the tournament. I have no experience with that, so I'm going to have to turn to some friends for advice.

Round two tomorrow. They say it will rain hard all day. The first full day of rain here in about eleven months. I hope it pours. That's our kind of weather. And I will get to watch Jack again in his Carnoustie rain jacket.

DECEMBER 16, 2011

Four in the morning. I am remembering the Old Course, the evening before the British Open in 2010, when I walked all eighteen holes with Ray, who was caddying for Ricky Barnes. We had just finished, and I was rounding the corner of Golf Place, when I ran into a group of noisy, middle-aged women, twelve or fifteen of them, all worn-out-looking housewives in matching red shirts, who had flown to Scotland from the States to form a cheering section for Tiger Woods. I was stunned. By then the whole world knew that Woods had betrayed his wife and children. This didn't matter to these ladies. They loved him. They couldn't wait to get a glimpse of him the next day. I suppose no one loves winners the way Americans do. It's fine if you have no love in your heart, but if you end up living with your family in a Studio Plus hotel, you cannot be pardoned in America. Finishing in the money is what counts.

I can remember when Jack was six or seven and he first began to excel at hockey and baseball and I told him that no matter what kinds of wild celebrations took place after winning, he had to be the quiet kid who just walked up to his coaches and shook their hands and thanked them for the chance to play. And I remember the spring evening he hit his first baseball over the fence at Bailey Field when I told him that all the truly great athletes know that you learn more from losing than from winning.

That's not going to help him today. Whatever lesson he might learn from losing today, he's not interested.

It has just begun to rain.

By 9:00 a.m., it is a cold rain on gusting winds, like a hundred Scotland mornings I remember. All the golfers on the practice range look a little stunned, as if someone were playing a trick on them. The only thing I say to Jack are the words we memorized years ago from *Band of Brothers*. Captain Winters to his men in the 101st Airborne just before they board the planes the morning of D-day. "Listen up. Good luck. God bless you. I'll see you in the assembly area."

But when Jack doesn't acknowledge me, I'm a little annoyed and I call to him. He turns back. And I decide in that moment that I will keep my silence. I will just be his caddie today, not a philosopher or a father, though most caddies I knew in Scotland are about the best philosophers I've ever met. And a lot of them are damned good fathers too. I am thinking in this rain that I wish Malcolm were here to roll my cigarettes for me in the wet today, a skill I never mastered. And I am thinking about Davy Gilchrist, my caddie master at Kingsbarns who gave me my first chance. He remains one of the most decent people I've ever known. I watch Jack walk away. It's cold and wet enough now for him to be wearing his proper rain jacket. The beautiful light blue Duke's Course jacket I bought him with the first tips I earned as a caddie. I am thinking of David Scott, who runs the Duke's and has such great insight into golf and life. I wish he were here today. And old Glen up in Canada. I have a bad feeling standing in the rain. I just wanted Jack to be grateful this morning for the round he played yesterday, but when I tried to talk with him on the ride in, it didn't go so well. All he had to say was "I played nine good holes yesterday. And nine lousy ones."

"We made the cut," I said. "We're back to fight another day."

"Not good enough," he said.

I went on. "I just think if a man is grateful in this life, then his heart is set in the right place."

"I don't buy it," he said. "In golf it's about making the swing. If you make a good swing, you play well. If not, no excuses."

"You don't have to buy it," I said. "I'm just an old man now, and nobody cares what an old man thinks about anything. I'm just telling you what I believe. If a man isn't grateful, he can't be calm. And in this game if you're not calm, you're dead."

That was the end of the talking.

I wish we could have spent the day talking instead of playing golf. It was that kind of day, starting with the first drive, when Jack made the worst swing I'd seen him make in Texas. The ball flew perhaps 100 yards, never more than two feet off the ground. With 260 yards left to a narrow green perched on top of a mound and surrounded by bunkers, Jack hit a miraculous shot and saved par. He hit another miserable drive on the 2nd and then made another miraculous par save after hitting a towering seven-iron—a completely blind shot— over a stand of tall trees blocking our view of the green.

We dropped shots on 3, 4, and 5, then recovered with a nice par on the 6th hole before the wheels fell off in a miserable run of bogey, bogey, double bogey. Yesterday in round one we finished the front nine at four under par. Now we stood at seven over.

I suggested we just try to make some birdies coming in for Colleen, and though he was trying his best, things just got worse. I stopped keeping score after eleven holes. I think we hit two good shots from there on in. It was another embarrassment for Jack. There are many ways to lose a golf tournament. You can stink on the first day and fail to make the cut. You can have one blowout hole. You can putt like an idiot. You can drive the ball out of bounds. For us, it was none of that really. Just one poor shot after another, shots that missed being good by a yard or two. A slow bleeding away of our hope and expectations.

Standing alone in the fairway on the 15th hole, I thought again about Scotland. Suddenly my mind was soaring across the Atlantic, back to the ground that I love. When I was last there, I was writing hard on a new novel from 4:00 each morning until I got on the bus to the course to go to work. My agents had sent the novel out to Hollywood—how many weeks ago was it now? I'd lost track. But the silence could mean only one thing.

"You don't understand how it feels," Jack said to me when we were walking back to his truck. "It hurts bad. Playing that way."

"I do understand," I told him. "You spend three years writing a novel, and then you realize it's not nearly good enough. That's been my story for the last thirty-seven years."

"I don't know, man," he said.

Instead of music on the ride back to the hotel, we talked. It came down to me telling him that he has all the shots and enough talent to play well on this tour. "It's in your heart," I told him. "What I said to you this morning about being grateful. That's what I'm trying to learn now as I grow old. I think the only way you can grow old gracefully is to be grateful enough to be calm. And that's funny, because when you and your sisters were little, that's the one thing your mother insisted on. That you all were grateful."

"I have to start all over when we get back here after Christmas," he said.

"No, you don't," I said. "We'll take what we've learned and do the best we can on the second half of the tour. But you don't have to start over."

Maybe I didn't believe that when I said it. I wasn't sure. We have a long struggle ahead of us, and we might never climb the leaderboard again. I know that I have wondered before if someday I'm going to look back on my time as a father and see it as a long run of fixing things. I am pretty certain that I've learned here during our first run on the tour what is broken in Jack. I know he's going to have to fix it himself.

DECEMBER 17, 2011

We are halfway through the tour now and facing three days of practice rounds before the two-week Christmas break. I am trying to take inventory early this morning. And trying to figure out what the hell happened yesterday. One reason golf is such a brutal game on the mind is that it is a game of uncertainty. But I think that part of my job as Jack's caddie is to cut through all that is uncertain and try to nail down some essential truth that we can carry with us onto the second half of the tour. If such a truth exists.

And I believe it does. I studied my notebook from yesterday's disaster and discovered that on seven holes where we earned bogeys and worse, we might have had quite simple pars if we had gone to the center of the green instead of at the flags, where missing left or right by two or three yards, as we did, placed us in great difficulty. That might have been a swing of seven to eleven strokes. The difference between a humiliating score and a respectable score, which is all that Jack was fighting for after the poor opening nine. Going for the flags is Jack's game, and that is what accounted for his outstanding four under par on the front nine of the first round. But it may also have accounted for the disappointing four over par on the back nine. Which makes it a difficult equation with reasonable arguments on both sides. Just as you might argue that a writer who spends three years trying to write a novel determined to reveal some important truth about the human condition that no one ends up reading would be wiser to spend those three years in law school. So what can we conclude with certainty here? We began this sixth tournament planning to just be content with the center of the greens, but when the rain softened them, Jack decided to go for the flags. That is his game. It has always been his game. But the figures from today's round tell a certain truth, I think. When you drive the ball as well as he has, and putt as well, maybe you consistently shoot respectable rounds by just going for the center of the greens. And so, it may be that when we return after our two-week Christmas break, Jack will have to consider changing his game.

I fell asleep last night thinking of an old, dear friend whose father loved and played golf into his nineties at the Rochester Country Club. If he had been caddying for Jack yesterday, I think I know what he would have said to him as they walked to the 3rd tee: "Son, you just made two outstanding pars on the 1st and 2nd holes and you are near the top of the leaderboard with sixteen holes to play, and you may think you have your 'A' game today and that you can fire at every pin, but I saw your first two drives on those holes, and I am here to tell you in no uncertain terms that you *do not* have your 'A' game today. So from here on out, you are going to have to dial it back if you want to shoot a respectable score and win some cash money."

We are going to have to regroup these next two weeks and then get back here and fight on. I have no idea how it will all turn out in the end. That is just more uncertainty. But tonight before we turned out the lights, I said this to my son: "Whatever happens from here on out for the rest of the tour, you had the courage to try to do something most people, most very good golfers, would never try because they couldn't face the disappointment and the failure that you have endured here. I will always respect you for that. You never made excuses. You never gave up. You played every shot as hard as you could even when you were defeated and humiliated. Even if this is all you win here in Texas, I hope you will take that with you for the rest of your life and be proud of yourself and grateful that you had the chance."

We'll be home for Christmas, as the old song says.

I have cooked up a secret plan for Jack. Barry O'Neill, the lad from Ireland, has agreed to work with Jack through our final six events on the tour, playing practice rounds with him every free day he has. Jack has never had the opportunity to have a coach before.

JANUARY 11, 2012

In Maine we got to sneak onto the Prouts Neck golf course again and hit a few balls for Teddy to chase. It was one of those perfect winter afternoons with the lowering sun throwing blazing bands of red and pink light across the fairways and through the tall dark fir trees. It was far too warm for December in Maine, and when Jack checked the temperature in Houston on his iPhone, he told me it was ten degrees colder there. We talked for a while about going back. He said he felt good about it. "We've got half the tour still left to play," he said. "I feel like I'm just getting started."

"Well," I said, "we learned some things in the first half. We played a few lousy rounds, a few solid rounds, and for a while you were at the top of the leaderboard. So I guess we hit all the highs and lows."

"I guess so," he said. Then he looked out across the harbor for a moment before he told me that during the round when he was four under par through nine holes, he was thinking that maybe he might go further than the Adams Tour. "It felt so good to finally be playing to my potential," he said. "I thought about trying to find a sponsor to cover my expenses so I could enter Monday qualifiers for the Nationwide Tour, you know?"

"It's something to think about," I said.

"Yeah," he said. "We'll see."

Then I told him that when we returned to Houston, I was going to be stepping into the background.

"What do you mean?" he asked.

"Barry O'Neill, the Irish lad, has offered to play practice rounds with you."

"Really?"

"Yes. He's happy to help out."

"Sounds good," he said. "I can learn a lot from him."

Much of the time back home in Maine, after hearing from Barry, I thought about shadows. Until I worked as a caddie, I never thought about my shadow before. But a caddie must always be conscious of where his shadow falls. You don't want it to lie across the line of the golfer's putt. Or pass over his stance, or distract him in any way. In Scotland, where it stays light until ten thirty at night in the summer months, it takes a while to get used to having to think about your shadow at so late an hour. Sometimes, I suppose, metaphors match the physical world. As Jack's father, I wonder if maybe I must fall back a little ways now for the rest of the tour. We know that a son has to be released from his father's shadow. I wonder if it is the son who must step free or if it is the father who must move aside. Or if it is a little of both.

Back in Houston now, as Jack took a place on the practice range at Panther Trail beside more than twenty players on the tour, I was thinking about the pink light in the winter sky above the Prouts Neck golf course when we were there together over Christmas, and the hope in Jack's voice when he spoke about the possibility of this tour leading to another tour if he could find a measure of consistency in the next six events. I had said nothing about what I was thinking then. I would never talk with my son, or with anyone else, about how I wished that this winter together would turn into a spring and summer together on another tour. But I would give anything to help Jack achieve that measure of consistency in the weeks ahead of us this winter so that maybe, just maybe, we can go on further. All the players on the range with him want the same thing that Jack wants. To achieve that elusive measure of consistency that will carry them on. I know this. Just as I also know that golf is a leaking ship of dreams. And you board at your own peril.

Jack and I talked about this last night for a while in a conversation that began with the physical layout of the golf course but soon veered off to the metaphysical. It turns out that nothing in my son's life has made him question his nonbelief in God the way Tim Tebow has. Jack has believed in him from the time he won two national championships in college, and when the Denver Broncos fired the coach who had drafted him and then benched him early this season, Jack began telling me that someday all the Tebow doubters in the world would be proven wrong. "I think I've figured out what it is with you," I said to Jack. "You don't believe in God, but you want to believe. And right now Tebow is making you doubt your own doubts. It was the same for me when you and your sisters were born. I mean when I held each of you for the first time."

"That's interesting" was all he had to say.

"Well," I went on, "as far as God and golf are concerned, I can't be the first caddie in St. Andrews to have discovered this little insight. Make a vertical list, by name, of the six golf courses in town":

Balgove.
Jubilee.
Old.
New.
Eden.
Strathtyrum.

"Now, take the first letter of each name, line them up horizontally, and you get":

B JONES

"And given that most of these courses were named long before Bobby Jones came into the world, I used to tell my golfers that this was proof not necessarily that there was a god but most definitely that there was a golf god."

"I guess we believe what we need to believe," Jack said.

We left it at that. And then he told me that he'd received a text from Barry. "He's not going to play in this tournament. After the long break he needs more time to practice. But he says that he'll catch up with us for the next one."

"That's okay," I said. "I wonder how he'd play number 18 if he needed to make a par." The 18th hole featured another island green, but this one was so small that anything more than a high-lofted wedge or nine-iron would never hold. And because the hole was a sharp dogleg left from the tee, you needed a perfect drive to set up the shot into the green.

"You have to go for it in two," Jack said.

"I'm not sure about that," I argued. "If you don't nail the drive, you can lay up on the second shot, fly a wedge to the pin, and make a one-putt par."

He sighed. He wasn't buying it.

<hr />

JANUARY 12, 2012

<hr />

Four in the morning. We start the second half of the tour today with an early tee time. Eight twenty. Which means I will be waking Jack at 6:15 so we can begin our drive to the course at 7:00, up Route 45 in the dark. I am more than a little concerned about what lies ahead today after playing a ragged practice round yesterday. Jack hit every fairway and had only one three-putt green, but the best he could manage was seven over par. We teamed up with two other players from the tour. One of them, Gabe from Iowa, had won his state title as a freshman at age fifteen. He was thirty-five now and still trying to chase down his boyhood dream, though after all the years he had enough perspective on life and the game to play with a mirthless smile on his face. I had wanted a disciplined and rigorous practice round, but it turned out to be a lighthearted affair. Maybe that is what the boys needed after the long break. We'll see. It is now thirty-three degrees and the wind is high. It will be long underwear and a wool cap for me. I've been scrolling all the greens through my mind since I opened my eyes this morning after misreading four putts yesterday. There was a lot of rain while we were away, which made the Bermuda rough very sticky. Jack left three wedges short yesterday. I was hoping we'd have time to hit a hundred more on the practice range, but it was dark by the time we finished our round. Today we are going to have to land the greens in regulation in order to have a decent chance. I don't want to try for anything more than fairways and greens. Keep it simple. Fairways and greens. If we make pars, we'll make the damned cut.

Hole 1. A 365-yard par-4.

"Here we go, Jack," I say. "Freezing cold. Gale winds. If it was raining sideways, it would be just like Scotland. Play well, man." With twenty knots of wind in our faces on the 1st tee, a dogleg left with water down the left side and out of bounds right, we can hit a three-wood today instead of the four-iron we hit yesterday, when the wind was squarely behind us. What we need to do is survive the first few holes. Just get it in play, Jackie boy, I am thinking to myself. And he does. But his second shot from 168 yards bleeds right in the wind, and he has to sink a six-foot putt to save a bogey.

One over after one.

Very quickly it becomes "House of Horrors golf." The guys in front of us are in the woods, in the water, climbing over hills into the hell of out of bounds. Our playing partners are not faring any better, but somehow Jack is keeping the ball low, under the wind, and in the fairways. After he sinks three six-foot putts to save bogeys on the first three holes, I tell him, "Not as poor a start as we had at Houston National, buddy. Keep fighting." And he hits the fairway again on the 600-yard par-5, then plays solid the rest of the way on this hole to make his first par of the day.

"It's like Carnoustie," I say as we climb to the 5th tee. The wind is still in our faces, but Jack nails a six-iron to six feet on this 197-yard par-3.

His first golf shot of the day. He's looking at his first birdie putt. "Just lay it on the left edge," I say. He agrees. Bang! Center of the cup. We get one stroke back.

Two over after five holes.

Hole 6. A 435-yard par-4.

We have to keep it up the left side here off the tee. Water all the way down the right. Great drive, but the ball kicks right, and now we have a second shot of 165 yards, over water all the way to the green. It's a lovely seven-iron, but the ball spins off the green, and it takes us three strokes to finish. Another bogey.

Three over after six holes.

Hole 7. A 228-yard par-3.

"Put a good swing on this one, Jackie," I say. He does. Fifteen-footer for birdie. He hits it way too far, and now we have a seven-foot comeback, downhill, to save par. He looks confident. It's a good roll. And it's dead center.

Three over after seven holes.

I tell him, "Three over will be in the money in weather like this."

"I hear you, man," he says.

Hole 8. A 322-yard par-4.

Yesterday this was a green we drove. But in all the wind today, we've still got 130 yards left to the hole after a nice three-wood from the tee. He has to hit a touch shot here, and his hands are blocks of ice. I'm worried. Very nervous. He nails it! Six feet left for birdie. The putt breaks left instead of right. We both saw it breaking right. He's fuming mad now. "I can't miss those putts," he says. "I have to make those putts." Be grateful, I am thinking; it's a par, be grateful.

Three over after eight holes.

Hole 9. A 571-yard par-5.

"It's like Carnoustie here because the wind is never behind us, Jackie," I tell him as I hand him his driver. He hits a righteous drive, 311 yards into twenty-five knots of wind, but it kicks left into the trees. Oh no. Oh no, I am thinking all the way to the ball. Just give us a damned shot, please. And we have one. Jack very smartly does not try to reach the green, which is guarded by a pond in front and right. He punches out a low six-iron. Then hits a masterful wedge from there to four feet, and we have our second birdie. "A working-class birdie," I tell him. "I prefer those, coming from where we do in this world." He smiles.

Two over after nine holes.

It's getting colder, and the wind is picking up. Jack records three bogeys and a par through thirteen, and we're sitting at five over. And I am thinking, If we hold on, we are going to make the cut and be playing tomorrow. That is all I'm asking for.

Hole 14. A 529-yard par-5.

Straight into the wind, this has to be a three-shot hole to the green today. Jack stripes his drive right up the right side. There is a big holdup. All three players ahead of us are in the swamp and the trees. I walk up ahead, leaving Jack with 211 yards left to the hole on a narrow green with water left and right. I know this next shot will make or break our round. The last thing I say to Jack is "We're going to be waiting fifteen minutes here. Take plenty of good hard practice swings."

I'm up waiting just right of the green when Jack plays his second shot. I know it will spray right, I know it. And it does. It then rolls onto horrible ground. Roots and dead branches. Jack says nothing. He studies his lie, then asks for his sixty-degree wedge. He keeps his head down, and the ball flies true, lands softly, and stops four feet from the hole. Another birdie. Another working-class birdie.

Four over par after fourteen.

I want the match to be over! Get us in at four over par and we will be at the top of the leaderboard unless the weather improves for the late tee times. We throw away a stroke with a needless three-putt on 15 and make solid pars on 16 and 17, and here we are facing this damned island green on 18. Jack hits a drive up the left side, and it should cut back into the fairway but it doesn't. I'm thinking, That's in the water. It has to be. But when we get there, we're on good ground, fifteen feet from the water. He hits a nice wedge from here, but it spins back off the green, and it's rolling down the hill toward the water. Don't break my heart, I'm thinking. And somehow it stops one foot from the water. We're safe. From here Jack hits a lovely wedge, but it rolls past the hole, across the green, and it's headed for water on the back side. No. No. It stops again. "Let's just get up and down and get the hell out of here, Jack," I tell him. He does. A bogey. We finish at six over par.

"You made the cut, Jackie boy," I tell him when we shake hands. "You played well. It could have been a bloodbath."

"Thanks to Glen," he said.

"What do you mean?"

"He sent me an e-mail about my pre-shot routine. It helped me today."

I smiled to myself and said nothing. Before Christmas, I wrote to old Glen in Canada and asked him if he would send an e-mail to Jack about the importance of good practice swings before each shot. It was something I'd learned in Scotland and had relied upon as a caddie. Back in our hotel room, Jack showed me what Glen had written to him:

Jack, Would like to make a suggestion. This is from an old caddie who has looped for a number of pros. I was looking at all the scores of the boys on your tour. Not a single player's scores fluctuate as dramatically as yours. I realize there is the good and the bad but what needs to be avoided is the great to the really lousy! Here is a thought for you if you want to turn this around after Christmas. Your father mentioned something in an e-mail to me that has bothered me. Shot preparation and that brings me to the practice swing. You need to start taking a good, *meaningful*, practice swing before each shot. Not a half assed, not committed one, but one that sets your swing in the proper groove and then repeats when you do hit the shot. If the first one does not feel right, take another *committed* one. Every good or great player I have worked for has utilized this technique, without fail. This might be a missing piece in you getting to the next level and it will breed consistency which I think must be presently lacking. The greatest player in my lifetime whom I have spent time with is Jack Nicklaus. You may have heard he can remember *every* shot he ever hit in a tournament. That is true. He remembered the details of at least 20 important shots I quizzed him on. He explained to me that, like many other successful players, he visualized every shot before he hit it and was thinking about that visualization during his *practice swing*. You obviously have all the shots to play this game at a pro level. No pro ever succeeded without this technique. Try it. My Christmas gift to you. Don't throw it away. Fairways and Greens. Merry Christmas, Glen

JANUARY 13, 2012

Five in the morning. Cold again, but the wind has fallen off, and it will be much warmer by the time we tee off at ten. We finished yesterday at seven strokes behind the leader heading into round two. If Jack plays well today, he can move up and maybe win some money for the first time. I know that matters to him, but honestly some things happened yesterday that mean a great deal more to me. I saw that Jack is winning back some belief in himself here. By fighting hard in difficult conditions to make the cut and to finish high on the leaderboard, he earned back some of that belief. I could see it in the way he was carrying himself out on the course yesterday. Of course I could ask for more. God, yes, it would be terrific to see him gain the consistency in his play that would take him onto another tour so I could caddie for him until the day when I can no longer walk. Let this run on for fifteen more years so I can die with my boots on! Let them come and drag me off the course when I'm so senile I'm begging the beverage cart girl to marry me. Or worse. I would love that as any father would. But just to see Jack believing in himself again yesterday is worth more than gold to me. And there was something else. Before we left the course, Jack spoke with one of the players he has come to know here, a young man who has fought bravely to overcome drug addiction. He had not played well, and he had missed the cut by one stroke. Jack was really sad about this. Then late last night on the Adams Web site he discovered that because of the brutal weather conditions, the cut line had moved and the young man had made it to today's round. I heard the excitement in Jack's voice when he told me, and I could tell that he wouldn't have been happier if it had happened to him. To be sure, this kind of generosity of heart is not what made Tiger Woods such a winner in this game. But I think it has made Jack a good fellow. And I'll take a good fellow for a son over a winner any day.

A friend wrote to me yesterday and asked how come the players on the tour were not all shooting par or better. I wrote him back:

> The reason you are asking me how come these guys don't all go out and shoot par is because all you know about golf is what you have seen on TV, and TV is never real. TV won't show you the guys out there who make triple bogeys and fail to make the cut. Each week on the PGA Tour, there is a lot of failure you never see because it doesn't look pretty on TV. I am guessing that you have no idea how often Tiger Woods is fined for failing to abide the pace of play rule. Rather than play by that rule, he plays at his own pace and pays the fines. The same is true of his cursing on the golf course for which he is routinely fined.

My time in Scotland taught me something about the game. It taught me that today Jack may lose some of what he earned yesterday, and then he'll have to fight to earn it back the next time out. But as for Jack's generosity of heart, he got that from his mother, and it runs deep in him, and I think it will stick.

Round two. Panther Trail Open. When you work as a caddie in Scotland you learn that every round of golf is another story. And the story of today's round is that if you play well enough in round one to make the cut and finish well up the leaderboard, there is the chance that you will get paired up with one of the top golfers on the tour as Jack was today, playing alongside young Dustin Morris, who has won money and finished high in every tournament on this tour. And despite being three over par through eight holes, Jack was on

Dustin's heels, just two strokes behind. On the 9th tee of the 578-yard par-5, Dustin striped his drive. Then Jack hit his first bad drive in weeks, spraying it up the right side. It hit a tree and kicked out of bounds. Meaning he is now hitting his third shot from the tee. He stripes it and has 259 yards over water to try to land the green in four and make a one-putt par save. He nails his hybrid, and it is perfect, never leaving the flag the whole way. But when we get to the green, we find that the ball has rolled across the green and is stuck on the side of a bunker in such a ridiculous lie that Jack has no stance. No chance. He doubles, and good old Dustin drains the putt for eagle.

As we headed to the 10th tee, I said to Jack, "Let's give him a run for his money on the back nine, what do you say?"

Dustin promptly birdies 10 to follow up his eagle. And Jack drains a fifteen-foot birdie putt of his own to match him. All square after ten. Jack drops a stroke on number 12. Down one. Then Jack birdies the par-5 14th to pull even. But only for about five minutes before Dustin drains another eagle putt. So he's two up on Jack on the back nine, but Jack isn't giving up despite a bogey at 15. Now Dustin is up three going to the 16th tee, where he hits his first poor shot of the day and has his drive up the left side pinned against an iron fence. Jack nails his drive right up the center about 320 yards. Dustin has no shot. All he can do is turn his club backward and hit a left-handed shot that advances the ball only twenty feet. Jack is looking at 258 yards to land the par-5 in two. He takes his three-wood and rips it. It's a heat-seeking missile that never leaves the pin. But it's ten feet short of the green. Seventeen feet from the hole. Our eagle chance. Jack takes the putter instead of trying to fly a delicate wedge onto the green. A good call, I think. But his first putt rolls into a hole and almost stops. Leaving him ten feet to make birdie. He runs the putt six feet past. He takes a four-putt for bogey to match Dustin's bogey. Dustin pars 17 and so does Jack, sinking a tricky six-footer. And now the dangerous 18th with the island green. Dustin drives straight up the middle. Jack does too, maybe 4 yards farther. Dustin lands the island green on his second shot. Jack's ball lies 10 yards right, and so he has a completely blind shot to the treacherous green. He nails a seven-iron, and the ball lands five feet from the hole and sticks. He's eight feet inside Dustin, who three-putts and then watches Jack drain the birdie putt. Not bad. Not bad at all. We finished at five over. I took a minute to tell Dustin that he was one of the finest golfers I'd ever watched. Then Jack and I bought a couple of beers and sat in a cart behind the 18th green to watch his pal Gabe finish. The sun was on our faces, as warm as summer, and Jack was singing those words from an old U2 song: "I am not afraid of anything in this world."

JANUARY 14, 2012

I slipped onto the Walden on Lake Conroe golf course in the late afternoon shadows after all the golfers had dispersed so that I could walk the ground the way I preferred to walk a new course for the first time—alone, and kicking a golf ball the entire way from the 1st tee to the 18th green while I paced off the yardages and wrote down distances in my notebook. This was a practice I invented in Scotland as a way of preparing to caddie at a course for the first time, and I had spent my share of Sunday afternoons when the Old Course was closed kicking a ball around while I committed the contours of the ground to my memory.

Walden is what is called target golf. Tight, tree-lined fairways with out of bounds left and right off almost every tee and with greens so small you could fit eight of them on the 13th green of the Old Course. Plus, enough water to make you feel even more restricted. With his power game, Jack will feel extremely uncomfortable here at first; instead of a slugfest, he is going to feel as if he's stuck at a tiny card table playing bridge for the afternoon in his great-aunt's parlor.

I don't think I've ever seen a course with five par-5s and five par-3s like this one has. And there are eight tee shots that are shrouded in deception; you stand at the back of the box, and when you look up the fairway, there appears to be plenty of room out there to land a driver. But when you pace off the distance, you discover that the fairways all end with trees, bunkers, or ponds at around 265 yards, which means that I will be handing Jack his three-wood on these tees and telling him to hit low stingers that will catch the downhill slope at around 240 yards and roll another 20 yards.

Even if you're just walking alone, kicking a ball along, you can learn a lot out on a golf course, and only a small fraction of it is about the game of golf. I came down over the hill on the par-5 number 11, and as soon as I saw the first flash of blue on Lake Conroe, I thought of the ocean at home and I missed Colleen so much that I sat down on a bench and called her. The moment I heard her voice, I knew that I *needed* to talk with her about Jack. "It's the same old story," I said. "The history between Jack and me—it's still hurting him. I'm almost certain that every time he looks at me standing beside him on a golf course, he has to remember that he was kicked off his team and let me down."

"Why are you still worrying about that?" Colleen asked.

"Because I feel it, that's why. He's the only golfer on the tour with his old man standing beside him and all that damned history."

"But you've already told him that it doesn't matter anymore."

"Talk is cheap. If you or I had been unfaithful sometime in the last thirty-two years, sure we could talk our way through it and maybe we'd still be married, but it would never be the same. The betrayal would still be there."

"He didn't betray anyone."

"He did. When he left home for college and made the golf team, I told him that I didn't care if he never got to play in a single match as long as four years later, when it was over, his coach told him that he'd never had a player work harder."

"That was you talking, Don."

"I know. But Jack promised me."

She listened to me for a while longer, then told me to talk with Jack. I knew that I wouldn't do that. Instead, I wrote to Barry tonight. I told him that I had decided not to tag along for his practice round tomorrow with Jack. Then I wrote:

Maybe you can find out how Jack feels. I would be very grateful for this. Jack has five tournaments left now, and this might be the last time in his life that he can find out how well he can play this game. I might be standing in his way, Barry. If so, I need to know. And I don't think Jack would tell me. Maybe he'll tell you. Thanks.

JANUARY 16, 2012

On the range at 10:00 a.m., a few words with Barry, to thank him for playing a practice round yesterday with Jack. "We were even through seventeen holes," he says. "Then Jack drove into a bunker on 18 and let me beat him. I enjoyed playing with him." I told him to play well. "We'll talk soon," he said.

When we tee off at 11:20, Barry is two groups out ahead of us. My nerves are shredded this morning, and it really pisses me off. Why am I so nervous? Why can't I just enjoy this? And here is Jack striding confidently onto the 1st tee in his dark banker's trousers and his Oakley shades, and in front of all these people he goes first and nails his drive straight up the turnpike about 340 yards, and I am saying to myself, don't ever forget this, you dummy. Don't ever forget how Jack was able to do this. And I am certain that this is going to be his day. On this 460-yard par-4 all he has left is 135 yards to the green, and he lands the right half easily and is looking at an easy two-putt par for a strong start. But somehow he drills the first putt nine feet past the hole and misses the comebacker and he's one over par, and four hours later we are both stumbling around Walmart like two blind men, searching for Chicken McNuggets and some understanding of what the hell happened on the golf course. I hear Jack say, "It's just so damned hard, man. I left ten lag putts at least eight feet short. Jenna could have done better."

"I know, I know. You don't have to tell me. You ran that first putt nine feet past the hole, and you were spooked the rest of the round."

"It's pathetic. Really stupid."

"I know. Your mother could have putted better, but, Jack, look, you had one easy par all day. You were getting hammered out there, and you could have hung your head and missed the cut."

"I should have been one under after four. I mean, easily. I'm seventeen feet from the hole in two on the par-5, and I make a bogey because of a stupid first putt?"

"I know all that, believe me. I know. But you fought hard. I've never seen you fight harder. You made the cut. We live to fight another day. So tomorrow go out there and play the best round of your life. Shoot under par. Climb back up. We'll eat our Chicken McNuggets if we can ever fucking find them, then we'll watch the Celtics and it will be okay."

"I'm hitting a hundred lag putts tomorrow before we start."

"Fine, we'll pull your truck up to the practice green and putt in the dark with your headlights if we have to. I don't care. Whatever you want to do. Okay?"

"Okay."

"You made the cut, Jack. You didn't give up. You didn't make any excuses. One of the guys in our group was throwing his clubs all over the course. The other guy gave up. But you held on. I was proud of you. Round two tomorrow. Bring your 'A' game and let's see what happens."

JANUARY 17, 2012

We have the same tropical conditions on the putting green at 9:30 as I encountered five hours earlier when I stepped outside the hotel. Hot and humid, with a dull and steady rain falling. Jack and I watched the Celtics game last night in a kind of stunned silence. We are both sick and tired of getting kicked around. This morning every golfer is wearing the same mask, hoping to conceal that he is praying to God or whatever he believes in that today, for just once, he might have a stress-free round. And what is that in precise terms? Hitting the fairways off the tees. Hitting the greens in regulation, then rolling the first putt close enough to tap in for a par and move on to the next hole, or if you should miss the green, finding your ball in benign ground so you can fly a wedge close enough to the hole to make your par that way. Yesterday we hit fourteen fairways with splendid shots from the tees. One missed fairway cost us a stroke. The others, Jack found a way to scramble for pars. We missed six greens and lost two more strokes to poor wedges. These three mistakes should have given us a round of three over par, right at the top of the leaderboard. But Jack left twelve putts short. I mean ten feet or eight feet short. He sank six of these for rather heroic par saves. The other six cost us another seven strokes. I have been wondering if perhaps the small greens threw off his perception in some way and this is why he left so many putts short, because he never lost his putting stroke or he would not have been able to sink those six long putts to save par. He was shy and putting scared. On the practice green this morning he rolled the ball hard. I watched while sitting in a buggy, drinking coffee. For the record, we will be riding in a buggy for a while. My stupid knee popped out of its socket during my practice round on

Saturday. It did this once before, but this time it took me a long time to snap it back where it belonged. In all the other tournaments there were only two or three golfers walking along with us. Everyone else was in buggies. I left it up to Jack this morning.

"Let's ride," he said, more for me than for himself.

"Are you sure?" I asked.

"Absolutely," he said.

I know he prefers to walk, to impose his own pace on the game. He's making this concession for me. There wasn't time for me to feel lousy about this. I took a seat and felt a little grateful to be able to get out of the rain. Everyone is concealing something in this world, and I suppose we can be defined more by what we hide than what we reveal. In my case I have worried here in Texas about looking so old that it might frighten Jack, sort of like the daughter whose mother has one of those giant double butts—one in back and a matching one in front—because the daughter knows that this may be her fate. Here, living in the same room with Jack since late October, I have been careful to dress and undress only in the bathroom so he doesn't have to see my pathetic potbelly. And I can hide my stupid bald head under a baseball cap. But now I have the limp, and I can't hide that. I am really turning into an old man now, and if Jack hasn't already acknowledged this, he will before we are finished here this winter. He will glance at me and say to himself, my father is an old man now. And with that acknowledgment, a certain immunity will be lifted from his head because he will know that he is next, that no matter how much time he has ahead of him, one day he will look as old as his old man.

Enough, I thought. Enough of that.

Jack finally began a round with an easy par after hitting a beautiful drive and a fine eight-iron to the green, the ball coming to a stop seventeen feet below the hole. Just what he needed for his first long putt after yesterday. And he put a good roll on it and then tapped in for a par. I saw an ironic little grin on his face. "Much better putts today," I said. "Just follow through right to the hole."

He hit a decent three-wood off the tee on the short par-5 2nd hole. Rather than trying to reach the heavily bunkered green in two, he laid up wisely with a punched five-iron. So he was left with 85 yards to the hole, an easy wedge. He put a good swing on it, but to our astonishment the ball airmailed the green and also the big bunker behind the green. The ball went so far that Jack had to hit a provisional in the event that it ended up out of bounds. "What was that?" he asked me. "I don't know," I said. He asked me if he had hit it thin, and I said, "No way. It didn't sound or look thin at all." So he ended up taking a stupid double bogey on an easy hole. And then the battle was on, and I don't mean the battle for golf; I mean that same old grinding battle to try to keep believing in himself enough to play the next shot well. Though he was disgusted, he made a solid par on the next hole, then made what I thought was just a harmless mistake on the par-3, by flying the ball ten feet past the hole into the Bermuda rough. When we got to his ball, it was clear that this mistake was anything but harmless. His ball was sitting down in deep rough, and he was looking at a green sloping steeply away from him right to the edge of the pond he had just carried on his tee shot. A mistake here and he was in the water. "Keep your head down, Jackie boy, and put a good swing on it," I said. But he couldn't advance the ball more than two feet. Then he left the third shot short of the green as well. We took our second double bogey in the first four holes. I could barely breathe. All I said to him was "Keep fighting, man. Don't give up."

That same damned fight, that same battle to believe in himself, was right in front of us now. And let me say this: for the next three hours I never saw a golfer fight harder than Jack did. After losing one more stroke on the next hole, Jack played the remaining thirteen holes at even par to post a respectable 77. That's not the whole story, though. In those thirteen holes, he made such splendid drives and such solid iron play that he set himself up for seven birdie putts inside ten feet. Only two of them fell for him. He should have made five. Hell, he could have made all seven. Still, he was holding his head up the whole way in, and he earned back just enough to face the Bentwater Open in two days.

JANUARY 19, 2012

I will be waking Jack at 6:00 a.m., and we will be driving an hour north in the dark for our 8:40 tee time in round one of the Bentwater Open this morning, and somewhere along the way I will tell him that those six poor wedge shots he hit yesterday in our practice round with Barry and two of his mates from the tour were all caused by fear. At first I thought he was just hungry; I had forgotten to pack our peanut butter and jam sandwiches. But it was fear, and each shot had cost him a stroke. I am going to tell him that when he strides defiantly up to his next shot, he always nails it. But when he is tentative, and timid, the wheels fall off. This Johnny Miller–designed course is what you would expect from Johnny, who could never putt terribly well but who had some of the most brilliant iron play ever. Flat, simple greens, accessible only through narrow passageways between towering pine trees and big bunkers. If you want to land these greens, you must be precise. Fall short and you might lose your ball in a ravine. Push your shot even slightly left or right and you are in the trees or, at best, looking at one of those delicate wedge shots from the Bermuda rough, which has been so ruinous for Jack, who never laid eyes on that type of grass before we arrived in Texas. I believe that today's round will come down to how Jack can play those shots. Unless of course *he doesn't need to play those shots*—because he hits every green in regulation like one of the fellows whom Barry brought with him to the practice round yesterday, a young Canadian golfer, winner on both the Nationwide and the Canadian Tours and a consistent money winner on our tour this winter. He played a flaw-less round of seven under par. Barry almost caught up to him on the 15th but finished two strokes behind while he and I talked about the Troubles in Northern Ireland, which he was too young, at age twenty-eight, to recall. I told him that here in Houston and in every American city now, all the young black men walk with their heads down and their shoulders pitched forward in defeat, like the young Catholic men I'd seen in Londonderry who could be hauled off the street at any time simply because they had the misfortune of being Irish. Barry misses the old country, but he has made his home in the States since he arrived here when he was eighteen and found work as a caddie at the St. Louis Country Club to earn his way through college. The pro there spotted his talent and encouraged him to play for St. Louis University. Six years later, he is here now trying to take his game to the next level. He told me that he dreams of returning to Europe to play on the big tour and to one day play in the Irish Open. I told him that this was as fine a dream for a young man to be chasing as I'd ever known of.

Round one today began unlike any other tournament we have played here. Jack birdied the par-5 1st hole (after hitting his second shot, a 254-yard hybrid over trees eighty feet tall just off the green, and then a beautiful wedge to four feet) and then birdied the second as well after hitting a 143-yard wedge to three feet. When he fol-lowed those two birdies with two strong and easy pars, it suddenly felt as if we were in this match not just to make the cut, or to post a respectable number, but to try to win. But in time those little wedge shots from the Bermuda rough that I had feared caught up with Jack, costing him two double bogeys. He fought hard and birdied the par-5 16 after reaching the green in two with a brilliant four-iron, but it wasn't enough to compensate for his mistakes, and he finished at a six-over-par 78. When it was over, he was as disgusted with himself as I've ever seen him. Let me just say that it was a rough ride back to the hotel. A wall of silence. And the whole way I was wondering how Jack was going to resolve this. When we reached the parking lot, instead of getting out of the truck with me, he took a deep breath and said, "I'm going to the range to hit two hundred wedges from the rough. I'll be back later."

Fair enough, I thought.

In the room I read an e-mail that had come from Barry in response to my asking him yesterday if he had ever considered playing on the EuroPro Tour in Great Britain as a way of breaking into the European Tour. These lines really broke my heart: "That would be a dream. I would like for my father to see me play in one professional tournament because I know he has never believed I can make it to next level, unfortunately."

I read those two sentences over and over before I fell asleep.

JANUARY 20, 2012

Round two. We drove in darkness again for an 8:40 tee time this morning. While Jack was on the range, I spent some time helping one young man change the spikes on his shoes. At age thirty, after chasing the dream for nine years, he is under pressure now to prove it for his sponsor, who called him last night wondering how he managed to post an 80 in round one. "Hit my drive into the water on number 4," he recounted grimly. He was teeing off just before us. The whole time we worked on his shoes I kept wondering why it was taking us so long. Then I looked down and saw that his hands were shaking badly.

There is pressure in this game, to be sure, pressure in every variation. But Jack looked very calm as he made his way up onto the 1st tee and hammered his drive 347 yards up the left side into perfect position to hit a high cut over the trees on the left and land the par-5 in two. An eagle putt of forty-seven feet. Not a strong lag putt, but the birdie putt was solid, and the ball dropped into the cup and then danced out. A par. I expected him to be disgusted with himself again, but for some reason he was smiling when he handed me his putter. "Did you see that?" he asked.

"A three-putt?" I said sarcastically.

"No, man, I ripped my pants, bending over to read the first putt." The only black trousers he's ever owned, the ones his mother bought him during his sophomore season in high school.

"If I wasn't so damned broke, I'd buy you another pair," I told him.

"No problem," he said.

As we headed to the 2nd tee, I said, "I mean that, you know? I'd love to be able to buy you a new pair of trousers."

"Why trousers?" he asked. "What happened to pants?"

"In Scotland pants are underpants."

"Hey, man, you're not in Scotland anymore. Remember?"

I apologized, then watched him hit his second drive just like the first one. Yesterday he hit every fairway but one from the tees. It has been this way for the last six tournaments. Now we were left with just 85 yards to the green on this par-4. I can't explain how he could have airmailed the green with his wedge. But he did. And then it was another ruinous wedge left short in the Bermuda rough, and another wedge bladed across the green and two putts. "You can't make double bogeys when you're 80 yards from the middle of the green," he said, disgusted now, as he should have been.

It was funny, though, the feeling that came over me. I know in the early tournaments here on the tour, Jack battled hard but could not recover from this kind of early adversity, but today for some reason I never doubted that he would come back. It slipped away for a while. He made two bogeys in the next three holes, but he never slumped his shoulders or lowered his head. Instead, after being four over after those first five holes, he hit shot after shot and made four birdies and seven pars in the final thirteen holes to finish at two over for the day. It was quite a run. On the day, he had five eagle putts on all five of the par-5s and another on the 302-yard par-4, which he drove to seventeen feet from the hole with a high fade that landed delicately. The one shot I will remember is the 257-yard hybrid he hit into the par-5 number 12, starting the ball out over the water on the left with a cut that brought it back to a soft landing thirty-seven feet from the hole. We couldn't be sure the ball was on the green until we climbed up over the hills and saw it there. There was something different about Jack's demeanor today, and I didn't realize what it was until I was handing him his putter as we walked toward the 18th green.

"It must be about noon," I said.

"I don't know," he said. "I don't even know what hole we're on."

"Are you serious?" I asked.

"Yeah," he said as he looked around for a moment as if he were seeing the place for the first time.

"This is the 18th. You have a four-foot putt for birdie."

I was astonished really. He didn't say anything. He took his putter from me, walked onto the green, knelt down behind his ball for a moment to check the line, then knocked it into the hole. While I watched, I remembered the feeling I'd had when he was four over par in this match after the 5th hole, the feeling that he was not worried, that he knew this time he would come back, that the remaining holes would be opportunities to win back strokes. Then I realized that he had been concentrating today in a way he never had before. He had reached the deep down world. I wonder if the time he has spent playing practice rounds with Barry has already helped him become a slightly different person on the golf course. More centered and calm. The rough edges smoothed a bit.

When it was over, all he could talk about was the three three-putts and the double bogey. "I gave away five strokes," he said as we walked to his truck. "Five strokes yesterday and five more today."

"You fought back," I said. "You really played well the final thirteen holes."

"I'm getting tired of fighting back," he said. "I want to fight to pull ahead."

"I know," I said. "You will. Trust me. Before we're finished here in Texas, you will."

The rest of what I told him, he had heard me say before. The bit about how this is his first professional tour, and after he had played no competitive golf for three years, I didn't know if we'd ever make a single cut down here. "Look, Jackie," I said. "You haven't caught the great players on this tour, but you've played well against the good players, and you've beaten a few of them. Now you have some time off before we head into our final three events. Maybe give yourself a little credit. What do you think?"

"I have to work on my short game," he said. "I have to learn to hit from the rough here."

"Or land every green in regulation so I'm only handing you a putter instead of a damned wedge," I said.

"I'm not satisfied," he said. "I guess I had higher expectations than you, man."

"That's okay," I told him. "That's good. Keep going."

I didn't say anything to him about what one of the fathers had said today out on the course. He was a sweet man who had been following his son on these tours for seven years. He came up to me off the 17th tee and asked me about Jack. "How far does he want to go with this game?" he asked with a melodious Texas drawl.

I told him that this experience was probably just about Jack trying to learn a few things so that someday he could become a good coach. "Man," he said as he watched Jack climb onto the tee box. "Not many players can do the stuff he does out here. You should tell him to keep going."

This wasn't the first time someone on the tour had talked to me about Jack and his future this way. When we said good-bye off the last green and the father told me he hoped that this tour was just the first of many for Jack, I thanked the man and said exactly what I'd heard Jack say before when he was asked. "We'll see."

We picked up a couple of Walmart steaks to cook for supper and then drove back to the Studio Plus, to the room we've shared since late October, which now feels like home to both of us. Jack told me that Barry had offered to practice with him during the break. He was pleased about this. "Have you ever seen a better player?" I asked him.

"Never," he said. "He's the real deal."

"What a great story," I said. "He has to leave Ireland when he's eighteen years old because his dream is to become a player and his father doesn't believe in him. He comes to America by himself and works his way through college as a caddie."

"I'll tell you this," Jack said. "Anyone who puts up money for him now is going to make a lot on their investment. I'm certain of that."

"If I had the money, I'd sponsor him, and I'd buy you a couple pairs of *pants*," I told him. "And I'm going to write to everyone I know. Maybe I can find five guys who will each put up four grand so he can make his run."

"You should," he said.

"Maybe I'd go with him as his caddie," I said.

"Hey, man," he said. "You thought this was going to be your last run. But it won't be. You'll be over there with him if he makes the European Tour."

"You think so?"

"I know you, man," he said.

FEBRUARY 5, 2012

We've had two weeks of practice as the days unfolded and then folded into each other while I watched Jack improving and gaining confidence in himself. These were some of my best days in Texas, out on the golf course with him, watching him learn a new way of hitting balls out of the Bermuda rough, following Barry's instruction to open his left shoulder so that it would lead him through the shot. I loved watching the two of them joking around together one minute and then suddenly turning dead serious as they bore down on their shots. Colleen has told me for years that she wished Jack could have had a brother along with his three sisters, preferably an older brother to guide him. Now he seemed to have found one in Barry, whose composure on the golf course was what I admired most about his game. Nothing rattled him. He just proceeded calmly with due diligence. He had achieved that elusive consistency in his game, and now at age twenty-eight he was right up against a choice: He could continue to play on these small professional tours and earn a modest living. Or he could put himself up against the hurricane, by returning to Great Britain to make a run for the European Tour and the chance to reach his boyhood dream of competing in the Irish Open.

Jack and I spent a lot of time talking about Barry. Talking about *his* dream and *his* story always gave us the chance to put off talking about our story for a little longer. Our story, which I suppose I knew was drawing to a close. But tonight, as we sat around the hotel pool, it suddenly presented itself. We were discussing the layout of the course at Cypresswood, and then there we were talking about our story. That's the way it is: you start out talking about golf, and pretty soon you are talking about life again.

I said, "You know that your mother is upset with us for never exploring Houston. I told her all we've seen is this hotel, the airport, the highways, the Walmarts, and the golf courses." There was a bright scatter of stars above our heads that seemed to mark this night. We were living it up, so to speak, now that the hotel had acquired a grill over the winter. We were cooking steaks that were advertised as "Nolan Ryan's Steaks" this time. A step up for us, we both agreed. "Living large" is how Jack defined it. It was nine o'clock, my bedtime, and we were relaxed in each other's company. Even the noise of the highway traffic seemed muted as Jack said he wished we could have flown his mother down to see him play here.

I agreed. "She loves it when you make birdies," I reminded him. "I checked the stats from the tour, and right now you're sixteenth on the list of sixty-seven golfers for birdies. I sent her the Web page."

"I wish I'd done better here," he said.

We had been together for almost four months and had never spoken about what would happen when the tour was over. I felt this was a good time. "Everyone always feels that way," I said. "You competed to the best of your ability."

He looked at me and then nodded slowly. "I don't have enough ability to make it any further," he said.

Our eyes met. I began scurrying down the corridors of my mind to find something to tell him. "Hell," I began. "All my life I wanted to write books like F. Scott Fitzgerald. I tried, but I never had enough ability. I just couldn't do it. No one on this tour drives the ball better than you. You know that. And not many players can hit three-woods like you can. Two hundred and eighty yards over water, uphill into the wind, with a fade that lands the ball softly on the green. I've watched you do it again and again, and you make it look easy. Your swing never changes. That's real talent. It's stuff you can't teach. The chipping and the putting—a seventy-year-old man can learn that. You can learn it. We could try to raise some money for another tour. Maybe get you a coach and keep going. I'd be up for it."

"I think I'd rather be a coach, you know? Help some other kid chase his dream. But we'll see."

I didn't press him. He got up to flip the steaks. "What was the best thing when you look back?" he asked me.

"The whole deal has been cool," I said.

"No, I don't mean here. I mean when you look back over your whole life."

I didn't have to think about my answer. "Babies," I said. "Without a doubt. Having babies and little children around. You don't want to miss out on that."

"Babies are expensive," he said.

"No they're not. Don't be afraid of that. Have as many babies as you can. Babies press you right up against the miracle of this world. You look in their eyes and you see—everything that is possible."

"That's cool," he said.

"Let me do the math," I said. "If you get married to Jenna tomorrow and have a baby in nine months, in twenty-one years, after he or she finishes college and wants to play on a pro tour, I'd be an eighty-three-year-old caddie. I guess there has never been an eighty-three-year-old caddie on any tour."

"I think you should caddie for Barry. I hope he makes a run for it."

"Yeah. We'll see," I said.

"Want to give Mom a call?"

"I do," I said. "Maybe you'll change your mind, Jack."

"What do you mean?"

"About going on further. Maybe you'll just wake up some morning after we're finished here, and you'll want to keep going."

"Let's see what happens from here to the end," he said as he handed me his phone.

I held it to my ear. It was already ringing in Maine. "Do you remember when you were trying to persuade us to get you a cell phone?" I asked him. "Your mother got into bed one night and said to me so earnestly: 'I think maybe it's a good idea, Don. It would be nice to check up on him and know where he is all the time.' I said to her, 'Colleen, he could tell you he's in church when you call him. I mean *every time* you call him.' 'Oh, right,' she said."

For some reason I couldn't fall asleep that night. I went back outside hoping to see the stars again, but they were gone. And the highway traffic was wound back up to full volume. Be grateful, I said to myself as I rolled a cigarette. Remember? Gratitude. You've had this time with Jack. You don't have to ask for more.

FEBRUARY 9, 2012

The hallway outside our door measures 113 yards long, which is the exact length across the 13th green at the Old Course at its widest point. I'd taken this as a good sign when I paced it off our second night in Texas. I was looking for signs then that Jack and I were on the right track coming here together. The Katrina kids in the hotel use the hallway as their playground, but late at night after their mothers have rounded them up for bed, Jack and I take over for our heroic putting battles, and we are always reminded that this is how golf began for us, putting across the floor of the family room when he was eight years old. As the years go on, I may forget the courses we played here in Texas, but not the hallway where we talked strategy and rolled the longest putts in the world.

But out there in the middle of the night, alone, I was suddenly traveling across time, back to the room off another hallway where I had lived alone for years before I met Jack's mother, trying to teach myself to write. As I pictured that room and my black Royal typewriter on the table by the window, it suddenly struck me for the first time in my life that I will probably live alone again in a small room as my time is running to a close. Because I am ten years older than Colleen, there is a very good chance that at the end of my life she will still be part of the wide world where people chase after dreams, and escape hurricanes, and are much too busy to wonder what their lives will be like at the end, while I am already there, *knowing* what it is like. If that's the way it turns out, I hope I'm still trying to learn to write in my little room. And though I don't know where that little room will be, if someone can smuggle in a putter and one golf ball, I know that each time I step out into the hallway, I will be stepping out into the long hallway in Houston, Texas, looking for Jack, and remembering this place and the time we had here.

I was surprised when I went back in the room and found Jack awake. "It's your back, isn't it?" I said.

"It's keeping me awake," he said.

Too much practice, I thought. I've never been a great believer in hitting a million balls on the practice range, where anybody can look like Jack Nicklaus. I got him two aspirin. It was just after three in the morning. "Try to get some sleep," I told him.

"I've been trying," he said. "Why are you awake?"

"I was worried about the extra putter in your bag."

"I would have remembered."

"Yeah, I know," I said.

When he got back into bed, I asked him if I'd ever told him my theory about life.

"Which one?" he said.

"Funny," I said. "No, this is important. When I was about your age and I was finally beginning to figure out how the world worked, I realized what a man needed to be content in this world. Whenever I'd drive by these tar-paper shacks in Maine, you know, the desperately poor people who somehow survive, I would remind myself that all a man needed in that shack was some work to occupy his mind and a darling girl who desired him more than her next breath. If he had that, he had enough."

"What about his health?" Jack said.

"Yeah, okay, three things then," I said.

I didn't say the next thing that was on my mind—how I probably wasn't going to get all three in my little room at the end.

We were in trouble in the first round of the Cypresswood Open today before we even reached the 1st tee. I watched Jack laboring through his swings on the practice range. His back was too sore for him to make his turn. All his shots were bleeding to the right.

It got worse out on the course. I honestly don't know how he made a single par, but we didn't say anything about his back until we walked off the 16th green. "I'm sorry," I said to him.

"No excuses," he said. "People play this game in pain all the time. I haven't executed a single shot today."

So there we were with two holes left to play and knowing that we had to birdie both of them to make the damned cut.

We were paired with Gabe from Iowa again today, and he came up to me and put his hand on my shoulder while Jack walked onto the 17th-tee par-5. "Don't worry, Dad," he said. "He'll make it."

And somehow he did. A birdie on 17, and then another birdie on 18. Not the prettiest birdies you'll ever see, but good enough to make the cut and live to fight our way back tomorrow.

After a year of almost no rain in this part of Texas, the long drought came to an end at just the wrong time for us and washed out the second round at Cypresswood. Jack and I showed up for our 8:00 a.m. tee time only to be sent home an hour later with no hope of finishing the tournament. The bright side of this was that Jack had the day off to rest his back. But I needed a long walk, and I was pretty sure that

I knew the one person in Texas who would play eighteen holes in the rain with me.

Barry was just one of a number of players whose chance to finish the tournament in the money had been washed away. But he was in good spirits, even though his $500 entry fee had turned out to be a very expensive round of golf. "Five hundred dollars for eighteen holes," he said. "Just like Pebble Beach, I guess." He had been a tour player long enough, selling his old equipment on eBay for gas money to drive to the next tournament and doing whatever was required of him to keep going a little further, to take all setbacks in stride. "Ah, you get used to it," he said. "But it's a struggle."

I joked with him that if he'd been a struggling writer instead of a struggling golfer, all he would need was some paper and a pen.

Our shoes and pants were spattered with mud, there wasn't another soul out on the course (just my kind of golf), and as soon as Barry walloped his first tee shot way the hell out there, we started talking about Jack. "He's told me that you're a dreamer and he's a realist," Barry said.

I caught the trace of irony in his voice when he said this, and then the look in his eyes told me that there was something more he wanted to tell me. And he was willing to tell me, but he wasn't so sure that I was willing to listen. I jumped in rather desperately and said, "You know if Jack decides he wants to go further after this tour, I'll work seven nights a week stocking shelves at Walmart for the money if I have to."

"I'm sure you would," Barry said. Then he patiently laid it out for me while we walked side by side up the fairway. Jack could play on these tours for another year or two, working harder on his game than he ever had before, and with his natural ability he might make it through Q school. "But I don't think that's what Jack wants," he said. "I think maybe you want that more than he does, Don. And I'm not blaming you. What Jack wants is to love his girl and hold down an honest job. That's his dream now. It's not a bad dream. Every day

I think that should be my dream. I shot five over par the other day at Cypresswood, and then I'm in my car asking myself why I ever believed that I could make it. What kind of fool am I? This game breaks you in pieces, Don."

"You're not a fool," I said. "It goes with the territory for dreamers. Most of the time you don't feel real. I've been writing for thirty-five years, every day, seven days a week, and I've only had maybe twenty days when I've ever felt real."

"Exactly," Barry said. "You see what I'm saying then about Jack? Maybe he saw that, and he wants something different."

"I see," I told him. And I really meant it.

We played our way around, talking about Ireland and how I was going to try to raise the money for him to make his run for the European Tour. I told him that all winter in Texas, I had been trying to come up with a metaphor to explain the mental torture of golf. "Tell me what you think of this," I said. "Let's say you rode your bicycle every morning to the little corner store for a newspaper and then you rode back home. And every single day you knew with absolute certainty that somewhere on that little trip you were going to be thrown over the handlebars. Without exception. That's golf."

He laughed. "Yeah, pretty good, Don," he said.

I had to break both of Barry's arms to let me fill his car with gas on the drive back to the hotel. "You can get to the next two events on me," I told him.

"I'm really grateful," he said.

"I know you are," I said.

He was going to try to make ten or fifteen birdies this coming week so that he could start chipping away at his credit card debt. On May 1, his visa expired, and he would have to leave America and Denise, the girl he loved. She called him while he was driving me back to the hotel. I could tell by the way he spoke to her that she believed in him. "That's the truth," he said. He recalled the first time he'd won some decent money, in an event on the Hooters Tour. "I'll never forget how it felt when I called her and told her," he said.

"It was one of those twenty days," I said. "You felt real."

"I guess that's true," he said.

I told him that he couldn't stop now. "When you have someone who believes in you, you have to keep going even when you don't believe in yourself."

I'd had that with Colleen for all these years. And that was probably the only reason I hadn't quit.

Back in the room Jack asked me to help him write a letter to Sherwin-Williams in Cleveland, where he and Jenna wanted to live so they could be near her family. Someone had told him about a management training program, and he wanted to try for it.

As evening came on, we worked on the letter while we watched golf on TV and I complained when CBS turned the tournament into the Tiger Woods Show again. He was in third place, but there was almost no coverage of the two golfers who were ahead of him because CBS knew that America wanted to see only Tiger. "How can he even show his face in public after what he did to his wife and kids?" I yelled at the screen. "And not only that, Jack. Take a look at the big-shot bankers who get invited to play. They're the same morons who fucked up the economy and cost your grandfather every penny he worked all his life for. No one bailed him out when he lost everything. But look at these guys, they're back on top, playing golf on TV again." Jack turned it off and got up. He grabbed the putters, and I followed him out into the hallway. "Let's go," he said.

FEBRUARY 13, 2012

We are scraping the bottom of the barrel now, and so, after playing a practice round at half speed yesterday afternoon to rest Jack's back, we swung by Walmart and loaded up on enough fifty-cent chicken pies to get through our final five days. I've been awake for hours listening to the rain this morning and thinking about the road through Q school for the PGA Tour. You pay your $4,600, and then, with the prequalifying and qualifying stages, you basically have to shoot sixteen rounds of under-par golf under extreme pressure to have a chance. It's like someone saying to F. Scott Fitzgerald, "Okay, you're a great writer, but in order to earn the chance to become a *real writer*, first you have to stand up on a stage under a spotlight and correctly spell every single word in the dictionary."

Fine, I thought. Bring it on.

Then Jack's phone rang with word that we were on a four-hour delay for round one of the Lakes Classic, waiting for heavy thunderstorms to pass through Houston. "Are you going back to sleep?" I called to him across the dark room.

"I guess so," he said.

"I hope you get the job at Sherwin-Williams," I said.

"We'll see," he said.

"And if you decide in a year or two that you want to give golf another run, I'll do what I can to help you."

"Thanks," he said.

"You never know," I said.

"That's true," he said.

I wanted to raise the stakes a little, maybe say, "If you shoot a round under par in one of our final two tournaments this week and win some money, then you were meant to make a run for the PGA Tour." But I didn't.

We were set for a 1:30 shotgun start after the rain fell off this afternoon. But the course was too wet, so we were sent home and will now play both rounds tomorrow. The ground will be so wet that balls will disappear in the fairways, and I am planning to go out ahead to watch Jack's shots land. If you lose a ball, it's a stroke penalty plus distance, and we can't afford that. There is one ruling that could make things easier tomorrow. It is rule 25-1, "Abnormal

Ground Conditions," which stipulates that if a ball disappears under these conditions, the golfer gets relief and can drop a ball, no closer to the hole, at the outermost limits where it entered the abnormal ground. I will have to speak with the tournament director about this before we tee off.

FEBRUARY 14, 2012

I got a text from Colleen early this morning wishing me a happy Valentine's Day and telling me she loved me. You can't ask for more than that. Well, you can ask, I suppose. But I'll take it with gratitude.

As we were driving to the course today, I told Jack about Barry's father, who had worked most of his life as a glassblower at Waterford Crystal only to have the company go belly-up before he could retire and claim the pension he'd paid into for four decades. "I guess that's why I was never able to hold down a real job," I said. "I must have lacked the faith or something. Maybe I just never believed in the system, I don't know. But I always had the greatest respect for people who just wake up each morning and go to work. They're the people who keep this world held together. Your mother will tell you how I always said I wished I could be a mailman who carried his work in a sack each day. When the sack was empty, he could go home and feel good about himself. I just never had what it takes. I never had what Barry's father had."

Jack didn't say anything for a while. Then, as we pulled in to the parking lot, he said, "When this is over, you need to finish your mom's screenplay and get that movie made, man. That's your Q school."

"You're right," I said. "I suppose that is my Q school."

All the brilliant young boys on this tour looked weary this morning after being sent home in the rain the last two rounds. I was hoping that Jack would find some inspiration and jump out to a lead while the rest of the players were trying to find their legs.

As we made our way to the 1st tee, I called to him. "Jack, I was thinking early this morning about your philosophy: 'It is what it is.' I've never agreed with that, but I never really knew why until just now. I don't think in this life *it is what it is*. I think it is what you make it. So why don't we try to make this a special day for your mother."

"All right, man," he said.

I am going to write down every shot today and send it to Colleen for Valentine's Day.

Jack has the honors, and he rips a three-wood up the left side of the fairway into perfect position. A hundred and forty yards left on this 414-yard par-4. If his back is sore at all, he won't tell me, but it will show eventually. He hits a lovely wedge that lands softly six feet from the hole. A great birdie chance. We both see the same break, one cup right to left. But the green is wet, and the ball doesn't break at all. It's a tap-in par.

Hole 2. This 521-yard par-5 requires a perfect drive through a narrow opening between the trees to reach the right side of the fairway so you can fly the corner of the dogleg on the second shot. We're up the left side instead with 240 yards to reach the green. It's an impossible second shot, and I'm hoping Jack will lay up and go at the green in three to try to make a birdie. But with only 240 yards left, he won't hold back. He nails a three-wood and is calling for it to draw as it races across the sky. It falls short about forty paces from the green. We need a good wedge here to set up the birdie putt. And he hits one. Six feet left. It's an uphill putt. The ball drops into the center of the cup for a birdie. One under par after two holes.

Number 3 is a narrow 414-yard par-4. Uncharacteristically, Jack's drive bleeds right into trees. He can only punch out from there and scrap together a bogey. We are even after three holes. "We've had worse starts," I tell him as we walk to the next tee.

"I have to play better," he says.

Number 4. A 212-yard par-3, all carry over a small lake. He lands a six-iron twelve feet from the hole, and after his birdie putt falls short by three inches, it's a tap-in par. Even after four holes.

Number 5. A 545-yard par-5. The course opens up here, and it's "bombs away" from the tee. A lovely big drive up the left side. The sun is finally out now, a good sign after all the rain. It's 11:45 and I hand Jack his first peanut butter and jelly sandwich for the day. We have another six and a half hours out here today before dusk, and I've packed him four sandwiches. After the big drive he has only 220 yards left, but he puts a poor swing on it, and he's short of the green. From there he hits a nice wedge to set up a five-foot birdie putt. He wants this one. He's fought for it. But the ball stops one revolution short of the hole for another tap-in par. "How do you leave a five-foot birdie putt short?" he says when he hands me his putter. "Patience," I tell him. "We'll have our chances." Even after five holes.

We are both still fooled by the greens on numbers 6 and 7, where we missed birdie putts from five feet and fifteen feet for two more tap-in pars. He is shaking his head now, and all I can do is remind him that we have plenty of holes left to make our birdies.

Even par after seven holes.

Hole number 8 is a simple 182-yard par-3, but Jack makes a poor swing here, and his ball is short of the green in a bunker. His first sand shot of the day is perfect. The ball stops eighteen inches from the hole, and it's another par. Even after eight holes.

On the 402-yard par-4 9th hole he hits another poor wedge from a solid drive, and he has to save par from another bunker to stay at even par after the first nine holes today. He does.

Hole 10. This is a wicked hole. A 546-yard par-5 bending sharply left around a lake, with trees blocking the path to cut across the elbow of the dogleg. I want to play safe here after he strikes a good drive up the right side, but with only 203 yards left, Jack isn't hearing any of it. He bombs a five-iron at the trees. It climbs high and then higher, but it gets caught in the top branches and falls right behind a big tree. From there he scrambles and saves a par. But that was a hole he could have birdied if he had played it a wee bit smarter. Even after ten holes.

That last hole unnerved Jack. He knows he made a bad mental error there. And on the 440-yard par-4 11th hole, he is in trouble right from the tee. The ball sails up the right side of a very narrow fairway into the trees. All he can do from there is hack it out into the fairway, hit a nice wedge, and make a two-putt bogey.

One over par after eleven holes.

Hole 12 is a 372-yard par-4. A dangerous, very narrow fairway to a landing area that isn't more than 30 yards wide. Jack nails a perfect three-wood and has 90 yards left. He hits a high wedge that drops and stops dead four feet from the hole. He jars the birdie. Back to even par after twelve holes.

Jack cruises through numbers 13, 14, and 15 with relatively easy pars, landing the greens in regulation and just missing birdies on 13 and 15. "Disturbing," he says to me when the birdie putt on 15 stops just an inch from the hole. I change the subject and tell him that his mother and I are thinking about getting a pup when Teddy turns ten next year. "That would be great," he says.

Even par after fifteen holes.

Hole 16. A 430-yard par-4. I'm not going to tell him again to be patient. I've said that enough. He hits his drive here too far left, and it clips the branch of the only tree on that side of the fairway. The ball falls straight to the ground, and we're miles from the green. "How far?" I ask him. "Two hundred and forty-seven yards," he says. He takes his hybrid and hits it right into the mayor's office. The ball never leaves the flag the whole way. "That was a golf shot," he says. It sure was. From where we're standing, we can't see how close we are. But it's only five feet from the hole. And it's another missed birdie. Another tap-in par. Silence this time. On to the next hole. I wanted that one for Colleen. Even par after sixteen holes.

Hole 17. A 447-yard par-4. A great drive, but a poor second shot, and then our first chunked wedge in the Bermuda rough, and it's a two-putt bogey. Jack is not a happy camper. I start talking to him about Teddy again: "Maybe we'll get a yellow Lab to keep him company, what do you think?"

"Yeah" is all he says.

One over par after seventeen holes.

"I need to make birdie here," he tells me as we walk onto the 18th tee of this 532-yard par-5, another dogleg left over water on the second shot. He hits his best drive of the day and then nails a three-wood that lands softly on the green. We have a forty-two-foot putt for eagle here, and somehow after that putt falls three feet short, it takes two more putts to finish the hole. Another tap-in par. Should have had an easy birdie.

We finish the first round at one over par. Could have been better. Could have been worse, I am thinking. There's no time to look back. We are heading right to the 1st tee to get in as many holes on round two as we can before the sun sets.

"I feel like we've been here before," I say to Jack on the 1st tee. He nails a three-wood to perfect position but somehow airmails the green with his wedge and has to settle for a bogey. One over par after one hole in round two.

He fights back from the bogey by landing the par-5 2nd hole in two and dropping the birdie putt into the center of the hole. Even after two holes. He misses a six-foot birdie putt on 3 but taps in for a par, then drains a twenty-foot birdie putt on 4, and just misses a thirteen-foot eagle putt on 5 for a tap-in birdie.

So here we are on round two—two under after five holes, with three birdies that will make Jack's mother happy.

We take a stupid three-putt bogey on 6 and then settle down for a par on 7 and are one under after seven holes.

On the simple 182-yard par-3 8th hole, Jack and his two player partners take a total of nine putts. "Just stupid," Jack says to me. He's right. We gave away a stroke there and are now at even par through eight holes. Everyone is running out of gas.

It is getting dark now as we finish the 9th hole with a solid par and head to the tricky par-5 10th with that second shot bending left around the lake. We've been out on the course seven hours now, and after Jack hits a great tee shot, I am arguing for a lay-up. No way. And Jack hits the trees for the second time today, and he's in trouble. It's a dumb bogey. One over after ten holes.

There is just enough light left to record a stupid three-putt bogey on the 11th hole.

Two over par through eleven. Tomorrow is another day.

We have an 8:00 a.m. tee time to finish the round tomorrow, and so we were in bed early. "We're three over for the tournament," I said just before I fell asleep. "You played some good golf today, Jackie."

"Decent," I heard him say.

FEBRUARY 15, 2012

We left the hotel in darkness and fog. Standing on the 12th tee, I told Jack that if he finished the final seven holes of round two under par, I would buy him a steak dinner. He looked tired, and I thought this might give him a jump start. He didn't need it. He played the best golf I've ever seen him play. Every single shot he took never left the flag by more than a yard or two. "I'm dialed in," he kept saying to me, "and I'm still not making birdies." True. He played the last seven holes with five tap-in pars, one birdie, and one bogey, finishing the second round at two over par and the tournament at three over par. His best finish on the tour.

Whenever you play a really good round of golf, you can look back and count three or four strokes out on the course that could have made it a terrific round. Three of those birdie putts could have dropped into the cup instead of burning the edge. But it was still fine golf, and I was elated. Jack disappeared at the clubhouse, and I sat outside in the rain that had returned, thinking to myself, One more year. Give Jack one more year on this tour, and he will be ready to make his run at Q school. I could feel it all drawing close, and I wanted to say something to Jack when he met up with me on the 1st tee of the Forest Course to play a practice round in preparation for tomorrow's event there. I really wanted to say something, but I didn't. We were on the 2nd tee when he said very casually, "I had a call from Sherwin-Williams. I have an interview next Wednesday."

It sort of took my breath away. "A week from today," I said.

"Yeah."

"Well, that's good, right?"

"I hope so," he said.

I watched him murder another tee shot. Here I am, I thought, in a world of dreams, and here's my son in another world. His own world.

FEBRUARY 16, 2012

Five a.m. We are down to our last two days together here in Texas and our final tournament. Tomorrow after we walk off the 18th green, we will get into Jack's truck and start the long drive north straight from the Forest Course at Kingwood, where he rolls his last putt. I have been thinking about dreams this morning while Jack sleeps across this room that we have shared since late October. His dream, my dream. And for some reason, the American dream. I think most intelligent people recognize that the American dream died quite some time ago in an economy that required both parents to work full-time instead of raising their children, that forced people to hold down awful jobs at poverty wages simply for health insurance, and that strangled college students with debt. I suppose the American dream was laid to waste by money. I've always thought that the greatest writing ever done about this American dream was Arthur Miller's *Death of a Salesman*, a play I must have taught at five universities to perhaps eight hundred young students. Hundreds of scholars have written hundreds of books contending that poor Willy Loman is killed by the American dream. I never bought that. Yes, there is the stunning portrait of poor Willy Loman, who buys into the same business world that crushes him with its sickening superficiality and breathtaking indifference. But I always argued that Willy, despite his failure in the business world, is already living the dream because he has a wife who is devoted to him and respects him, and two sons who admire and love him. I used to tell my students: Make that your dream. Not some dream that is measured in material wealth.

The other thing is that very few people are prepared to meet the price of their dreams. Years ago an editor in New York told me that when the last collection of Fitzgerald's stories was put together at the end of his career and the publisher asked the author for a title, Fitzgerald said, "The Price Was High." And he might have been thinking not only about the price he paid but about the price paid by those who stood beside him.

And even now, living this dream with Jack, I can hear fathers asking me: You mean my son might be good enough at golf to play on a professional tour someday and I could caddie for him? Where do I sign up for that? What do I have to do? My answer would be: Well, at age fifty-eight you have to leave home for six months and go live alone in one room in Scotland with no car, no TV, no Internet, no telephone, and you have to start at the bottom of the pile and work 187 days without a day off, walking about a thousand miles, most of it in brutal weather. For starters. And then you have to go back to Scotland a second time at age sixty and do it again. The same drill. Only this time with a bad right knee. I won't know any other way to answer. There might be a shortcut, but shortcuts also carry a price. In fact, in *Death of a Salesman* it is the affair Willy has that costs him the love of his favorite son. And you have to dig deeper to see why he has the affair. The woman he is sleeping with is a secretary to the big buyers, the guys at the top who can buy what Willy is so desperately trying to sell. It's complicated stuff. And in two hours I'll be happy to stop thinking about it and just concentrate on golf.

Jack is fast asleep as I write this. Just after he turned out his light last night, I took the advice of a good friend, a former student of mine, and asked him if he wanted to play this last tournament on his own. I called to him across the dark room. "Hey, Jack, I was thinking . . . you might want to have this round tomorrow to yourself."

"What do you mean?" he asked.

"I mean, you're the only golfer on this tour who has played every round, every shot, with his old man standing beside him. I was thinking I might sit this one out. I'm kind of tired, and it would give you some space. You've earned the right to have the round to yourself if you want it that way. I promise you won't hurt my feelings. I just want you to walk away from Houston on your own terms here, however you want it to sit in your mind. I was here; I saw it. I'm proud of you and what you've done. I'm leaving with fond memories. So, sleep on it, Jack, okay? You can tell me in the morning."

"Okay, man," he said. "We'll see."

This morning, just after seven, when Jack stepped out of the shower, he said to me, "I want you out there today, Daddy. We started this together, and you've been with me all the way, so let's finish up together."

"Good enough, Jackie," I said.

Of course I was relieved that he had made this decision, especially when we were informed by the tournament official at the start of our round that a forecast of heavy rain tonight would likely make the course too wet for a second round tomorrow. Meaning I would have missed my last chance to walk beside Jack on this tour.

At 8:20, Jack made a poor swing on his first drive, and the ball sailed up the right side of the fairway into bad ground. He recovered on the next shot and landed an eight-iron seventeen feet left of the hole. The greens were soaking wet, and his lag putt fell three feet short, leaving him a downhill second putt with a left-to-right break. He struck the putt a touch too hard, and the ball fell into the left side of the hole and then jumped out. A disappointing three-putt to start the round. One over par after one hole.

He was discouraged but not beaten, and he recovered to record pars on the next six holes. But I could tell by the dirt in the grooves each time I cleaned his clubs that he wasn't flushing the ball. He was striking the ball off the toe. After another three-putt on the par-4 8th hole, disaster struck when his drive from the 9th tee, a 247-yard carry over the marsh, turned left instead of fading back into the fairway and landed in the water. He tried to recover, hitting his second drive onto good ground, but he couldn't steady the ship from there, and he posted a triple bogey. I think only the second one on this entire tour.

We talked then about how there is almost always pain in competitive golf, and I reminded him that he had already proven many times that he could fight his way back from disaster.

He proved it once again, recording six pars and a birdie in the next seven holes. But on the 17th, a 600-yard par-5, he blocked his drive into the woods. For the first time on the tour I found myself looking for a ball that my son had hit, and I wanted in the worst way to find it. Nothing rips a caddie's heart out like failing to find a golf ball. As I was walking through the woods with my head bowed, I tried to concentrate on the task at hand, but I kept recalling all the times in Scotland I had somehow found my golfer's ball. This time I failed. We had to play Jack's provisional shot from the tee, and it was stuck in thick grass off the left side of the fairway. All he could do was hack it out into play, which left him 187 yards from the green as he took his fifth shot. "I've got to save a bogey here, to have any chance at all," he said. "I know," I told him. It came down to a nine-foot putt from the right side of the green. He looked down the line carefully, then settled into his stance and drained it. I put my hand on his shoulder and said, "That damned hole was a struggle. This is the first time your shirt has come untucked here in Texas."

He tucked it back in as he climbed onto the 18th tee box, then striped his drive and set up a lovely nine-iron that never left the flag all the way to the green. We both thought it would be maybe four feet from the hole, but when we got to the green, we saw that it had rolled seventeen feet past. And then, for the second time today, his par putt sat on the lip and wouldn't drop for him.

A six-over-par 78 was a great disappointment to Jack. You figure when you make twelve pars and a birdie in a round that you will post a better number. But there wasn't time now to look back; the tournament director was waiting for everyone coming off the 18th green with word that we would play a second round in half an hour because the forecast was so poor for tomorrow. I couldn't have asked for more.

But there was one catch: every player in the thirty-four-man field had to agree.

It came down to one player refusing to play and an ugly scene. One player after another begged him to change his mind. But he wouldn't budge. He had played well enough in this first round to win some money if the second round was canceled, and he wasn't going to jeopardize that, even if it meant disrespecting every other player in the tournament. Barry took it upon himself to use that great word from the old country and called him a wanker to his face. It was a moment I will always remember. And because I've had difficulty all my life walking away from an asshole without first telling him the truth about himself, I let him know that I had witnessed my share of wankers on golf courses in Scotland, and his behavior was the most compelling display of poor sportsmanship I'd ever seen.

And that was it. We are now waiting for the rain to start tonight. If it is raining when I wake up at four in the morning, I know that Jack and I will have played our final hole of golf here in Texas. God, I'm hoping for a miracle with the weather so that Jack can have one more shot at a great round here and so that Barry can go out there tomorrow and beat the miserable wanker.

Jack will get a text from the tournament official at seven in the morning, and then we'll start packing the truck for the drive north. We'll leave this room where we have eaten and slept and talked and laughed and lain awake worrying and counted our blessings just for the chance to be here.

FEBRUARY 17, 2012

There were flood warnings last night as we were packing. But here it is Friday morning at 5:30, and there has not been a drop of rain. When I looked out the window and saw the parking lot was dry, my heart began to race, and it felt as if a miracle had taken place. With two and a half hours until our tee time, our chances of playing improve as each minute passes without rain.

Last night it hit Jack and me at the same time that there was only one way to resolve the injustice of what happened yesterday. And so I wrote an e-mail to the director of the tour, a fellow who is known to be fair and also to read his e-mails:

Tyler,

Sorry to bother you. I hope I get to meet you someday and thank you. Jack and I are sitting here, packing up for the long drive back to Maine and licking our wounds after the injustice of this day. And we are just thinking that the very best thing that could happen now for every player in this last tournament except the one player who refused to play the second round today would be if you let us play tomorrow no matter how bad the weather is.

Just let the boys play, Tyler. I've seen great competitive rounds of golf played in St. Andrews, Scotland, in the worst weather you can imagine. In fact, I've seen some of the most heroic golf played in those conditions.

That would be a terrific way to wind up the tour.

Thanks again.

Somewhere outside Memphis. We finished our round at 11:30 this morning in light rain that never threatened the tournament. Before we left, while Jack changed his clothes, I had a chance to talk a bit with the two boys from our group today. Noah was twenty-four years old, and this was the end of the road for him. He had a beautiful game and hit the ball a mile like Jack. "No," he said solemnly, "I gave myself this tour to see if I could putt. I never sank a single putt the whole time. I'm through." Brian, on the other hand, was planning to play thirty events on the Adams Tour this summer.

"Q school for you in the fall?" I asked.

"You got it, sir," he said.

"Good for you," I said.

"What about Jack?" he asked. Even as I was explaining that Jack was not a dreamer like his old man and that he was ready to go back to the real world, I was doing the math in my head. He had finished his last round on the tour at three over par, hitting sixteen greens in regulation to match the sixteen he had hit yesterday. He had hit every fairway from the tees except one again. No one on this tour had better accuracy from the tee, and only a few players had hit more greens in regulation, and this was a triumph to me for a kid who had not played any competitive golf in almost three years before Texas. But Jack wouldn't see it that way. In today's round he had seven tap-in pars, which to him meant seven more missed birdies to add to the seven he had missed yesterday.

But that isn't what I am going to remember from our last round of golf together. I am going to remember Jack giving Barry a couple of hats from the Inverness Club. And Barry very sweetly trying to persuade Jack that he had a future in golf. "You play fearlessly, Jack. You were only behind me by a few strokes these last couple of events, and I've played in a hundred tournaments. Think of the progress you've made. I'm just saying, think about it. Look ahead five years and think what you could accomplish in this game."

And there was Jack thanking Barry and telling him how he saw things. "I never played up to my potential here, Barry. There were three or four rounds when I embarrassed myself. I have to be honest about this. You're either the real deal in this game, or you're just a pretender, lying to yourself. I don't want to do that, man. I came here and, yes, I made some progress, but I never played up to my potential. I wish I had. But I didn't."

I watched them shake hands. In that moment I understood something about my son. He saw the grace in an ordinary life lived honestly. Something that big dreamers like myself almost never see.

I am going to remember Jack rolling in his last putt for a par with a golf ball that had his girl's initials on it. And how he cheered on his playing partners through the round, even though they were his opponents. And then the moment today when I looked up through the mist and rain and saw Jack walking toward me, wearing the black jacket that I had bought him that winter day at Carnoustie five years ago where this journey of ours began. Five years ago, I thought; like anyone, I wanted to get those years back. And in a way I got them back this winter in Texas.

I am going to remember all of it for as long as I can. The handshake on the last green. The quick embrace. And the walk to the parking lot when Jack said, "That's that, man. It was real, wasn't it?"

I was a step behind him. "Yeah, Jackie," I said. "It was real."

By noon we were on Route 59 heading north out of Texas into winter, just another father and son in this world who would soon say good-bye without any clear idea when we would ever see each other again.

ACKNOWLEDGMENTS

In the curious geometry of life, it turns out that some of the best philosophers and psychologists in the world carry golf clubs for a living in Scotland. They are as tough and determined as sled dogs, and they are also generous teachers and spiritual advisers, raconteurs and even meteorologists when they are called on to be. One of the great privileges of my life was to work for two seasons in their company, and though I poured everything I had into this work and tried to measure up, if I were to return there and work for ten more seasons, I would still be learning from Neal, Big Brian, Wee Brian, Adam, Andrew, Gary and Jimmy, Kenny, Paul, Alan, Colin, John, Scottie, No Chance, Pots and Pans, Billy the Bullet, the Beast, the Goose, Donuts, Stretch, Johnny, Connor, Kim, Stevie, Kevin, Mark, Sean, Arthur, Gavin, Robert, Ian, Duncan, the wise old veteran Glen, and half a dozen Malcolms, including the incomparable Malcolm of Stirling, who held me up on my sixtieth birthday, and big Malcolm, aka the Whale, who once in a sleet storm took my glasses off for me and dried them when I was too cold to move.

I am grateful to my caddie masters for every round of work, especially Davy Gilchrist, who got me started, and good old Kenny McLeod in his red jumper up the road at St. Andrews Bay, who should be called by central casting if Hollywood ever needs a caddie master.

Every caddie needs a home, and I am grateful to Philip Rolfe, who runs the Scores Hotel to perfection and who always made me feel welcome in the Chariots bar, where my journey began and my long days often ended.

Long ago, after Bryce Roberts first showed Jack how to swing a golf club, there were some fine young golfers at the Algonquin in St. Andrews-by-the-Sea, New Brunswick, who taught my son a lot about the game: Marty Mitchell, Peter Young, Chad Parks, Matt Myers, Todd Duplessis, and Timmy McCullum, who could hit the ball almost as far as Jack grew up to hit it.

David Scott, a glorious golfer and one of the best people you'll ever meet, was the first person I caddied for, and though I got all the yardages wrong, he never held this against me. While caddying for my son, I often turned to David for advice, as I did the fine Canadian golfer Gordon McGarva, who, in the summer of 2011, won the Victory Cup in St. Andrews, and Ray Farnell, an outstanding caddie on the PGA Tour who took a walk with me on the Old Course the night before he caddied his first round of a major. And there was the brilliant young Irish golfer Barry O'Neill, who helped Jack and me on the Adams Tour. I know that someday I will watch Barry play in the Irish Open, and if there's any justice left in the world by then, he will be paired up with Rory McIlroy in the final group, on Sunday afternoon.

The friendship of John Carr, Zac Sherman, Charlie Woodworth, Mike and Pat Ciesla, Brian Durocher, Colin Harrison, David DeSmith, and the matchless writer Daniel Asa Rose carried me through this book. I owe them for this, as I owe Jim White of Toledo, Ohio, who was the first person to tell me that I had to go to Scotland if I wanted to learn to be a caddie, and his son, Jimmy, who has been such an important person in Jack's life and in mine. The whole time I was away from home, I had the support of my old friends Glen York, Jim Sullivan, Jeff Sullivan, Ed Beem, Mel Allen (my first editor, "back in the day," as Jack says), and Doug Eisenhart and his dear wife, Gilly, who grew up in Edinburgh and moved to the States and thinks me perfectly daft for loving her Scottish weather. It meant so much to me after Jack moved away when Jono Sexton would come to Maine from time to time and take me golfing out at Prouts Neck.

For the years when I was living this story, and then writing it, I had people in New York City whose belief in me made all the difference. Thank you, Victoria Pryor, Rich Morris, Lynn Nesbit, Jason Kaufman, and Robert Bloom.

Of all the fine philosophers I worked with in Scotland, Stevie Morrow, who walked me through some early season jitters, delivered the best caddie line I ever heard. "Don," he said one sunlit morning as we made our way to the 1st tee of the Castle Course, "when I get stuck out there with a real wanker, I give him the bronze treatment instead of the gold, which means the same lousy reads but without the smile." I have a deal with Stevie. When I am old and facing the end, I am going to ask Colleen to take me back to St. Andrews for one last walk on the Old Course with some of the old caddies who were still young when I knew them. I will wear my black rain jacket with the Links Trust emblem over my heart and the word CADDIE on my left sleeve. Stevie will help me out to the 11th green, and then we'll turn and slowly make our way back toward the timeless embrace of the old gray town, and I will remember.

FROM JACK SNYDER . . .

I would like to thank everyone who helped me chase my dream. I was overwhelmed with the support from so many friends and family. Not only financial support, but the emotional support and encouragement from everyone were greatly appreciated. I wish that things had gone better and I had performed at a higher level, but the experience was life-changing and something that I will carry with me the rest of my life.

In particular I want to thank Dave and Susan Snyder, Randy and Callie Curtis, Carl Patrick, Mark and Laurie Murphy, Marty Scarano, Jim Sullivan, Peter Waldor, Mike and Melissa Field, Doug and Gilly Eisenhart, Johnny Guarino, John Carr, Steve Kapelke, Colin Harrison, Chris and Julie Tansey, my three sisters, Eryn, Nell, and Cara, and my grandmother, who made the journey to Houston possible.

I would like to extend a special thank-you to Jenna, my girlfriend of five years, who stood by me while I chased my dream. You have always been the most supportive person, and encouraged me every step of the way. Thank you so much for always being there for me. I would also like to thank two very special people, my dad and of course my mom. If it weren't for your support and love, I would never have been able to believe in myself enough to even try. I love you both and am so thankful to have you two in my life.

I am grateful to Sherwin Williams for giving me the opportunity to work for such a great company.

Don J. Snyder is the acclaimed author of *The Cliff Walk* and *Of Time and Memory* and many novels, including *Fallen Angel*, *Winter Dreams*, *Night Crossing*, and most recently, *The Winter Travelers*. He wrote the screenplay for the Hallmark Hall of Fame movie *Fallen Angel* based on his novel. He lives with his wife, Colleen, in Scarborough, Maine, where they raised their four children and where he is at work on his mother's screenplay.